FIONA O'LOUGHLIN

ME OF THE NEVER NEVER

Fiona O'Loughlin spent her childhood in the tiny country town of Warooka in South Australia before moving to Alice Springs with her husband Chris – and five children later, she started doing stand-up comedy. Her hilarious stories of housewifery and motherhood were an immediate hit – Fiona's first festival show earned her the Best Newcomer Award at the 2001 Melbourne International Comedy Festival, and she's been enjoying sell-out seasons on the festival circuit ever since.

Fiona has taken her story-based stand-up around the world, headlining LA's world-renowned Improv Comedy Club and performing at the Edinburgh Fringe and Montreal's invitation-only Just For Laughs festivals.

She has also been a hit on television, with guest appearances on *Sunrise*, *Good News Week*, *Spicks and Specks*, *The World Stands Up* and a heap of Comedy Festival Galas.

When she's not performing on tour, Fiona divides her time between Alice Springs and Melbourne.

FIONA O'LOUGHLIN
ME OF THE NEVER NEVER

hachette
AUSTRALIA

AUSTRALIA

First published in Australia and New Zealand in 2011
by Hachette Australia
(an imprint of Hachette Australia Pty Limited)
Level 17, 207 Kent Street, Sydney NSW 2000
www.hachette.com.au

This edition published in 2013

National Library of Australia
Cataloguing-in-Publication data:

O'Loughlin, Fiona.

Me of the never never / Fiona O'Loughlin.

978 0 7336 3012 5 (pbk.)

O'Loughlin, Fiona.
Women comedians–Australia–Biography.
Women entertainers–Australia–Biography.

791.092

Cover concept by Razor, Sydney
Cover adaptation by Christabella Designs
Back cover quote: *Maroochy Weekly*
Cover photographs: Sean Izzard <www.seanizzard.com>
All text photos from author's own collection
Text design by Bookhouse, Sydney
Typeset in 12/18 pt Adobe Garamond Pro by Bookhouse, Sydney
Printed and bound in Australia by McPhersons Printing Group

MIX
Paper from
responsible sources
FSC® C001695

The paper this book is printed on is certified against the
Forest Stewardship Council® Standards. McPherson's Printing Group
holds FSC® chain of custody certification SA-COC-005379. FSC®
promotes environmentally responsible, socially beneficial
and economically viable management of the world's forests

CONTENTS

For Mrs Kennedy

NOTE TO THE READER

For as long as I can remember I have been the keeper of stories.

'Fiona! Tell them about your friend Jasmin from Tennant Creek.'

'Fiona! Tell them about the time we thought Aunty Mon had a heart attack in church.'

'Fiona! Tell us about the chemist shop uniform.'

I've relished the role of storyteller since it was given to me, or rather since I elected myself to the position. And apparently my paternal great-grandfather was an enthusiastic raconteur, so maybe it's simply in my blood.

It goes without saying that I am a woman of many flaws. None of my flaws are serious enough to be of any interest to the authorities, but I am unable to write another word for you before I come completely clean on a most relevant shortcoming when it comes to writing a piece of non-fiction such as this.

I just have a tendency to exaggerate, to change things, to make a story better. Which is all right, because everybody knows.

Right now I can see my mother in bed with this very book in hand, her glasses on the end of her nose and my father to her right in his blue checked pyjamas. She sighs, not unhappily, somewhere in the first chapter, and then lays the book on her white cotton bed cover.

'Good Lord, Denis.'

'Hmm?'

'She does go on with a lot of rot sometimes.'

* * *

This book is a record of moments, events and experiences that have humoured, humbled and heartbroken me, but just for the record it is not, and was never meant to be, an actual book of record. And all of it is true – but not always accurate.

PROLOGUE

I still find it amazing that I ended up carving out a life and a career in a place that, until I was about seventeen, I had never given a moment's thought to. I doubt I could have pointed to Alice Springs on a map but I clearly remember the first time it was ever referred to while I was paying attention. When I was a Year 12 boarder at Cabra College in Adelaide, I and thirteen other classmates were asked to attend the funeral of an eleven-year-old girl from the school who had been killed in a light plane crash on a return flight from Alice Springs. Her mother and uncle had died with her.

Our purpose was to form a guard of honour for the coffins and represent the college. I have never seen such a crowded funeral before or since, and I remember feeling so physically reticent during the requiem mass because we were strangers to this family and took up two precious rows near the front of the altar while friends and relatives who couldn't fit into the church filled a hall next door and spilled out into the street.

The little girl's name was Libby, and when I looked over at her six older brothers and sisters and their devastated father I almost failed to breathe and witness grief like that at the same time. I don't recall him particularly on that day but my husband was one of those brothers and, as raw and as tragic as it was, I'm forever glad that I was able to pay a small tribute to the mother and sister-in-law I would never know.

* * *

Nothing ever turns out as you plan, I guess, but I often think if I'd gone to a fortune teller thirty years ago and been told I'd marry a guy who makes false teeth, move to Alice Springs, have five kids and become a stand-up comedian, well, I quite possibly may have asked for my coin back.

That said, becoming a stand-up comedian has hardly been an accident. I've been at it like a dog with a bone for two decades. I couldn't put it down, couldn't leave it alone and couldn't bury it for the life of me.

Stand-up is one of the most exhilarating, joy-laden careers on the planet and also one of the most soul destroying. I was twenty-seven when I made a silent pact with myself that it was a job I would set out to conquer. Perhaps I might have done that faster had I been availed of a more conventional apprenticeship – you see, a stand-up is generally born in the city. Comedy clubs invariably have a try-out night for newcomers, which is an unpaid gig for about five minutes where a fledgling can spread their wings, fall down or fly – live or die – but ultimately hone their first set. A lot of comedians are on the try-out bill for months before they are elevated to a paid set. I only had one shot and I remember it like it was yesterday.

I had been married and living in Alice Springs for about four years, and ever since being involved in an amateur production of *Godspell* in the early eighties I had been loosely regarded as a performer around town. I'd been treading the boards between having babies – nothing professional, just community cabarets and emceeing the odd fete or fashion parade.

After emceeing one such cabaret I was given the nod by Shane Stone, the then Northern Territory arts minister to apply to his office for a grant to assist my career. But therein lay the problem: I had no idea what my career was. It was the director of the Araluen Arts Centre, Christine Dunstan, who pointed out that what I was doing at Witchetty's was a thing called stand-up. I had never seen a stand-up artist in the flesh so I took it as gospel and successfully applied for an arts grant to travel to Melbourne and observe comedy.

'Oh my God, what have I done?' I might well have asked myself that question, but I don't remember much more than the fear. I was in the front bar of the Star and Garter Hotel in South Melbourne with ten minutes between me and my first appearance in a stand-up comedy venue. With my $600 from the Northern Territory government I had done the unthinkable and left three babies under four at home with my husband and caught a bus to Melbourne, armed with a letter of introduction from the director of the Arts Centre and about four jokes.

Looking back on my career, which has had some exhausting peaks and some dazzling troughs, what I honour most is the courage of that first step. I would like to go back to that terrified young woman in the front bar of that pub puffing furiously on her Benson & Hedges and say thanks – thanks for starting.

That night I met my first ever stand-up, a big bloke called Brad Oaks. Someone from the bar directed me to him. He seemed to be running the night and I have since fathomed that Brad's initial friendliness was an instrumental moment in my expedition into the laugh business. Had it not been for Brad Oaks and his instinctive inclusion of me I believe without a doubt that I would have turned and headed for the hills, or in my case, the Macdonnell Ranges by way of a McCafferty's bus.

'So you're the stand-up from the Territory?'

I don't know how I replied but I've got a fair idea it would have gone something like this: 'Er, yeah . . . not really . . . well, I'm just starting out . . . I've got a letter . . . er, I'm just here to watch.'

'Jeez, I would have thought the first stand-up from the Northern Territory would have been a ten-foot truckie, but it's a girl! Want to get up and do ten?'

I immediately hid my fear, took a deep breath and said, 'Sure.'

So it was done. I was about to do a ten-minute set of stand-up in a real stand-up club in Melbourne, and there was only really one problem: I didn't have ten minutes of stand-up.

I spent the remaining time before my slot jotting down ideas and trying to memorise them. I remember the emcee Bob Franklin introducing me, and then stumbling onto the stage. I talked about trams, caesareans and clothes, and I dare say it was a very inexpert performance. I remember being horrified that one of my legs went off on its own tangent and shook uncontrollably for the whole time. But meanwhile something great happened. The audience laughed – not gut-busting guffaws by any stretch but they laughed and they liked me. I was hooked, and even though I was vaguely aware that I had a long way to go, I had solicited what I wanted, maybe even what I needed. I would be a stand-up.

That night brought back the memory of my first ever solo public performance. I was about ten years old, in the lounge bar of the Warooka Hotel just near my home, and I sang 'Molly Malone' to a smattering of locals at the insistence of Mr Kennedy, the Irish publican and my parents' great friend. I almost forgot myself that afternoon, concentrating on the lyrics, but more so on Mr Kennedy. It was the look of pure joy on his face that spurred me on to sing for him with all that I had and to do my very best.

I only realised much later that performance is at its finest when you abandon your ego, harness joy from your audience and ride it like a wave. That joy rebounds back to you, the performer, and I am, and will possibly forever be, addicted to that joy.

* * *

I'm sitting in a stairwell. It feels like my tonsils are beating, but it's my heart up high in my throat. I'm about to go on stage in Edinburgh, Scotland, and it's a stage like no other. They say it's the toughest gig a comic can do. I've been in the audience myself a couple of times in the last month and it's not unlike being a spectator at a rodeo.

Out comes the comedian and if nothing else he tries to stay on the horse and not get injured or worse. Tonight it feels like the Coliseum, the audience are the Romans and they're hungry for the Christians.

The venue is called Late 'n' Live and it operates every night during the Edinburgh Fringe. Hundreds of people pour in at twelve-thirty. They've either seen shows, performed in shows or just spilled out of the pub, but they are definitely here for sport above art. This is the room of heckling and the home of no mercy, and somehow I've ended up next on stage.

Even stranger, I suppose, is that somehow I've found myself to be a stand-up comedian and what seems a million miles from home in the first place. But I'll get to that later.

* * *

'You suck!'

'Get off!'

'Yer nowt funnay!'

A very young Russell Brand is on stage doing it tough and the emcee Adam Hills has just rushed past me and whispered, 'Fiona, they're a really ugly crowd. I'll try and shut them up before I bring you on.'

The noise from the audience is frightening and Russell is as pissed off as the crowd and has just thrown something at them.

Meanwhile someone from the front row has hurled a glass at him and luckily missed his head. So here I am, crouched on the stairs just left of the stage as this young English comic stomps past me and a wave of shattered glass follows.

'Ladies and gentlemen, our next act is all the way from Alice Springs, Australia. Please make her welcome . . . Fiona O'Loughlin!'

I can't go out there . . . not yet . . . there's a whopping piece of glass stuck through my pants and into my thigh . . . I take a deep breath and yank it out, then make my way to the stage and grab hold of the mike with sweat pouring down my neck and blood pouring down my leg.

* * *

I'd been in Scotland for three weeks with my show *Fiona and Her Sister (and some guy)*. I had left Alice Springs and my five kids behind on a Thursday morning and cried all the way to Darwin. Partly because I wouldn't see them again for a whole month, but mostly because I'd left my passport on the kitchen table.

I've never been a great sufferer of guilt but I was uneasy for most of the trip. Of all the performance genres, stand-up comedy must be one of the hardest to justify, especially if you're a wife and mother. Stand-up is so essentially self-oriented and self-absorbed. Sure, it's an art form, but at the end of the day it's just you and a microphone talking about yourself and the world according to you. I'm sure if I were a dancer with the Australian Ballet or the Minister for Defence I wouldn't have spent such a large part of the long journey trying to validate my mission.

What sort of a mother would I be if I ignored my hankerings anyway? I'm setting a fantastic example to all of my kids: follow your heart's desires and take risks. I'm not abandoning them forever, am I? They're all safe. It's only a month. My mother played golf three days a week and it didn't hurt any of us.

My thoughts were interrupted about an hour out of Kuala Lumpur when the pilot announced that we were having technical difficulties and then mentioned something about circling for a couple of hours to dump fuel and then attempting a re-land in Kuala Lumpur.

This plane is going to crash and now my kids are motherless. How did she die? On her way to Scotland to tell jokes about them.

I took the subsequent safe landing as a very favourable sign from the gods. Eventually I was in Edinburgh and didn't have time for self-recrimination. Anyway, I had a show to put on – me and about two thousand other performers.

The city swells from five hundred thousand to a million people during the Edinburgh Fringe Festival and you really have to see it to believe it. Every few yards there's a performer shamelessly handing out fliers to promote his or her show and everywhere you look there are jugglers, musicians, singers, poets, comics and dancers gigging in the streets.

The backdrop to this mayhem of colour and noise is ancient Edinburgh, grey-cobbled and awesome. Literally two worlds collide: one of the oldest cities in the world, with its architecture and castles demanding tribute to its age of tradition, playing host to an international fusion of the most contemporary of performing arts.

I'm here because I too have a story to tell, and I'll tell it via stand-up.

CHAPTER 1

WAROOKA DAYS

Our house in Alice Springs is chock-a-block with photos, thanks to my husband Chris and other friends and relatives. Personally, I have never owned a camera nor taken a shot that was good enough to frame. I have, however, since I was very young made memories and frozen them like stills in my head whenever I've come upon a moment that mattered.

Forgive my evasion of exact times and dates in this memoir because unfortunately I don't have a head for it. I don't have a head for a lot of things. Right at this moment I would not be able to lay my hands on my own birth certificate in under thirty minutes if the future of the planet depended on it. I have lived a disordered chaos for more than forty years but I remember with clarity my baby brother Justin's dimpled legs when he walked up the passage for the first time, and I can still see my grandmother's hands in a twisted tangle of bulging veins and rosary beads at her only son's funeral.

And the memory of when I was thirteen years old in the living room at Warooka, South Australia: the theme song from *M.A.S.H.* just beginning, and the warm, sweet smell of a summer breeze hand in hand with daylight saving wafting through the sunroom, knocking on the screen door like a favourite cousin coming for a sleepover. We had a cold collation for dinner that night: leftover corned beef, beetroot, chicken wings, potato salad and button mushrooms from a can. Mum was, and still is, a first-rate cook and would never have fashioned such a graceless meal, but she had not long had her seventh baby and I was the chef that night. My first culinary effort – and everybody ate it.

I don't know why that is one of my happiest memories, but I guess I felt useful. I guess I was just plain happy. But I have never eaten a button mushroom or heard the theme song from *M.A.S.H.* again without a sense of happy recall.

Dad had land in and around the town, and commuted to his various blocks each day. Most of our properties were within about a five-mile radius except for some scrub land at the 'bottom end' that was some twenty miles south of Warooka. We lived in the town in a 'modern' brick house on a huge block on the eastern corner of Warooka. It was largely designed by my mother when she was only twenty years old. I look at the house now and marvel at the talent she had. My parents still live in that same house, and while it isn't and never was a grand place it has stood the test of time and is a pretty classy (albeit eclectic) home.

There were two huge open-space living areas, each with raked ceilings and a wall of windows, a large kitchen that still never seemed to be large enough for nine people and a beautiful breezeway that divided the business end of the house from the sleeping quarters – and that is where my appreciation for the house ended.

Three bedrooms and one toilet. What were they thinking? Two young Catholics, building a house and starting a family in 1959. Unfortunately, neither God nor the stork had given any thought to numbers or the distribution of sexes when they generously delivered seven bundles of joy to the Tahenys in Baker Street, Warooka. (We didn't actually have a street number. We were, and still are, the only house in Baker Street.)

The girls in the house drew the short straw, and all five of us were allocated one room. It only ever had four beds, but Emily spent her first three years in a cot and then a foldout bed at the foot of Mum and Dad's (this not only served to lighten the load in the 'girls' room' by a small margin but quite possibly had the added advantage of preventing an eighth Taheny). And by the time 'Milly' was finally promoted to the 'girls' room' at least two of us were away at boarding school.

We rotated sleeping quarters continuously as kids and, having never had an exclusive cubiculum for more than a year or two, any bed was very much a temporary thing. In fact as we all got older and came and went from Mum and Dad's, the reality was that we were always one bed short.

* * *

My memory can serve me uncannily well at times but it can also cruelly let me down. I lost my laptop three times in the writing of this book and I would like to begin by thanking two taxi drivers in Melbourne and an unknown man in Sydney who lived next door to my sister Emily and found that one in Upper Pitt Street.

I do know that I was born in Adelaide in 1963 so maybe that is just as good a place to begin as anywhere.

Calvary Hospital is a pretty handsome two-storey building overlooking the North Adelaide golf course and I enjoyed all of its benefits when I had four of my own babies there: a private room, menus for every meal, an ensuite bathroom and wine with dinner. We had a balcony room where the midwives in white uniforms came running at the touch of a buzzer. I remember talking out loud to my own six-day-old baby girl in 1988 as I was packing up ready to be discharged.

'You poor little bugger. You thought you lived in a castle with servants, didn't you? Well, the party's over, baby girl. We live in an ex-housing commission house in Alice Springs. It does have a nice golf course, but you can't see it from our place.'

Legend has it that I was born smoking. I was Mum's third baby, and before she married Dad, Mum was a nurse at Calvary herself. During my delivery the midwife (who was one of Mum's old nursing mates) discovered that I was a footling breech.

'Oh shit, Deirdre,' she said. 'There's a pair of purple feet sticking out. Here, you have a cigarette and I'll go get the doctor.'

I was the only baby Mum had that was born feet first and she told me after I'd had a thirty-hour labour of my own that

I had been her easiest delivery. I wondered if maybe all babies should enter the world feet first to give the midwife something to tug on.

The nuns at Calvary sewed a blue smocked dress for me with a tiny round collar and little puffed sleeves, which I probably wore home from hospital. I remember Mum showing it to me when I was about twelve and I couldn't take my eyes off that little dress. It's a rare thing in a big family to have an heirloom all to yourself and I was absolutely in awe of it (although deep down I have to admit I would have preferred pink).

I came home to a three-year-old sister Genevieve and a twenty-month-old brother Richard and enjoyed fourteen months of baby status until I was joined by Catherine.

Justin followed three years later and Sarah rounded things off a year or so after him.

That is until eight years down the track when the seventh Taheny was born – little Emily Brigid.

* * *

The first six of us were pretty much born in three sets of pairs and I was forever maddened that neither Cate nor I had been born male, which would have made the Tahenys exactly like the Brady Bunch, except, of course, for their manicured house and garden, a housekeeper, a mum in hotpants and a dad with a permanent wave.

In my childhood I wanted everything in my reality to be more like it was in the movies or on the telly. Consequently I was perpetually disappointed. Dad was and still is a cereal and sheep farmer and we lived in a small, nearly coastal town on the

Yorke Peninsula in South Australia – a town so small that one day during the Easter holidays, when I was about twelve, my sister Cate suggested that we walk up the main street to 'see if we could see a stranger'.

There was one pub on the corner opposite the bank, two general stores, one service station, one garage, one butcher, one haberdashery and a deli.

Looking back now I guess Warooka had more than its fair share of characters. Mary Koop from the service station was one of the nicest ladies in town. She wore pleated skirts that she teamed with grey bobby socks and leather sandals.

'Hellooooooooo!' She always half sang the same greeting as she waddled out to fill your car. We used to call her 'Lazy Mary' because she never seemed to take a day off, or even a lunch break for that matter, and would obligingly open the shop at any hour for our little community. 'Try Mary Koop's' was an option for anyone in town needing anything from a pint of milk to a double A battery at inconvenient times.

I absolutely adored Sammy Murdoch, who owned the strangest little shop that I have ever seen before or since, directly across from the pub in the main street. Long before the Mitre 10s of this world, Sammy's shop was not much more than a yard and a half wide, about twelve feet long and was completely made up of hundreds and hundreds of little drawers behind the big, long wooden counter.

You could literally buy one nail, one bolt or one screw from Sammy's shop and I have no idea how he made a profit. Not being in the market personally for bolts, nails or screws, I, and just about every other kid in town, would wander into

Sammy's shop at some time during the week to say hello to Sammy and be given two cents to spend on lollies up at Mrs Koop's service station.

'Shaky Smith' was another lovely local, and to this day I don't know why he shook or why the whole town thought it not inappropriate to refer to him as 'Shaky Smith' in his presence.

'Morning, Shaky.'

'G'day, Shaky.'

The first time I met Shaky Smith was in the grocery store and he and Dad were talking about a headline in that day's *Advertiser*. I was a bit intrigued by the man's heaving shoulders, which seemed to have a life of their own, causing his arms not so much to flap about as jiggle uncontrollably.

Dad and I were in the ute heading home when I asked the stupid question: 'Why does that man shake so much?'

'I don't know. Maybe because his name is Shaky Smith.'

The Johnsons were Jehovah's Witnesses and lived in the centre of town right next door to the grocery store that was diagonally across from the pub. Most of the kids in Warooka were nothing short of intolerant and cruel to the Johnsons, myself included.

Indeed it was a creepy house with a massive fig tree in the front yard with roots that burst through the cement like buried anacondas. The tree was so huge it gave the old stone house an almost black shade, and though I never set foot in the Johnsons' abode I knew without a doubt that it was exactly the same as *The Munsters* on TV. The Johnsons must have been very poor as they went without shoes most of the time. From memory there were five kids and every day for the Johnsons must have been torment. Ignored by the whole town for the most part, they were openly referred to as the 'Jovvas' on the school bus morning and afternoon, and then spent the weekends accompanying their mother and having doors firmly closed in their faces as they attempted to spread the word.

Without a doubt there were worse things in Warooka than being Catholic. We lived in a mainly Protestant community, and when I truly look at it for what it was I'm pretty sure that the Catholics I knew were every bit as wary of Protestants as vice versa. But except for the unspeakably rotten treatment of the Jehovah's Witnesses, I don't believe anyone set out to actively persecute anyone else on a religious basis.

We were caught between two eras, I guess, no longer with an argument but with a lingering wariness from past generations. I remember believing that the Freemasons meetings held in the town hall hatched plans to eventually get rid of all Catholics, and a girl who lived up the road told me on the school bus one morning that she couldn't be friends with me anymore because of all the blood I'd drunk from Jesus. Suffice to say there was not much more drama than childish misunderstandings on both sides. So much was to change, and the change was rapid and wonderful by the time I reached adulthood. In one generation the intolerance had wiped itself out between my experience of white Yorke Peninsula and our differences. Sadly, white and black Australia had barely gotten started.

Mrs Lennell owned the deli, and she had one eye that came considerably further out of her head than the other one. I used to be freaked out by Mrs Lennell's eye and tried not to look at it if it was my turn to run up to the deli and buy a packet of Viscount cigarettes for Mum.

We lived on a corner of the main street running through Warooka and Mrs Hough lived across the road from us. I liked Mrs Hough a lot. She was a painter and had a grown-up daughter called Jenny who was an artist as well and a son called Jimmy who never seemed to tire of playing 'What's the time, Mr Wolf?' with any little Taheny who wandered over to their place. Mrs Hough didn't look like the other ladies in Warooka. She had long painted fingernails and sometimes wore bright silky scarves in her hair like movie stars did.

I remember visiting Mrs Hough once in a new hand-me-down dress from one of the Kennedy girls from the pub. We were heading to Maitland to visit the dentist, which was about a fifty-mile drive, and I think we were dropping off baby Sarah at Mrs Hough's to be babysat.

I detested the dress I was wearing and had been complaining all morning about the really stiff net petticoat under the skirt that pricked me every time I sat down.

We pulled up out the front of Mrs Hough's and Mum told us to wait on the front verandah while she went inside. We rarely saw the inside of a house when we were kids. We laugh about it still, and have a saying that we grew up with our faces pressed against glass panes. Back then kids weren't far above cats and dogs in the pecking order, and one of Mum's favourite catchcries was 'Kids outside please!'

Mrs Hough wanted Mum to have a listen to a new record she had bought, so the wait for us on the verandah was long enough for me to start a fight with someone. I don't remember if it was Richard or Cate, but by the time Mum had finished listening to Simon and Garfunkel's new single 'Bridge over Troubled Water' I had been pushed into Mrs Hough's garden, right on top of a cactus plant. Mum had seen none of this and when we piled into the car I screamed with pain when I sat down, at which point Mum just about threatened me with my life if she heard 'one more word about that damn petticoat'.

About twice a year Mum and Mrs Kennedy would pack a tribe of kids into the car and head to Maitland for a day of fillings and extractions. The trips to the dentist in Maitland were arduous excursions enough, even without half a cactus plant stuck to your arse.

Mrs Kennedy was Mum's best friend and she and her husband ran the Warooka pub. Mrs Kennedy had two daughters before she had been widowed young and then married an Irishman called Michael Kennedy. After they were married they bought the Warooka Hotel and went on to have four more girls and one boy, Michael Patrick, who was the youngest and the same age as me.

Unlike country pubs nowadays, the Warooka Hotel heaved with customers every weekend and kept up a steady trade even during the week. Local farmers, fishermen, and the football, cricket and netball teams all gathered there – it really was the heartbeat of our town. During the holiday seasons the pub needed elastic walls to keep up with the onslaught of city visitors who came in droves (and still do) to their shacks all along the coastline of the Southern Yorke Peninsula.

The Warooka pub nowadays is a much more temperate locale, and I have no doubt our pub's glory days came to an end (as they did for many others) with the introduction of drink-driving laws. Not that anyone could argue with such laws. Our community had certainly suffered its share of heartache with the premature deaths of more than a few behind the wheel with a belly full of beer.

But change always comes at a cost, and for publicans in the early eighties, particularly rural publicans in towns with no taxis, the price was high. I still suffer the stab of nostalgia for times gone by when I step into the Warooka Hotel these days.

While the exterior is the same as it always was, the inside has been 'tavernised'. There are archways where doors used to be and laminate where there once was timber. Fortunately Alby Goods and Kevin Detman are still in the front bar, ready for a yak and a laugh as they have been since I can remember. But Alby has to step outside for a smoke these days and shut the door on the hubbub behind him. And the babel, which once was made up of booming conversations in shouts and laughter, has been replaced with the endless sounds of Sky TV and poker machines.

As much as Mrs Kennedy seemed to revel in her role as the hotelier hostess, she loved the trips to the dentist as much as Mum did. It was nothing short of an outing for them and they made the most of a rare day off from the pub and housework. Mum had been born and bred in Maitland and Mrs Kennedy had lived there previously herself, and so while we were all having molars pulled out of our heads or amalgams put in, our mothers would either be catching up with someone at the Maitland Hotel or ducking in to visit the Mannings, the Harrises, the Darmodys or the Honners.

At the close of dentist hours we would usually call in on Pam and Bob Honner, who lived on a farm just outside of Maitland with their eight sons. The grown-ups would have a great catch-up while an assortment of Taheny and Kennedy children with swollen faces sat in uncomfortable silence staring back at the eight faces of the 'Bob Honners', as we used to call them.

Mrs Kennedy and Mum were never overly keen to hit the road for home on the dentist days and we invariably suffered in silence until well after dark. One visit was cut short though when my brother Richard had half his ear bitten off by one of the 'Bob Honners' dogs and we had to go home via the Maitland Hospital to have it sewn back on.

I have a throwaway line that I use on stage: 'People are having fewer children these days and they must mean more to them.' While it's a flippant thing to say, it makes me laugh when I think back to Richard's dangling ear.

'Mum! Richard's ear's half off!'

'See you at the wedding then, Pam.'

'Bye then, Deirdre. Thanks for calling in.'

'Mum! Oh my God, is it off? Is it off? Is my ear off?'

'Don't be ridiculous; of course it's not off. Genevieve, hold that towel on his head will you? Bye, Pam. Say goodbye to Aunty Pam, everyone.'

'Mum! There's blood everywhere. He's got blood on me!'

'Oh for heaven's sake, would everyone please be quiet! Bye, Pam! Thanks again for the towel.'

I grew up with relations all over the Yorke Peninsula. My mum was an Honner and Dad is a Taheny, and both families originally came from Ireland to the Yorke Peninsula three generations ago. Consequently first, second, and even third cousins are easily identified.

If you're an Honner and you live on the Yorke Peninsula then you're related to all the other Honners somehow and the same thing applies to Tahenys.

These days I really do appreciate the beauty of the Yorke Peninsula, but as a kid I liked very little about my environment and I would look out of the bus window every morning on the thirteen-mile trip to school with contempt for everything in my vista.

Despite Mum's protests I read far too many Enid Blyton books. I stashed Enid Blyton editions under my mattress like a teenage boy hiding *Penthouse* magazines. Mum worked in a school library for years and has never been a big fan of Enid Blyton. She insisted we read Australian narratives but I couldn't get enough of the adventures of the Secret Seven and the Famous Five and the English landscape. And if one absolutely had to live in the country, in my opinion, it could at least be like the countryside in those books.

I wanted brooks, knolls, mountains, forests, willow trees and streams. But to my eternal frustration all I got was the Peesey swamp (a rift valley of salt lakes), gnarled old windblown tea trees, Mallee scrub, flat paddocks and 'the boy's waterhole'.

'The boy's waterhole' was a natural spring on my dad's property, supposedly named after a boy who had drowned in it a hundred years ago or more, and when I first heard about it I made a plan to take a picnic there one day. In my imagination it was an enchanting pond surrounded by green grass and maybe a big old shady tree.

Except of course for the dead boy at the bottom of it, 'the boy's waterhole' was a very romantic place in my imagination and when I finally did hustle my dad into taking me there I was more than a bit disappointed. You can't really even see the water for the long bull grass on top and around it. It looked more like a booby trap billabong than anything else and I remember thinking no wonder the poor little bastard drowned.

The southern end of the Yorke Peninsula boasts some of the most ruggedly beautiful coastline in Australia but I never felt any real connection to the ocean as a kid. The peninsula was predominantly settled by farmers and I've only just noticed in recent years how so many original homesteads were built facing towards roads rather than the ocean. Had fishing been the primary industry in settlement times I guess you would see a greater homage to the sea reflected in the positioning of those homesteads, but being grain farmers our forefathers must have given their ultimate nod to the highway.

* * *

There is a theory that a career in stand-up is the perfect antidote for an unhappy childhood. I loathed childhood but not because my circumstances were particularly miserable. I was just in a continual state of frustration at the lack of options and privileges available to a minor. To this day I've never quite gotten over the thrill of being grown-up. Simple pleasures like not having to share my milkshake with anyone and reading till 3 a.m. still give me enormous satisfaction.

I didn't much like most of the adults in my world. Mothers and fathers had wooden spoons and the nuns had leather straps. Trouble was always just around the corner, and I grew up in an era where kids had very little power, which was fine if you had safe parents, but I saw kids who could have done with a much fairer go.

I had a kind of justice barometer inside of me and I knew that it wasn't right that the man down the road belted the hell out of his kid with a plank of wood, and I knew that another man up the road was a possible pervert and kids shouldn't be in the house with him alone. And without a shadow of a doubt I knew that a lady in the next town who made her kids line up naked outside of the house to wait for their turn in the shower after having thrashed a couple of them with a belt was a stark raving lunatic.

Just a sign of the times maybe? My memories sense it to be more sinister than that. Kids certainly have a louder voice nowadays and they're twice as precocious for it. Maybe all that my generation has done is swap physical safety for moral safety, but whenever one of my kids ramped up to an age when they could scream at me and stomp through the house slamming doors, a part of me did want to strangle them but a much bigger part of me was inclined to celebrate their liberty.

The world may well be going to hell in a handbasket, but I really believe that the liberation of children is one of the great unobserved revolutions of our era. 'Leave them alone and they will come home, wagging their tails behind them.' Hear, hear! I say.

I wanted the universe to hurry up and come and get me as a kid. I had a morbid dread of nothing happening, and for a lot of the time nothing much did happen in that windy little town. Mum was flat out cooking, cleaning and looking after kids and Dad was flat out farming.

Life was a monotonous business at times but every now and then I would hear the sound that I loved the most – gravel, under the tyres of a car in the driveway. My head would dart up like a Jack Russell's at the sound of car tyres. Who knows? It might be visitors. It might also just be the milk lady on her milk run and we'd fish around in Mum's purse for some change and head out with the dented old metal pot and ask for 'Six pints please, Mrs Trengrove.'

But it might be visitors.

It might also just be our Great-Aunty Mon, who rolled her Rs like an English baroness and never got out of her car but just tooted the horn and waited for someone to come outside and take a message for Dad.

'Tell your father that therrre are some lambs out on the Yorketown rrroad just acrrross from the Detmarrrs place.'

But it might be visitors.

It might be our grown-up second cousin Michael, who worked with Dad sometimes. He would stand in the doorway of the kitchen scratching his head, giving Dad a rundown of his day in the shearing shed or out in the paddock, and just about every second word was 'fuck'.

Apart from the odd 'bloody' or 'shit' from Mum at times of heightened botheration, nobody swore in our house with endorsement back then, so it was beyond thrilling when Michael Taheny stopped by. One morning we were in the middle of saying the morning prayer when Michael's six-foot-plus frame sauntered into his position in the entrance of the kitchen.

'Oh my Jesus, through the most pure heart of Mary, we offer you our prayers, works, joys and sufferings of this day for all the intentions of your divine . . .'

'Yeah, Denis, the fence by the boy's waterhole is pretty fucken rooted, and I reckon the shearing shed roof has shat itself.'

Us six kids must have stood there with our eyes open as wide as our mouths, and for my money Michael Taheny was nearly as good as a visitor.

Two of the most hospitable people I know, my parents Denis and Deirdre would invite Gaddafi inside if he stood on their doorstep. I loved it when people dropped by because the routine stopped in an instant. More chairs would be squeezed around the kitchen table and Dad would hand around beers or open a bottle of wine and Mum would say 'stay for dinner' or 'stay for lunch', and I would sit as near as I could to the action and hope for what I always hoped for: that 'funny' might happen.

One night something even better than 'funny' happened. Ludicrous, you might say, and downright flabbergasting. Mr Kennedy, who rarely left his post behind the front bar at the pub, had wandered down to our place after closing with a visitor in tow and more than a handful of locals bringing up the rear to witness the spectacle.

In through the front door he walked with none other than the most famous premier South Australia had ever known. The Right Honourable Don Dunstan was standing in our living room! We abandoned the kitchen table this time and chair upon chair was brought into the lounge while we all stared gobsmacked at the man in the safari suit who we only ever saw on the telly and whom our cousin Michael referred to as that 'fucking idiot poofter'.

The staunchest of Liberal voters, Mum and Dad proceeded to kill the fatted calf, so to speak, for their number-one political enemy, and the party was on. Beers, wine, speeches and recitals went on until the wee hours and culminated in Don Dunstan playing our piano while everybody sang along.

Years later, I had a flashback to that night and for a moment thought I might have imagined the whole thing.

'Mum, did Don Dunstan come to our house once?'

'Yes, it was hilarious wasn't it, Denis?'

'Uhuh.'

'Why was he in Warooka?'

'It was the year Mr Kennedy stood for the Labor Party, so he came to support him.'

'Mr Kennedy stood for the Labor Party?'

'Yes, of course he did. Mr Kennedy loved the Labor Party. He never had a chance of winning, though.'

'How come?'

'Turned out he was never an Australian citizen.'

Another interesting visitor turned up one day but was nowhere near as warmly welcomed by Mum.

A circus had come to Warooka and as far as I know it was the first and only circus we'd ever been host to. The excitement sadly didn't reach as far as the Denis Tahenys, as for some reason none of us were allowed to go. I'd say that it probably wasn't so much the cost of the tickets but more that Mum and Dad were aware that it must have been a pretty lame circus if it had found its way this far off the beaten track, and from memory everyone took the disappointment in their stride except for my selfish self.

I hated missing out on anything, and still do for that matter, but luckily a part of the circus came to us the morning after the town had paid to see it.

'Oh shit, Denis.'

We were all at the kitchen table and Mum was standing at the stove staring out at our front drive.

'There's a bloody camel in the garden.'

And sure enough there was a massive one-humped beast eating Mum's tulips not six feet from where we were all sitting. An extraordinary sight, as you can imagine, but even more extraordinary, don't you think, was Mum's reaction? Never before had any one of us kids laid eyes on a real live camel and yet Mum simply sighed heavily as if a camel in the garden was nothing more than yet another irritant in her already overloaded day.

'Shoo it out will you, someone? Quickly please, this porridge is burning.'

* * *

Mum and Dad had a lot of funny friends and relations, and in a way I started my apprenticeship in stand-up comedy around that cramped kitchen table. All families have their traditions and I guess ours was and still is the telling of, and listening to, stories around the table.

I didn't have a lot to say myself until I was in my teens but I watched and listened not just to the storyteller but also to the audience. I found an instinct for the rhythm of stories and I could tell when someone's anecdote was about to go belly-up.

I remember being as young as ten and thinking if Aunty Pat had just told the story about the dead kitten differently she would have gotten a bigger laugh. She should have started out with the bad smell coming from the car shed and not given away the bit about the fur under the bonnet of the ute until the end.

I recognised great comic timing in my dad at a very early age, and yet he was regarded as the quiet one out of him and Mum. I came home furious after my first day in a public school when I'd learnt about evolution for the first time in Year 8 science.

'Dad? How come nobody ever told me we came from the apes? Apes! Did you know we came from apes?'

He didn't even look up from the *Stock Journal* he was reading.

'Well, you can speak for yourself.'

My dad's always been funny, and yet I've never seen him once hijack a conversation. My two brothers have inherited the same virtue and I value them for it. To be a good storyteller demands that you be an even better listener, and Denis Taheny has always been proof of that.

I have a snapshot in my head of Dad at the kitchen table in the week leading up to Cate's wedding. He was having his breakfast alone with Biddy, his first granddaughter, on his lap and she was babbling away in sixteen-month-old-speak.

'Is that so?'

I stopped short of the kitchen and spied the scene from the next room.

'Yaggabuddagubbadoggabuddabun.'

'You don't say?'

He was giving her his full attention and reacting to her as if they were having an in-depth discussion on farming techniques.

'Buddigabuggadubalubligum.'

'Yes, well, that does make sense when you think about it.'

'Unduggubuggugudduyung.'

'Indeed and indeed, and as I said before, we had one of them once but the wheels fell off.'

We loved nothing more than one of Dad's stories, especially when he or we accidentally stumbled across one we'd never heard before, like the one about him and a friend going to the pictures when they were teenagers and Dad genuflecting in the aisle and his mate flying right over the top of him. Or the very first time he ever went to see the theatre.

He was only sixteen and along with his classmates had gone to see a production of *Macbeth*. His mate had never seen live theatre before and yelled out to one of the actors at the height of the suspense, 'Watch out! Watch out! The bloke behind you's got a knife!'

Some of Dad's stories were just plain old interesting more than funny and I was all ears when he told us about his first taste of Coca-Cola.

'I was on my way back to boarding school on the bus, it was just before the war ended and the bus stopped at the Port Wakefield service station. I'd heard a lot about this black drink from America and couldn't wait to taste it for myself.'

'Did you like it?'

'I thought it was the most delicious thing I'd ever tasted in my whole life and I drank it all down in about two or three swallows. And as soon as the bus got to Adelaide I went straight to the nearest deli to buy myself another bottle.'

'Did you still like it?'

'Yep, even more than the first time. I drank it all down in a couple of seconds and you'll never guess what happened after that.'

'What?'

'I threw up all over the floor of the shop.'

* * *

One of my mother's best friends was particularly hilarious and could put an irreverent spin on just about anything. One afternoon they were having a wine when Margaret nudged Mum and pointed to her youngest child, who was falling asleep in front of the TV with her mouth slacked open, looking positively gaga.

'Have a look at that, Deirdre. That's old sperm and old eggs if ever I saw it.'

It's been hard to explain at times when I've come under fire for openly exposing my own maternal shortcomings on stage for laughs, but it's a culture I grew up with – a culture where therapy sessions didn't exist, self-help wasn't yet a catchphrase, and yet it truly did exist in the form of laughs and self-deprecation.

One of my enduring memories is of Mum and Mrs Kennedy, wine in hand, doubled over with laughter as they tried to stick Smarties back onto the melting icing of a birthday cake that was still hot from the oven. The cake was servicing all the

Kennedy and Taheny children who'd had a birthday anywhere near July, and I'm pretty sure Alice and Deirdre were thumbing it at 'better' mothers who wouldn't be caught dead putting on such a lame celebration.

They were laughing at themselves and not one of us kids had any complaints at all that day.

Though Alice and Deirdre only lived a few hundred metres from each other, it was hard for them to find the time to kick up their heels together as often as they'd have liked when we were little. Although about twice a year it was possible to get off the school bus and walk into an empty house with not a mother in sight. We would look to our eldest sister Genevieve for an explanation.

'Where's Mum?'

'I'm not sure.'

'Maybe it's St Patrick's Day.'

'Yeah.'

'Or Melbourne Cup?'

It didn't matter if it was St Patrick's Day or the Melbourne Cup as the end result was usually the same: Mum and Mrs Kennedy around the piano up at the pub on their third or fourth rendition of 'Danny Boy', joyously downing a drink or five.

But there is one memory of Mum that I never understood for years. Once a week she would head to Yorketown for a pretty big grocery shop and not every time, not even nearly every time, but every so often she would sit in the car on her return and do nothing. For the longest time, she sat in the car and was statue still, doing nothing.

I was happy for her to stay in the car for as long as she wanted. The longer she was out of the house the longer I had to fight with Richard, antagonise Genevieve or help myself to more than my allotted two Scotch Finger biscuits, because as soon as the front door banged her re-entry, order was restored at once. But I did wonder what she was doing sitting so still, doing nothing.

'Mum? Mum! MUM! What are you doing?'

Fast forward to 1999 and it's me sitting in the car and Biddy is knocking on the window. I've just come back from Coles.

'Mum? Why are you just sitting in the car?'

'Go away!'

I'm crying, sitting in the car, doing nothing. Because the car is warm, and quiet, and peaceful. Inside the house Tess is screaming at Henry to give her back her pencil case and there's a load of washing on the kitchen table that's all turned pink from a red footy sock and little Bertie is standing on a chair looking at me through a window bawling from an ear infection that should have been seen to by a doctor but I was too tired to organise it and Mary-Agnes is still in her afternoon sleep which is Okay for now but that means she'll be awake until eleven o'clock and I have no idea what to cook for dinner or how I'm going to keep everything going until I can crawl into bed and my immediate chore is to lug eight bags of groceries inside with me and so I don't move.

* * *

Sunday mass at Warooka was in St Brigid's church, which was about a two-minute walk from our place. We never walked, though; it was always a mad rush in the car as, much to Dad's eternal frustration, we are one of the tardiest families on the planet.

St Brigid's was such a tiny church it was more like a chapel and we always sat in the very front row on the left.

Aunty Mon sat directly behind us, the Brian Tahenys about five pews from the front on the right and the Detmars across the aisle and one pew down from us.

Our great-aunty played the organ, my dad took up the collection and often he or Mum did the readings. Richard, Justin, Stephen Fooks or John Taheny were the altar boys and for about eight years our great-uncle was the parish priest.

We sang hymns like 'Faith of Our Fathers', 'Sweet Sacrament Divine' and 'Firmly I Believe and Truly', but my all-time favourite was 'We Stand for God and for His Glory'.

Sarah used to call it the Catholic war cry and we'd do our best to sing it and not get caught laughing and doing Nazi impressions at the same time.

Laughing was a major taboo during mass because of the presence of the Blessed Sacrament, but the temptation was usually too much for me, especially if Justin or Richard was serving on the altar. They would kneel sideways with their profiles to us and, since we were in the front pew and the church was so small, we were only inches away. I would just about pull my face inside out trying to make them laugh.

If I had no luck with the boys I had a stock standard boredom buster that would work on Sarah, and later Emily, every time: singing hymns in my own made-up form of Russian, just loud enough for them to hear and just quiet enough to get away with it.

The highlight of mass for me was watching people going to and from communion, which is another fairly large transgression. At that time of the mass you are either supposed to be praying for worthiness to take communion yourself or be praying in thanks for just having received it.

I used to pray thanks in record time and then peer through my fingers at the procession to see what everyone was wearing. I was particularly interested in what the Kennedy girls had on. The Tahenys were at the receiving end of all of the Kennedy girls' hand-me-downs, and one morning I was desperate at the sight of Julia Kennedy in a hideous horizontal-striped green and mission-brown dress that I forlornly estimated would be on my own back in about three years time.

One Sunday in the middle of mass there was a huge crash right behind us and then some of the heaviest breathing I'd ever heard. Genevieve grabbed me by the arm and warned me to keep facing the front.

'Don't look, Fiona. I think Aunty Mon just had a heart attack.'

I had no ability to resist looking and turned around to see my cousin Josephine with her head and neck slumped over a pew and one leg in the air. Genevieve was keen for information but kept her attention towards the altar. By now Uncle Brian and Mr Evans were carrying Josephine outside and we would have to wait until the end of mass to find out anything more.

'I think Josephine's dead.'

Mum told me to be quiet and face the front.

'She's not dead, you idiot. She fainted,' Genevieve informed me as we all stood around outside the church like we did every Sunday. Then Aunty Mon piped up for all the world to hear, 'Josephine is nearrrrly thirrrrteen. What a wonderful day for her. I suppose today is the day that Josephine has become a woman.'

Honestly, we may as well have all been wearing hooped dresses and holding parasols.

Poor Josephine, as if life wasn't embarrassing enough without the whole congregation knowing that you had your period. That story will give you some indication of how small our church was. Except for Easter and Christmas holidays anyone's absence was very noticeable.

I once made an innocent observation out loud after mass when we were all sitting down having Sunday breakfast: 'I notice Mrs Clarke doesn't go to mass much anymore.'

I was only about eleven at the time and was oblivious to how angry Dad was as I took another bite of my jam and toast. The jam and toast flew through the air seconds later when I noticed Dad had left his post at the top of the table and reappeared menacingly close to me and thumped the table and bellowed: 'How dare you! Mrs Clarke might go to mass in bloody Broken Hill for all you know and whether she does or she doesn't is none of your damn business!'

I've rarely ever heard my dad say a bad word about anyone. He didn't explode much when we were kids but when he did it was impressive. If any of us ever kept someone waiting he'd go off his rocker. One thing he particularly hated was people being 'put out' on his or his family's account and another thing he detested was gossip, which became clearly evident to me after the Mrs Clarke and the jam and toast incident. I'd like to say that I refrained from slander from that day forward but the truth is I simply never partook in defaming anyone within earshot of Dad for a long while to come.

* * *

In many ways time had stood still in our parish for nearly a hundred years and the 'faith' that had been brought out with our great-grandparents was handled with care and passed on with precision. There was never any talk in our house of missing mass. Even as teenagers the thought never crossed our minds because missing mass could put your soul in serious jeopardy, and I remember not believing my ears years later when we had two Irish girls come for a visit.

Mary and Trish were in their early twenties and had come to Warooka on their Australian holiday as Trish was a cousin of the Kennedys. Both girls had bunked down at our house one Saturday night. We'd had a big boozy evening around the kitchen table and the whole house groaned in a united hangover when we heard Father John toot his car horn outside our place on his way to the church, as he did every Sunday morning.

Father John's alert always initiated various permutations from Deirdre and Denis.

'Nine o'clock mass! Action stations, people!'

'Ten minutes, everybody!'

'Jaysus,' groaned Mary as she rolled over for more sleep. 'Do you people still go to fecken mass?'

I wanted to stab her in the eye with a crucifix.

CHAPTER 2

THE DENIS TAHENYS

While we had hundreds of relations, it was Mum's brother Maurice's family that we were the closest to. They lived fifty miles up the road from us and had six kids. We spent every Christmas with them, either at their place or ours.

There were forty-three first cousins and seventeen aunts and uncles, with the tally of second and third cousins too great to count. We had a spectacular family reunion on my mum's side a decade ago. The Honner family reunion was held at Wirrinna Holiday Resort east of Adelaide and the hotel was completely taken up with about three hundred Honners.

My great-great-grandfather Richard and his wife Sarah emigrated from Ireland in the late 1800s and had seven sons who have to this day always been referred to as 'the seven deadly sins'. We are all descendants of a seven deadly sin, and my great-grandfather Joseph was one of them. At the start of the reunion we were required to collect our name tags, and they were all colour coded so people could ascertain at a glance which 'seven deadly sin' a person had descended from.

Our family had purple name tags and I remember getting a great laugh from my first cousin Mary when we hooked up in one of the bars for a quick champagne. Mary (whose mother was my mother's sister) was also wearing purple as we shared the same deadly sin in our great-grandfather Joe. But problematically my Auntie Genevieve had married her second cousin Joseph Honner after having been emancipated from the convent and consequently Mary was also wearing a blue name badge as she was also a descendant of James Honner, yet another deadly sin.

'Well, that's a bit confusing, Mary.'

'Tell me about it. But I'm having heaps of fun. I just met my third cousin, she's gorgeous!'

'Who is she?'

'Me!'

The Honner reunion was an incredible weekend. The Friday night was set aside for very informal meeting, greeting and drinking. There were far too many people to get to know individually, but it is a weird reality to be in a lift with a total stranger but because of his red name tag you know that you share a great-great-grandfather.

Saturday was probably the most bizarre part of the weekend as there were seminars being held all afternoon right across the resort. Each seminar specialised in the life, times and history of Richard and Sarah Honner or one of their seven deadly sons.

Saturday night was a huge dinner, which I happily emceed, and then Sunday morning was a mass held in a nearby oval celebrated by Father Jim Honner, and then beer and wine and plenty of it until we all finally parted company and left what was probably the biggest gathering any of us would ever encounter again in the name of family.

* * *

My grandmother on my mother's side used to come and stay with us regularly. Her name was Madge Fitzgerald. We called her Gammy, and I thought Gammy knew just about everything – she read the paper from back to front every single day and was addicted to crosswords. Gammy spoke in riddles half the time, and had a cryptic kind of language all of her own. People who had put on a bit of weight had 'been in a good paddock', the very ill were referred to as being 'on the blink', and the barking mad were summed up in a simple sentence: 'Nothing wrong with him I don't think.' If someone had died then they'd 'gone to their next address' and I remember being with her at the gravesite at Father Tuit's burial and hearing her say to herself as we headed out of the cemetery, 'Well, that's that then. No further worries with him.'

Gammy had chronic emphysema for the last ten years of her life and I remember a hip operation that she survived despite being well aware that there was a fair chance she could die during the operation. A few of us were standing by with lumps in our throats as she was wheeled into theatre, and she gave us a wink and said not to worry. 'I've been to bigger shows than this.'

* * *

I come from a long line of matriarchs and have been handed down some curious expressions that certainly add a bit of colour to the daily rantings of an overworked and overtired primary caregiver of the female persuasion. My personal favourite is one of my own mother's, and it was always delivered without a hint of irony: 'I might not always be right but by hell I'm never wrong!'

Lately I've started to impress myself with what rolls off my tongue in the heat of the moment: 'I saw you on your bike this afternoon, Albert, going hell for Sydney at the wrong crossing!'

'No, Tess, we are not buying another movie channel and believe you me, NO does not mean MAYBE!'

'Well, somebody has traipsed mud all through the living room . . . See eggshells, suspect eggs is how I know.'

'Where's Henry off to? Goodness gracious gorgeous me, it's none of my beeswax but is he going like that? He's done his hair with the leg of a chair!'

What I loved about Gammy is that you could argue with her. She loved a debate and seemed to be one of the few adults I knew who didn't take it personally if you didn't agree with her.

We all adored Gammy and she used to come to stay at our place for about a month every year and spend most days parked at the end of the kitchen table with the sewing machine, either mending our clothes or making us new ones. After 5 p.m. she'd be accompanied by a brandy but her cigarettes were with her around the clock.

Gammy was no stranger to grief, having lost both her parents as a young adult and burying at least six of her thirteen siblings before she was fifty. Gammy had had a pretty tough life all round, as my grandfather had died at thirty-three, leaving her pregnant and the single mother of two girls. She married again in her forties but was widowed for a second time about eight years later.

She actually didn't start smoking until she was thirty-one. On his deathbed my grandfather suggested she take up smoking – 'It'll be good for your nerves' – and she took to it like a duck to water. Eventually her beloved Craven As claimed her life at seventy-nine.

Gammy was deeply religious but was also as devoted to fun as she was to God. She told me once that life is something you mustn't take too seriously, and that you mustn't ever forget to laugh. I was about nine at the time, and it was on that same day that I found out purgatory was actually the same state as hell in a religion lesson.

'Sister, when you get to heaven can you have anything you like?'

'Yes, dear.'

'A bike?'

'Yes, but you won't want a bike, dear.'

'All the lollies in the world?'

'You won't want all the lollies in the world.'

'What will you want, then?'

'Just to be with God.'

'Sister, is purgatory like a big long waiting room?'

'No, dear, purgatory is the same as hell.'

'Then why is it called purgatory?'

'Because you won't be there forever.'

'Do you know you won't be there forever?'

'Possibly.'

'Are there burning flames in hell?'

'Worse than burning flames, dear.'

'What's worse than burning flames?'

'Hell is like a baby screaming for the mother it can never have.'

Thank God Gammy was visiting that day. She didn't dispute anything that Sister had said when I relayed it to her after school but she did tell me that hell was reserved for especially wicked people and that she personally had never known anyone who'd gone there. Everything always seemed better when Gammy was around.

She lived in Maitland with Mum's brother Maurice and his family, and whenever I stayed at her place I would sleep in the spare Queen Anne bed in her room. Gammy had an alarm clock with hands that glowed in the dark and it had a really loud tick. To this day the sound of a ticking clock at night reminds me of being tucked up in a bed next to Gammy and feeling as safe as a person can be.

My grandmother on my dad's side lived much nearer to us and, like Gammy, had been dealt more than her fair share of bum cards. Nana was orphaned at three and separated from her three younger siblings to live first with an aunt and uncle, only to be relocated six months after that to yet another aunt and uncle who had no children of their own.

Nana is still alive and well at ninety-seven, and is the mother of seven surviving children with four deceased, grandmother of forty plus and great-grandmother of eighty-eight and still counting.

I was visiting her a few years back and asked her if the people who brought her up had been kind to her. She became uncharacteristically teary and I don't think I've ever loved her more. 'Yes, dear, they were very good to me, but do you know, I don't ever remember sitting on anyone's lap or being hugged.'

The irony of how many babies had since been hugged and loved on her own lap hit me hard and then she pulled out a photo of her very young parents on their wedding day and spoke in a very quiet voice. 'I've waited my whole life to see them again. I know they're in heaven waiting for me and when I die I'm going to run straight to them. And if they're not there, then I'm going to turn around and come straight back.'

As you can imagine, Nana has known little else than hard work all her life, and mornings at her house were punctuated with a strip of light under our bedroom door and the sounds and smells of Nana making breakfast. She'd always get up before the sun and set the table and start the day and similarly to Gammy's ticking clock, a strip of light under a door in the early hours takes me right back to feeling safe and snug in the land of happy.

* * *

I don't think I was a very nice child if I'm honest about it. I felt repressed and angry a lot of the time and tended to take it out on my siblings. Genevieve was the eldest and had a very undemanding personality. She also had red hair and I teased her mercilessly for it.

'We're all invited to the Kennedys' shack tomorrow . . . Except for redheads!'

'Red-headed people usually get adopted out, you know, Genevieve.'

'You killed Gammy's husband, Genevieve. He lay down and had a heart attack right after he held you, because you were such an ugly baby.'

How she didn't kill me I'll never know. She was a wonderful big sister. I remember once when we were on holidays at the beach in Glenelg – it was not long after the Beaumont children were abducted and we had all been worded up on stranger danger – and Genevieve all of a sudden started panicking and screamed at all of us to get out of the water.

As we all huddled together on the sand she whispered to us, 'See that man over there? Next to the lady in the green bathers? Well, I'm not completely sure, but I think he might be a stranger.'

Genevieve was particularly close to Gammy and was the oldest grandchild on Mum's side. I was eternally frustrated at how satisfied she was by everything. I remember her yelling at me years later, one night at Cate's place at two o'clock in the morning. We had just finished a family party and I thought it would be a good idea to put a CD on and open another bottle of champagne.

'That's always been your problem, Fiona. You've never known when enough is enough!'

When we were kids it was always Genevieve who still had Easter Eggs left over, weeks after Easter had finished. She'd go to her drawer and unwrap one, have a few nibbles and then carefully wrap it up again, while I looked murderously on. When we built cubby houses she made us wait for ages until everything was properly finished.

She rarely joined in on the physical assaults we had with one another, but she nearly knocked me out once when she threw a medicine bottle at my head one Sunday afternoon because I'd gone into our latest cubby before she'd finished the curtains.

One day when we got home from school there was a huge cardboard box on the back lawn. It had housed Mum's new washing machine, which had arrived that day, and the box was ours to play with.

'Let's put Genevieve in it!'

Genevieve was happy to oblige and hopped inside the box. The rest of us had a riotously good time rolling her around and around the backyard until we noticed one corner had suddenly gone soggy. She'd laughed so hard she'd wet herself. One of the rare times she really let go.

I'm pretty sure I drove Genevieve mad for most of her years in Warooka. She was always pretty modest and was horrified one night when I took my bra off and waved it out of our bedroom window in the direction of the man up the road. We used to call him Mr Pervy.

'Yoo hoo! Yoo hoo! Mr Pervy! Is this giving you a thrill?'

'Stop it, Fiona. He'll see you!'

'He sees us every night, Genevieve. He's probably got binoculars, disgusting old bastard.'

As I mentioned, all of us girls shared one bedroom, which was particularly rough on all my sisters because my mess nearly choked the room, but it was also our close proximity that drove us all nuts. Some of us snored like drunken sailors until we had our adenoids taken out. I also apparently 'slurped in my sleep' and Sarah's and my sneezing used to send Genevieve into a tailspin.

Poor Sarah was a chronic asthmatic with a thousand allergies, and would sneeze ferociously, up to twenty sneezes in one round, every morning. My sneeze of choice was always the quiet internal sneeze that sounds more like an 'ahh-tth' than an 'ahh-choo!'

'Follow through! For God's sake, Fiona, follow through!'

'Shut up, Genevieve. I'll sneeze how I want.'

'It's dangerous sneezing like that. You can rupture your brain.'

I used to act out dramatic scenes in our bedroom at night in preparation for the famous movie star that I was sure I was going to become. 'Sarah? Can you pretend to shoot me so I can practise my dying?'

'No, I'm tired. Go to sleep.'

'Catherine?'

'No, you'll make a noise and get us all in trouble.'

'Genevieve, c'mon, shoot me and I'll show you how I die.'

'No, and stop talking. I'm saying my prayers.'

'Why aren't you kneeling down then?'

'For your information, Fiona, lots of saints used to prefer to pray in comfortable positions. I pray better in bed.'

'Bullshit. You're supposed to kneel down. You're just being lazy. Please just shoot me and I promise I'll only die once.'

'Believe me, Fiona, I'd love to.'

I absolutely adored my brother Richard and I thought he was the bravest, cleverest most handsome boy in the whole world but unfortunately he couldn't stand the sight of me. All

I ever wanted was to have his sole attention and I learnt pretty quickly that the only way to get it was to annoy him incessantly. The old adage that any attention is better than none couldn't be more true to describe my childhood relationship with my eldest brother.

The real trick to driving siblings out of their minds, I found, was to find their weak spots and home in hard. Richard used to be freaked out by other people's germs, and germs in general for that matter, and was forever sniffing things in the fridge and checking use-by dates.

One morning he had to interrupt his breakfast for a phone call and came back to the table to find me sitting uncomfortably close to his food.

'Did you breathe on my toast? You did, didn't you? You fat bitch, you breathed all over my toast!'

'God you're a dickhead, Richard! How do you breathe on someone's toast?'

'You better not have.'

I waited till he'd swallowed every last bite. 'Nice toast?' I could smell fear and he knew it.

'I'm gonna kill you!'

'Richard, I didn't breathe on your toast, okay? . . . Idiot . . . I licked it on both sides.'

Two nights before my wedding I had a shocking nightmare. An evil killer had my brother Richard and my fiancé Chris at gunpoint and made me choose which one he shot. Without hesitating I told him to shoot Chris and woke up convinced that it was a sign that I didn't love Chris enough to marry him.

I went straight to Mrs Kennedy's place to tell her about it and she totally let me off the hook. 'You'll never love anyone in the same way you love your brothers and sisters, Fiona. You've lived and breathed with them your whole life, but if you're lucky, one day you will love Chris as much as you love them.'

* * *

My sister Cate tended to wish for little more than a peaceful life when she was a child, and thanks to Richard and me she rarely saw it. Cate was and still is a beautiful girl inside and out with a bone-dry sense of humour that has inspired a lot of my comedy over the last twenty years. We lived in a parallel universe as children but often now when I see her with nine kids of her own I'm reminded of the little Catherine Anne in Warooka over thirty years ago. Tolerant, patient and unselfish, the antithesis of myself, I only remember Cate going off her trolley once in her childhood. I was coming home from a sleepover at Carmel's place and was struggling with too many bags to carry and Mum told her to give me a hand. She gave me a serve instead, and the rest of the house as well.

We all looked on in shock as she went screaming through the house yelling at the top of her lungs. 'You all think I have good days! You all think I have good days all the time! But I don't! Some days I have bad days too!'

Cate and I have become insanely close in adulthood. She's had horrendously long natural births with every baby, and I've sat by the phone in tears for every one of them. Especially Ned, her eldest, who took a very long time to be born, and was wedged like a cork for the last few hours. Cate is a whopping

48 kilos herself. I think she's actually given birth to things bigger than her.

I was staying with Cate and her husband Phil when she went into labour with Ned, and she asked me just before she went to hospital, 'What if my baby's really ugly?'

I thought that that was the strangest concept I'd ever heard. 'Well the thing is, Cate, if your baby's ugly, you won't know. Even if it is ugly, it'll be beautiful to you.'

About twenty minutes after he was born she was on the phone to me. 'Get in here, he's horrific!'

Poor little Ned, his face and his head had been through the wringer, literally, and I must admit that even I got a bit of a shock and struggled to put a positive spin on my brand new nephew. 'Wow, he's . . . he's . . . he's terrific, isn't he, Phil? . . . He's terrific.'

Cate was beside herself and I tried to explain to her that a lot of babies looked a bit odd after being stuck for so long and delivered by forceps. 'Really, Cate, in a couple of days he'll be perfect.'

I was still in the delivery room not long after when the midwife came in. 'Mrs Taylor, are you ready to breastfeed your baby now?'

And Cate's answer? 'How about I just pat it for a little while?'

I turned that whole episode into a stand-up routine at the Melbourne Comedy Festival in 2011. As a footnote to this story, if ever someone refers to your newborn as 'terrific', Anne Geddes ain't heading your way soon, and Ned Taylor, incidentally, was the cutest toddler you could come across and then a very handsome teenager and currently a very handsome young man.

I asked Cate recently to give me her spin on what it was like growing up with the rest of us, and she said that she doesn't have very defined memories of anyone when we were very young. I found that interesting and, having spoken to other people from large families, apparently it's not that uncommon. I guess each child is in his or her own private Idaho and in some ways as isolated as an only child.

Personally, I don't believe the joys of large families are necessarily at their height, either for the parents or the kids, when the house is wall to wall with small children. But I do believe a large family sows the seeds for a later joy that comes with having six or more people on the same planet as you who were soaked in the same marinade. I have a snapshot in my head of my dad at my brother Justin's wedding, when the seven of us were doubled over laughing, trying to behave for a family photo for Mum. Dad was holding a beer and gazing at us and I remember thinking that he looked like a millionaire who'd just doubled his money.

I also think that small families reap a reward that large families often don't. My first three were all born within thirty-five months of each other and their relationships have very much mirrored my own childhood sibling relationships: every man for himself, to a degree, and for God's sake get out of my way.

The last two, Albert and Mary-Agnes, were born three years apart and five years after the first batch, and with the older ones leaving home for boarding school and then university they haven't really lived the same chaos as their brother and sisters. I've noticed an intimacy between the little ones that was never there with the big ones. They play together like bear cubs and fight as much as any kids but don't seem to be threatened by a lack of their own space.

Each to his own, I guess, but I remain fascinated by family whatever form it comes in, and I love it every time one of my kids complains that our family is nothing like 'the Blacks' or 'the Taylors' or 'the Skipseys'. It reminds me of myself when I was a kid and convinced that 'the Tahenys' were the most deplorable, hideously embarrassing family on the face of the earth. It took me years to realise the truth of the matter: every family thinks this! It's probably the main thing they all have in common.

Cate did tell me that she could never understand why Richard and I couldn't just do as we were told and not ruin everything for everyone. I guess it's a fair question, and I have no idea why I couldn't keep the peace for any real length of time.

As I said earlier, I was terrified of boredom, and Sunday afternoons were my least favourite part of the week. On and laboriously on and on they went, with Monday morning and undone homework looming like a monster, the depressing sound of the wrestling on the television in the background and no fun in sight unless I invented some of my own.

Sarah was the youngest at the time and, being the most gullible, was usually my easiest target. 'Sarah, have you tasted the metal bar on the freezer door?'

'No.'

'It tastes just like a Wizz Fizz. You should stand on a chair and lick it.'

Sarah's screaming brought Mum running in from the clothes line. 'What the bloody hell's happened now?'

Genevieve was pouring warm water from a cup over greedy little Sarah's mouth. 'Her tongue's stuck to the freezer.'

Meanwhile, Richard's target was usually our other brother, and I gave him full marks one day on the farm when he asked Justin to grab hold of a new fence with both hands and shake it really hard to make sure it was stable. Great fun all round for everyone, except Justin of course, since it was an electric fence with quite a kick in it indeed.

Justin and Sarah had learnt from the masters (Richard and me) and turned on each other pretty spectacularly by the time they were pre-teens, and I recall being very proud of them one day when I was home from boarding school and noticed an unopened block of Cadbury's Dairy Milk chocolate in the fridge – a very rare find in the Taheny house. I ripped the wrapping off immediately, only to find it was a carefully wrapped old bathroom tile with a note attached, which said, 'Sucked in. Justin.'

I was always in particular danger of trouble on long family car trips, when we were cramped in like refugees. Richard used to threaten me with one of Veronica Taheny's 'dead legs' if my big fat revolting thigh touched his one more time, and I'd slap him back and tell him it wasn't my fault, that it was 'inertia, you idiot', and Dad would threaten to stop the car for the twenty-eighth time that day.

Once we were heading to New South Wales to stay with relations and consequently stuck in the un-air-conditioned Valiant station wagon for a couple of days. Justin and Sarah were very little then and two of the most adorable looking kids you could come across. Justin was a blond, blue-eyed angel who Cate was particularly close to, and Sarah was a funny, curly-haired, big, brown-eyed beauty who would have had to have been Mum's pride and joy.

Justin used to suffer badly from car sickness and often sat in the front seat between Mum and Dad on long trips, and I couldn't resist tapping him (although he'd have you believe it was more of a kick) in the back of the head with my foot every half hour or so to break the boredom. The pay-off was always pretty good as he'd bellow and turn around while I denied everything and Dad threatened to stop the car for the twenty-ninth time that day and Cate and Genevieve wished they were anywhere but a hundred miles from Wagga Wagga in a car with this particular family.

One thing I remember about Sarah was how much she loved money. She was fascinated by it when she was very little and then in awe of it as she got older. One long car trip when I was about thirteen was not long after my birthday, and Gammy had given me a brand new purse with a dollar note in it. I have a picture of that purse in my head: white plastic with three stick figures of African people on either side and a zip on the top.

Staring out the window at the Hay Plains, I opened the purse and noticed that Sarah was watching me looking at my dollar note for about the tenth time. All of a sudden I couldn't resist. 'Sarah?'

'What?'

'Watch this.'

I wound the window down about half an inch and let the dollar note get sucked out. I was more than satisfied with her reaction – she nearly jumped right out after it. I swear it's the best dollar I've ever spent.

'What did you do that for?'

'Well, I guess if I ever need a dollar I'll know where one is, won't I?'

* * *

Holidays were mostly visits to far-flung relations, with the occasional caravan park stopover on the way and even more occasionally a motel when we'd squeeze into one room and sleep top-and-tailing each other. Perfect if Justin's head was anywhere near the vicinity of my feet.

One year we went to Hornsdale in the mid-north of South Australia and visited an old schoolfriend of Mum's called Trish Noonan. Trish was married to a farmer called Michael and they had six kids. Mum and Trish hadn't seen each other for years, and Dad and Michael hit it off right from the start.

Somewhere around this time the 'Hornsdale Leprechaun Club' was born. The Hornsdale Leprechauns take a bit of explaining, but in its beginnings was made up of six or seven families all connected in some way to Trish and Michael Noonan. We would get together once or twice a year for anything from a week of camping to an afternoon barbecue.

There were dozens of kids at any given time and we were fascinated by the goings-on of our parents. I'd seen my mum and dad have fun before but never quite at this level. The Hornsdale Leprechauns was almost like living in a Monty Python sketch. In one massive piss-take the adults referred to each other as 'Brother' and 'Sister' constantly. They held important meetings where minutes were actually taken and various duties were distributed to various officials at the beginning of our gatherings and reports given in at the end. All of this went on amidst a lot of beer, wine and gut laughing.

My earliest memories of the Hornsdale Leprechauns was when they hired out a whole campsite at Point Turton, which was right by the sea about four miles from Warooka. We were staying in dormitory-style cabins and I was heading to the shower block one morning, listening in to their madness.

'Good morning, Brother Bullen.'

'Sister Deirdre! And a very good morning to you. Tell me, Sister, do you know who the latrine officer is?'

'Why I believe it's Sister Shanahan, Brother Bullen, but I'm sure Brother Beerworth can tell you for sure.'

'Ah yes, Brother Beerworth; I need to speak to him on another matter. There were teenagers in a car late last night and I'm afraid the morals officer had left his post.'

To this day my parents still meet with the Hornsdale Leprechauns at least once a year, and Brother Howard has the minutes of every meeting held for the last thirty-five years. One of the biggest family weddings on record was my sister Sarah's marriage to Matthew Shanahan, which is, to date, the only union of Hornsdale Leprechaun offspring.

Another semi-regular holiday was in the summer at Cadell, where we would stay with the Dalzells in a shack on the Murray River. Just down from the shack was a gorgeous pristine beach on the river, and across the other side was an enormous cliff face that seemed a mile high. Whenever I find the patience to meditate, that's the place I will go to in my head. I panic when I read about fears for the Murray because so far I have never seen another place so beautiful.

We adored our times at Cadell but one trip there was considerably less comfortable than any summer holiday I've had before or since. A group of dads, including mine, rose to the challenge of taking all the kids away for a week to give their wives a break and, as only blokes can do, took it upon themselves to cut some domestic corners to increase efficiency and save time.

We were read the riot act and I'm sure they thought they'd come up with some revolutionary concepts in childcare. After all, what the hell would women know?

'Okay, you kids! New rules this holiday. Rule number one: two meals a day. Watermelon and cereal at ten o'clock and then fill yourselves up on chops and bread at four. Rule number two: no sun block. Get yourselves good and burnt in the first couple of days and that'll toughen you up for the rest of the week. If anyone does get burnt, go and see Uncle Maurice and he'll organise a hot shower to take the sting out of it.'

As I mentioned earlier, every one of my great-grandparents came from Ireland and my skin considers me a 'full blood' colleen. Except for Justin, who we believe to be a Spanish throwback, we haven't got a pigment between us, and could burn standing too close to the toaster.

The pain of that sunburnt holiday was unforgettable. Cate turned to me as we were heading for home in the back seat of the Valiant and said, 'Fiona, have you got this bit?'

She was referring to the grooves on her face between her nose and her cheeks, and I checked to see if I had mine and indeed I did not. Our faces were swollen red balloons with holes for nostrils, mouths and eyes. I'd say it was probably the most peaceful car trip with kids that my dad ever experienced; we were too tired and sore to move, let alone speak.

* * *

One Saturday morning when I was about twelve, Mrs Wallace, who was the policeman's wife from Yorketown, dropped in with a bassinette for Mum and said something vaguely cryptic as she left: 'You'll never know when you might need this again, Deirdre.'

For a minute or so the penny didn't drop with me, but Cate was looking at Mum strangely and then all of a sudden it dawned on me. 'Are you having another baby?'

The look on Mum's face said it all. I was out of my skin with excitement that day. I guess even though there were six of us, a new baby was still an almighty novelty, as we'd all been born so close together. Genevieve was only eight when Sarah was born and the last time there had been a baby in the house the rest of us were not much more than babies ourselves.

I remember Mum calling out after Cate and me as we headed up to the Warooka Oval for the Saturday footy, 'Now listen to me, you girls! You don't need to go telling everybody you see today.'

I was bursting at the seams with our family's news and took Mum completely at her word. As in all country towns, people park their cars alongside each other all around the oval to watch the match, and we'd only just walked through the gates when I spotted the Souths' Fairlane and headed towards it.

'Come on, Catherine, let's go and tell Aunty Frances.'

'But Mum said not to tell everyone.'

'We won't tell everyone. We'll just tell every second car.' And around the oval we went, knocking on every second window on the driver's side, until we came across Aunty Mon.

'Aunty Mon, our mum's having another baby.'

'I hardly think that's an appropriate thing to be running around blabbing about, you rude little girls,' she snapped. Then she wound the window back up without another word.

The wind was taken out of our sails for a bit, but then we remembered that Sarah had already left for the football before Mrs Wallace had come around. We headed to the playground to find her.

'Sarah, guess what? Mum's having another baby.'

'She is not.'

'She is so.'

I guess the least likely person in a family to be excited by the prospect of a new baby is the baby of the family, and Sarah really took some convincing that afternoon.

'She really is, Sarah. Mrs Wallace dropped the bassinette off and everything, and Mum said it was true.'

Sarah actually looked like she was about to cry, and then in one last desperate pitch she called out after us. 'Yeah? Well, what if it's not a Catholic?'

I don't think Emily's birth was a terribly easy one for Mum. And being eight years between babies, times had changed a bit and Dad witnessed a birth for the first time. Mum had Emily naturally, but not without the help of an induction, an epidural and some giant salad tongs. I overheard Dad telling someone on the phone that 'if that's the most beautiful thing I'm supposed to ever see, I hope I don't live to see much more'.

I guess times had changed more than a bit. At my own birth, Dad got the call that Mum was in labour and drove himself to Adelaide. He went shopping for a sports coat and then walked into Mum's hospital room and asked if she liked his new jacket, to which she responded, 'It's a girl.'

'Hell, have you had it already?'

We were all besotted with Emily, or 'Milly' as we call her, from day one, and she changed our family forever. In a way she closed the generation gap a bit between us and our parents; they were far more easygoing with Milly and we couldn't believe how much she got away with. It's no surprise that she now works as a comic actress on various networks as she was born to perform and mimic, and can still make our dad laugh till he cries.

When we were little, one of the biggest crimes we could commit was missing the school bus, and we'd cower in the car while our furious mother drove down the Yorketown road in her dressing gown to chase the bus, threatening us with our lives 'if this damn car runs out of petrol'.

The rules had certainly relaxed by the time Emily was at St Columba's. I remember one morning Emily being in a major panic when she was about five because she'd missed the bus and Mum was actually consoling her.

'Don't worry, love. If you've missed the bus Dad will drive you to school.'

'No way, Mum. He's not driving me to school. It's embarrassing. All the kids at school say he's got a squishy face.'

'Well, you don't have to listen to all the silly kids at school, do you?'

'Well, it's true! Have a look at him! He has got a squishy face.'

One morning soon after that, Emily had had another run-in with Mum and Dad about God knows what, and she stormed out of the kitchen and then turned around for a parting shot.

'Anyway, great parents I've got! One's fat and the other one's ugly!'

Neither of them batted an eyelid, and Mum continued on with her breakfast while Dad went on reading the paper for about a minute and then looked up.

'I'll take ugly if you like, Deirdre,' he said.

Emily had really pressed Mum's buttons, though, one Sunday morning, and we all knew it when we overheard Mum call her a 'bitch of a child' under her breath when Milly refused to wear the dress that had been ironed for her. Poor Mum was mortified later that morning outside mass when Emily was asked by an elderly visitor to the church what her name was and she point-blank refused to answer.

The old lady tried another tack and said, 'Well, what does Mummy call you at home then?'

Sadly, Emily opened up.

We all had our own special relationship with our funny, elf-looking baby sister, but it was Cate especially who mothered her incessantly, and maybe she can thank Milly for nine kids of her own.

Seeing Emily for the first time was unforgettable. Dad had taken us into the city before visiting hours and we all walked up Adelaide's brand new Rundle Mall for the first time and had milkshakes, and for some reason bought Richard, and only Richard, a new pair of shoes.

Not long after that the six of us were waiting out the front of the hospital while Dad had gone in to see if the coast was clear for a visit, and the excitement must have been all too much for Richard. Genevieve was sixteen at the time, and I guess teenage embarrassment had started to kick in and reached a crescendo at the sight of Richard doing a tap dance on the front steps of Calvary Hospital in his brand new shoes.

Mum was only thirty-seven at the time, but we thought she was as old as the hills and very clever to be able to have a baby at her age, especially when only a few wards away from her was our cousin Karen Pledger who had just given birth to Vincent, her first son and Nana's very first great-grandchild.

Things weren't spectacular for a while after Mum came home with Emily. I think even she might say now that she had some level of postnatal depression, and from memory Emily wasn't an easy baby. Genevieve had left for boarding school by then but Cate and I were on hand for early morning feeds and Dad was ahead of his time as a hands-on father.

For a pair of farmers my folks were ahead of their time in a lot of ways. Dad bathed and dressed us, and I reckon he was the first cocky on the peninsula to eat home-cooked Thai curry or gnocchi for dinner.

Even back then my mum and dad had one of the most equitable partnerships I've ever encountered. Mum certainly would never have needed the counsel of Germaine Greer, as she was always well and truly liberated, maybe a mix of her matriarchal upbringing and my dad's simple decency, and I recall being flabbergasted when I first heard about the women's liberation movement.

Hadn't women always been equal to men? I couldn't believe that women en masse had been subjugated by men as I had never witnessed it myself and from what I'd experienced, if anything the scales were tipped slightly in favour of the ladies. Lucky me, I guess, and shame on those idiot bastards.

Emily's christening day was not without drama. We've all worn the family christening gown that was made by the Calvary nuns, and on the morning of the baptism Mum waited until the last minute to dress the baby because she hadn't pooed for quite a while. (Understand I'm talking about the baby and not Mum.) Eventually she had to go ahead and dress Emily while Genevieve was busy getting Sarah ready. Sarah was making her first Holy Communion on that same day at the Yorketown church.

Sometime during the mass I was horrified to look down our pew and see Dad whacking Sarah repeatedly on the back of the head. I couldn't think what she could have done so wrong to warrant being publicly smacked on her first communion day, and I was mortified for her and for the rest of us. Eventually Dad stopped, and the reason for the assault became apparent when Sarah walked up the aisle to receive communion. Whoever was sitting behind her had accidentally set fire to the back of her head with their candle, and before any of us could recover from the sight of a big black hole in Sarah's veil the banner of mortification had been handed to Mum.

Just as she stepped up to the baptismal font Emily decided to relieve her infant self and a bucketload of green baby poo squirted out of her nappy and down through the christening robe and poured spectacularly down Mum's arm, dripping off her elbow and onto the altar.

* * *

One obsession I had in childhood was my love of dogs. I shared a passion for them with my cousin MaryAnne South, and I remember us lay-bying an *Encyclopedia of Dogs* from the Yorketown newsagency one winter. It cost $9.95 and some weeks we could only manage as little as fifteen cents, and the lay-by was becoming dangerously close to expiring when Aunty Frances went in and paid the remaining $4.50.

I was worried about this and wondered if that meant that the book was more MaryAnne's than mine, but we took week-about turns with the encyclopedia and pored over the hundreds of different breeds, making a solemn pact with each other that when we grew up we were going to run a dog kennel together and never pluck our eyebrows.

I'm still not sure what never plucking our eyebrows had to do with anything but we both spat in each other's hands and shook on it outside the girls' toilets at St Columba's in about 1971.

My first dog was a Corgi bitzer called Sam, and while I loved him to pieces I think it was only a matter of months before he was run over out the front of our place. I remember very much enjoying my grief that night. Mum let me have Weet-bix with hot milk for dinner in the living room while all the others had to eat braised chops at the table, and Dad put his arm around me and promised to bury him in a nice spot near 'the boy's waterhole'.

The day after Sam's death I was having a race home from mass with Richard and tripped over a stump of wood at the very top of our block and went flying through the air and landed smack on my face. I went back to pick up the stump only to find that it wasn't as much a stump of wood as my dead rigor-mortis-ridden dog hidden in long grass, and I screamed bloody murder at the whole damned world.

Maybe Dad felt guilty, because not long afterwards I was allowed another dog that I called Ben. Ben was a mutt as well, with a black shiny coat, and he and I enjoyed each other's company immensely for two weeks and about five days.

I was in the bath with a head full of shampoo when Richard knocked on the door to tell me that Ben was dead in the middle of the road a bit further down from where Sam had been run over. I had a feeling Richard enjoyed being messenger boy and I screamed at him to 'rack off'.

Only that same week Richard had asked Sarah if she'd checked on her budgie Yellowie recently.

'Have you seen your budgie Bluey today?'

'It's not called Bluey, Richard, it's Yellowie.'

'Well, it's Bluey now.'

I'm sure Dad took to his undertaker duties more swiftly with Ben than with Sam and, while I wasn't as devastated this time round, I didn't knock back the Weet-bix with hot milk in front of the telly and I still managed to sob into my *Encyclopedia of Dogs* that night.

I swore off dogs for a long time after that, but a few years later I was recovered enough to loan my heart one more time. My Aunty Eileen had a Pekinese called Su-Yen who had had her wicked way with a Dachshund, and Aunty Eileen generously offloaded one of the pups on me. I named my new pet Phoebe and kept her indoors as much as I could, resulting in much better luck with her mortality.

Phoebe was magnificent and helped me through a horrible twelve months or more. By now I was in Year 9 at the Yorketown Area School, and my friend Mary-Anne Williams and I were inseparable. We were shunned by the nerds and the cool kids alike and we couldn't have cared less. We spent our days mocking the world and writing sketches for the school assembly and laughing till we ached.

Mary-Anne and I had conned the school principal into letting us have a regular five minutes stage time at the school assemblies, which were always held in the gymnasium on Wednesday afternoons. One recurring assembly skit that Cate also joined in on was a spoof of the Sullivans, from the long-running television serial. Mary-Anne played Dave, and Cate played Grace Sullivan, who sat at the kitchen table reading telegrams with terrible news from the war, and I played everyone from the postman to 'Aunty Rose'. Lord only knows what was funny about it but the auditorium would often be filled with laughs. In fact one assembly the audience laughed so hard it was quite literally too good to be true.

In a spoof of *The Midday Show* Mary-Anne was in character as Mike Walsh and I was playing the part of Jeanne Little. I was wearing a wig and a white satin dress and, though I do concede that I did a wonderful 'Daaaarling!', the roar that went up from the audience was a bit over the top, and quite surprisingly some of the loudest applause was coming from the revolting boys from Year 10 in the back row. Still, applause is applause, so we continued with the sketch until we simply couldn't be heard over the shouts of glee from our classmates.

Could this really be happening? I thought. It seemed the whole school was chanting my name and clapping at the same time.

'Fi! Fi! Fi! Fi! Fi! Fi!'

I glowed with pride and turned to look apologetically at Mary-Anne, as it seemed I was the star of the moment, but to my horror she had left the stage and was fleeing the building. I took a final bow or seven and then ran to comfort my upstaged best friend (in the toilets).

'You poor thing. Are you okay?'

Unfortunately it was Mary-Anne who asked the question, and now I was becoming more confused by the second.

'Of course I am, but why were they shouting my name?'

'They weren't shouting your name, you idiot, your skirt is completely see-through. Have a look in the mirror.'

A very apparent dark triangle reflected back at me. The bastards had been chanting the letter V.

But life couldn't have been better with Mary-Anne. One Monday morning, though, the ever present smile on my face was wiped off in an instant. Mary-Anne was waiting for me at the bus stop.

'We're moving to Jamestown in six weeks.'

Life at the Yorketown Area School was very grim for me after Mary-Anne left. We had systematically ostracised ourselves from everybody in our first two years of high school and I had never once considered the consequences of life without her. I was peerless by my own design and dreaded every day of school from then on.

My nickname was 'No-friends', and I copped it every morning as I walked past the lockers. Actual lesson times weren't so bad but at recess and lunchtime I would either sit in a toilet cubicle with a book or work in the library as a monitor. The only things that kept me going were the knowledge that boarding school was only sixteen months away, and my beautiful Phoebe.

Anyone who has ever loved a dog would understand the solace they can give their owners in rough times and some afternoons I would sit on my bed with Phoebe and stare into her big beautiful eyes and tell her all my problems without saying a word.

I know a Pekinese–Dachshund cross doesn't sound like a recipe for good looks but she really was a very pretty girl. The Dachshund part of her gave her a much nicer face than a Pekinese and the Pekinese part of her gave her a gorgeous coat and her lovely eyes. I adored Phoebe and was panic stricken when I came home from school one day and Mum told me she was at the vet's and had to stay there until the next day.

Mum was very evasive about what was actually wrong with Phoebe but eventually I managed to get it out of her that she was being de-sexed. What I didn't know until some time afterwards was that my poor little pup was pregnant to a Border collie and had undergone an abortion. The pups inside of her would have grown so big it would have killed her and while I knew that abortion was a major sin I was very relieved that dogs were exempt from the church's teaching on this issue. Phoebe was even more precious to me after that.

Nearly a year later Phoebe and I headed out for a walk in the July holidays. It was a rare cloudless, windless winter morning and I had recently been given new clothes for my birthday. I can still see that outfit now: a red ribbed polo-neck jumper with a denim skirt, red ribbed tights and pale blue leather lace-ups. I thought anyone driving by could almost mistake me for somebody from Adelaide, I was so fashionable, not to mention the fact that I had the best-looking dog in Warooka trotting along beside me. We were heading to the corner store and I had the twenty-five cents in my hand ready to buy the new *TV Week* that had a pull-out poster of Steven Tandy in the middle and I couldn't wait to get my hands on it. Steven Tandy was the actor who played Tom Sullivan in *The Sullivans* and I was in love with him and knew for sure that the feeling would be mutual if and when he ever got back from Gallipoli.

Out of the blue, when we were only metres from the shop a big black dog came from nowhere and Phoebe chased him into the middle of the intersection. Before I could even call out after her I heard screeching brakes and watched a brown Holden headed straight into Phoebe's path. I watched in horror as my little dog went under the front wheel of the car.

I screamed so loudly that even Gwen Thomson heard it from the kitchen in the pub, and I remember her running across the road to comfort me. The bank manager whose name I can't recall had been behind the wheel of the car and he also did his best to calm me down but I was frantic and had bolted to the middle of the intersection where Phoebe's lifeless little body lay.

I picked her up and as I did her insides fell entirely out of her belly and thudded onto the road in a pile of organs and intestines. I nearly passed out with the horror of it all and don't remember what happened directly after that. Mum told me that the bank manager came around later that night in a terrible state and said he couldn't get the sound of my screams out of his head.

I've always been a screamer, in childbirth, in horror movies, even watching a grand final. I'm a fine hollerer and I can also cry for impressive bouts at a time. After Phoebe's death I didn't let up for weeks.

The Weet-bix with hot milk came out again that night but this time it didn't come close to helping. I swore to myself that I would never fall in love with a dog again, and I only relented a few years ago when I took the kids to the pet shop to buy some guinea pigs and there was a Phoebe replica in a cage. Doug was supposedly a Shih tzu cross, and the kids offered to empty their own bank accounts to pull together the $200 asking price.

'Mum can we have him?'

'No, we don't have a front gate.'

'Please, please? He's so cute. We'll keep him inside.'

'No, he'll ruin the carpet, and you don't even like Weet-bix, Mary.'

'What's Weet-bix got to do with it?'

'Mum, what's a Shih tzu?'

'A zoo with no animals.'

I was playing for time in the pet shop but eventually I caved in and Doug was ours. We were all very proud of having such an exotic breed and were a bit confused when our new neighbours moved in and I asked them what their two dogs were.

'They're Shih tzu–Maltese.'

'Really?'

I looked at Doug and suddenly realised my kids had been swindled and our vet confirmed that our dog is about as pedigree as Les Patterson.

But it couldn't have mattered less to the kids, especially Mary-Agnes. Doug is the light of her life. He guards her all night and then sleeps all day until she's home from school. A very small part of me is closed off to him, though, and I'm at the ready with Coco Pops and tissues for the rite of passage she'll undergo if Doug breaks her own heart one day.

* * *

There was nothing like the joy of waiting for the Honners. Uncle Maurice always drove a big American Pontiac. He loved the room it afforded, and the sound of the car tyres on our gravel driveway sent us mad with happiness.

'The Honners are here! The Honners are here!'

And it was exactly the same if the Christmas location was reversed.

'The Tahenys are here! The Tahenys are here!'

First cousins have been one of the greatest joys of my life. As I said, there were six kids in the Honner family: Maurice, Felicity, Meg, Louise, Jane and Caroline.

Most of the Tahenys were lucky enough to have their own personal Honner to pair off with.

I had Felicity and we managed to spend as much time as we possibly could in each other's company. Whenever our families got together we would smuggle pyjamas and clothes into the car in the hope of being allowed to stay. Felicity was a fair bit taller than me even though I was a year older. She had brown frizzy hair, fair skin and the long straight honk that many of us have that is referred to as the 'Honner nose'.

Felicity and I lived to laugh, score lollies, tease anyone who was younger than us and annoy anyone who was older. I adored Felicity and gorged on her company, and thank God I never missed a chance to be with her, because she died before she turned sixteen. It feels like my early life is divided into two parts: the time before Felicity died and the time after.

The time before was without any real grief at all. My memory of Uncle Maurice and Aunty Shirley and our times with them is like playing any Australian home movie from the seventies in my head: laughing, pretty mothers, backyard cricket, pavlovas, barbecues, dads holding stubbies and kids everywhere.

Uncle Maurice wasn't born when his father (my grandfather) died, and he had no brothers. I don't know if that's why he was so sensitive, but he was a very tactile bloke who had no qualms showing his emotions, particularly after he lost his beloved Felicity or 'Sister', as he used to call her. He was the king of the bear hug and the empty threat, and I loved him nearly as much as my own Dad. He too had the classic 'Honner nose' and was also fairly short and squat (two other distinctive Honner traits).

Uncle Maurice died in his early forties from a stroke. We used to say that he liked a bit of bread with his butter. His diet definitely wouldn't have been endorsed by the Heart Foundation, and despite Aunty Shirley's protests he had a fried breakfast nearly every morning. I reckon there's a chance, though, that he may have died from a broken heart.

I only remember being afraid of Uncle Maurice once in my childhood. It was during the summer holidays, and I was staying at the Honners as I often did. Aunty Shirley had not long had the twins (Jane and Caroline), and if she said it once I reckon I heard her say it a thousand times in the first couple of years after they were born: 'If you wake those twins, I'll bloody kill you!'

Felicity and I were mucking around very loudly in the room next to the nursery, and I think our hearts stopped beating when we heard them start bawling. It was about ten o'clock at night and we dived into bed, hoping we could disassociate ourselves from the crime. Uncle Maurice roared into the bedroom with a face like thunder. 'Right, you two, you woke the bloody twins! Tomorrow it's the horsewhip!'

He switched off the light and left the room and stormed out, and Felicity started laughing again. She had a very big laugh, but this time I wasn't joining in.

I thought she was demented, laughing in the face of a god-damned horsewhip. I barely slept a wink that night. I mean, I didn't even know what a horsewhip looked like. The next morning was like waking up in the gallows. We went out to the kitchen and Felicity proceeded to hoe into cereal and toast as if she didn't have a care in the world. Uncle Maurice was reading the paper and everything seemed to be going on as usual. By lunchtime I was beside myself but I finally found the courage to ask, 'Felicity, didn't your dad say we were going to get the horsewhip today?'

She laughed. 'You are such an idiot! He says that all the time. We haven't even got a horsewhip.'

Aunty Shirley was a very groovy aunt for her day. She wore denim jeans and whistled incessantly as she whipped around the house with a ciggie in her hand. 'Look What They've Done to My Song' was her all-time favourite. She was a cross between beautiful and handsome, with short blonde hair, and she was very particular about her – and everyone else's – clothing. Aunty Shirley was one of the loveliest mothers I ever knew. She wore Elixir 21 and, to this day, just a whiff of that perfume reminds me of everything about her. I can't remember her ever lounging around doing nothing or vegging out in front of the telly. She was constantly on the move, either sewing, reading to the 'twinnies' (Jane and Caroline), cleaning up after everyone or simply talking to us.

I was alone with Aunty Shirley very rarely. I guess with families the size of ours being alone with anyone is unusual, but one Saturday afternoon she was making orange cupcakes.

'Do you want to lick the spoon, Fi?'

I had a big lick and so did she, and then another and another, and we sat at the kitchen table and ate the whole bowl of orange cupcakes before they managed to be cupcakes at all.

Somehow, maybe subconsciously, it was almost like Shirley knew that her kids wouldn't have her forever. She hugged harder and longer than most mothers, told them she loved them more often and literally lived her life for them.

I remember walking into the living room on the afternoon of the twins' christening to find Aunty Shirley alone and engrossed with Louise, her five-year-old, whose baby status had been upstaged by the arrival of two brand new babies. Shirley had a house full of visitors and relatives, and there she was on the floor with her 'Luscious Lu' as she called her. She was definitely ahead of her time in child psychology.

She died of breast cancer at forty-four, and was diagnosed a couple of years after Felicity was killed. From the day Felicity died, Shirley was never really the same. She still worked like a Trojan and gave everything she had to give, but it seemed like her eyes didn't smile all the way to her soul anymore. Losing Felicity wasn't just losing a daughter for Shirley. She had also lost her right-hand man.

I couldn't count the times Felicity and I would be interrupted in the middle of a game with the sound of Aunty Shirley calling out: 'Feliciteeeeee.' Felicity and Shirley together raised the twinnies, two of the most adorable babies you ever saw: blonde, blue-eyed and identical. It's hard to look at photos of them as babies without being heartbroken about all the loss that lay ahead, but until they were five years old they were smothered with adoration. Life got harder for my cousins after Felicity died. I can't imagine what it must have been like for them to lose so much and so often. I remember Meg saying under her breath as we were leaving the cemetery in Maitland on the day of Uncle Maurice's funeral, 'Maybe we should have just pitched a tent.'

Aunty Shirley put up a monstrous fight with cancer, and my sister Cate once witnessed her courage. Cate was about seventeen at the time and living with the Honners for a while to help Aunty Shirley after another round of chemotherapy. Ever swanky, with a groovy headscarf, and ever on the move,

Shirley put down whatever she was doing to take a phone call from her doctor.

That phone call was the moment Shirley found out that the cancer was going to take her life. She hung up and sat at the kitchen table with her head in her hands, and started to cry.

'My poor twinnies, my poor twinnies.'

Jane and Caroline were only seven years old, and Cate looked on helplessly.

Only moments later she stopped crying and stood up and looked straight at my sister. 'Well, Cate,' she said, 'we'd better get cracking. I haven't got long and there's a hell of a lot to be done.'

She was ever practical and mothered her kids until she took her last breath. One of her most ominous lines was issued a couple of days before she died. She was instructing Uncle Maurice on a thousand matters for after she was gone.

'. . . and for God's sake, Maurice, lose some of that weight. If you leave these kids orphans I'll bloody kill you.'

Shirley died at the Mary Potter Home in Adelaide and I remember saying goodbye to her there. She asked for a private moment with everyone and when my turn came Meg grabbed me and gave me a quick warning.

'She's making everyone promise to give up smoking.'

I was twenty at the time and it still feels like yesterday. She had lovely eyes and she stared right through me.

'Well, Fi, I guess I'll see you in the spring.'

'I love you, Aunty Shirley.'

'I love you, too.'

I headed out of the room, but just as I got to the door she said, 'Promise me one thing, Fi?'

I crossed my fingers behind my back. 'What's that?'

'Promise me you'll marry that boy.'

Aunty Shirley had only met Chris twice by then, but she was a big fan from the get-go.

I remember well the last day I spent with Felicity. I was catching the bus home to Warooka that afternoon and we were lounging around on hammocks under the pine trees in the front yard. Usually we were pretty morose when our times together were nearly over, but it was the beginning of the summer holidays and we would all be spending Christmas at another aunt's house in less than a fortnight.

Life was good. The whole summer stretched out ahead of us. I had just finished my first year at boarding school and at the end of the holidays Felicity would be joining me there. We were both reading books, I was reading *Seven Little Australians* and had just finished the chapter where Judy dies. I put the book down and said to Felicity, 'I wonder what it's like to be dead. I hope you can still see everything after you die.'

'What are you talking about?'

'Well, imagine your funeral. Wouldn't you want to be there some way and check out who's crying and who's not?'

'Feliciteeeee!'

Aunty Shirley was calling again and Felicity got up and headed for the house. She threw her book at me on the way inside and said, 'You're weird.'

I had an awful nightmare a few days after that. In my dream the phone rang in the middle of the night and somebody had died. Mum was holding the phone and crying and I was running as far away from Mum and the phone as I could. The house kept getting longer and longer as I kept running through heaps of rooms and doors until I got to a last room. There was a table in it, up against a wall, and I hid underneath it with my hands over my ears.

About a week after the day in the hammocks, that dream almost played itself out entirely.

The phone rang in the early hours of the morning and I could hear Mum crying and saying, 'Oh Maurice, no, no, Maurice, no.'

Just like in the dream, I ran to the top of the house and crawled under the dining room table with my ears covered. For a while I thought it might have been my grandmother, Gammy, which would have been bad enough, but despite being under a table and having my fingers in my ears I eventually heard Mum tell the household, 'Felicity's been killed.'

Felicity was thrown from a car on a country road on her way back from a friend's sixteenth birthday party. She apparently didn't suffer and died instantly. I don't remember very much at all about the rest of that night.

The next morning was like being stuck in a nightmare. Mum and her sister Genevieve were driving to Maitland and decided that I should come too. I sat in the back and as every mile went past I sank deeper into the corner of the back seat. I figured that I would be the last person Uncle Maurice and Aunty Shirley would want to see. I was alive and their daughter was dead, and as far as I was concerned that's what I'd represent for the rest of my life. By the time we were standing at the back door of the Honners' place I felt physically sick.

The door opened and there was Uncle Maurice. The first thing he did was hug me. He hugged me for a long, long time and said, 'You poor old sausage, you poor old sausage.'

The morning after Felicity was buried I woke up very early and walked into the kitchen. The house seemed incredibly quiet. Up until then it had been a moving sea of people, casseroles, cups of tea and rosary beads. Uncle Maurice stood at the kitchen sink, unaware of me. He was staring outside, a light rain was drizzling down the window pane and a torrent of silent tears was pouring down his face.

Whenever I hear on the news or read in the paper of a teenage road death, that's the first picture that comes to my mind: Uncle Maurice staring out of that window.

I try to imagine Felicity as she would have been now when I think of her, and it isn't very hard to do when I look at her brother and sisters in their grown-up forms. They remain some of my favourite people on earth, and just the sounds of their voices and laughter is soothing to anyone who knew their parents and sister. I've always said, and it is wholeheartedly agreed upon by my brothers and sisters, that the first sighting of our cousin Maurice at any family get-together makes the whole world seem safer.

My cousin Maurice was the eldest and only twenty-three years old when he became the legal guardian of his younger sisters. It's almost with a sense of shame that I think back over everything. It was so unfair that they copped so much grief and were left to fend for themselves while our family sailed merrily on with parents at the helm.

Uncle Maurice's death was sudden and devastating. It was six weeks before my wedding and, as Chris was still in Alice Springs, his father, Ivan O'Loughlin, drove me to the peninsula for his funeral. A kindness I have never forgotten. I could barely look at my cousins at the mass in Maitland so my only clear memory of that day is of our beautiful Gammy, already battered by emphysema, and now nearly broken with grief.

I remember meeting Jane in Adelaide for coffee when she was about nineteen. Jane has unusually wide feet and she was wearing an awful-looking pair of boots with the laces undone. I asked her why she was wearing them and she said, 'I can't find shoes that I can fit into. Mum used to get them specially made for me but I don't know where that place is.'

All of a sudden another aspect of their loss hit me in the face. When you lose your parents you actually lose parts of your own history. So many details go with them, especially with your mother. Gone are all of the little things that only a mum knows, from your dental history to the things you said when you were little, your first steps, the first time you laughed out loud, a million things.

Bloody sad all round.

CHAPTER 3

ST COLUMBA'S BIZARRE

Warooka was a predominantly Protestant area, and instead of attending the local public primary school we and about four other families boarded the state school bus every morning, per favour of the government, and attended a tiny Catholic convent school thirteen miles away in Yorketown.

I was forever running late and would most mornings be seen running up the main street panic stricken with my bird's-nest hair, still trying to stuff my lunch box into my satchel with one hand and clutching my Vegemite on toast in the other.

Before the driver put the bus into first gear he would look back through the rear-view mirror and ask, 'Is Fiona Taheny on the bus?'

'Yes, Mr Cairney.'

'Then that means everybody's on the bus.'

I would sit down next to my sister Cate and hate her with every inch of me. Cate was always up and ready for school about an hour earlier than I was. Her bed was made, her hair was in pigtails, her homework was done and her schoolbag didn't have the aromatic cocktail of mouldy bread and rotten banana wafting out of it like mine always did.

The local area school was in Yorketown as well, so the bus was full of secondary school students who made it their sport to torment us 'convicts', as they called us, every morning and afternoon. We were the only kids in the district who wore a full school uniform and the girls actually wore pinnies over the top of our tunics. By the time we were dropped at the gates of the Catholic church in Yorketown we had endured being tied to the back of the seats by our pinnies, or our plaits if our hair was long enough, had our lunch boxes thrown back and forth over our heads and been tripped up as we boarded and vacated the bus.

I have to say I loved every minute of it. I've always had a penchant for high drama, so I would imagine we were children being persecuted and I prided myself on our dignified courage in the face of our tormentors. At other times we were the children of Fatima being driven to our inquisition and were suffering for Our Lady. Whatever the scenario, in my imagination it was all being captured on film and I played my part with a rare and special talent – according to myself, that is.

School at St Columba's was about thirty kids in one room, and more than half of them were either my brothers and sisters or some manner of cousin. Every year level was represented in this one room but some grades were in very short supply. My sister Sarah went right through her primary schooling with only Matthew Luke for company.

The nuns who taught us were softly spoken gentlewomen who could transform themselves into a fury of flailing habits and leather straps in the blink of an eye. Some of the sisters availed themselves of their straps more readily than others. Sister Ridiculata (not her real name), I remember, could be particularly vigorous, and the sting that is left on the tip of your fingers after an ill-timed hand withdrawal from the leather strap is a sensation I will never forget. It stings like a bastard at first, then it almost goes numb for a while and then slowly, achingly, throbs back to life.

I remember as a kid wondering what sicko makes the bloody things? Who's sewing leather straps together for a living? Who's ringing up the leather strap shop and putting in an order? Where is the bloody leather strap shop?

At that time, in the late sixties and early seventies, most schools were phasing out corporal punishment, particularly for girls, but the new order hadn't quite reached St Columba's, Yorketown. By our numbers and proximity to each other we were a very close population and I clearly recall a communal sadness whenever someone got the strap.

I definitely remember some lovely nuns – Sister Judith, Sister Bernadette, Sister Margaret and Sister Antoinette, who must have only been in her twenties and was as beautiful to me as the sister in *The Nun's Story*. She only stayed a year though, and in my head she had gone on to an island in the Pacific to nurse the lepers and had taken ill herself and after a long convalescence had left the convent and walked off into the sunset to live happily ever after with Robert Mitchum.

There were only ever three or four nuns at the convent at one time. They had transient postings to schools throughout the state and could be with us for months or years at a time.

A new nun at the convent was both thrilling and frightening. I remember thinking we'd hit the jackpot when Sister Margaret Hehir arrived as our new principal. Probably in her early thirties at the time, she was the first nun I ever knew to share some personal history outside of her vocation. I was absolutely gobsmacked when she told us the story of when her mother had her last baby. Sister Margaret was a little girl and had no idea that her mother was pregnant until her dad woke her up in the middle of the night with a packet of snowballs and told her that she had a new brother or sister.

I don't know where I thought nuns came from but it certainly had never occurred to me that they had mothers and fathers of their own and had been kids themselves once who wore pyjamas and ate snowballs. To this day I've never seen a snowball without thinking of Sister Margaret.

My own mother's sister was a nun but I hadn't really even considered her as a physical reality, as she was a nursing sister who lived in a place called Sydney and I'd never laid eyes on her personally.

Aunty Genevieve was the only relative I didn't know and it wasn't until Christmas Eve sometime in the early seventies that she finally appeared in the flesh. The poor woman had left the convent after nine years and arrived back on the peninsula with not much more than the clothes she stood up in and the daunting task of beginning her life over as a layperson. Very much like Maria from *The Sound of Music* in my romantic head but truthfully the first thing that struck me about my long-lost aunty was how pretty she was. She looked a lot like Mum but younger than the two years that separated them.

Unfortunately one of us was insensitive enough to point this out to Mum on the way home from midnight mass.

'Well of course she looks younger than me. She's been in a convent and hasn't had all the bloody stress of marriage and six children!'

I swear Mum has no idea how funny she is sometimes and I hope I'm not painting her too much as a one-dimensional farmer's wife. My mother had and still has some extraordinary capabilities.

One of a few girls in South Australia to be accepted into university to study maths and science after her leaving honours, Mum could easily have gone on to be a mathematician or scientist, but I guess that was Dad's fault for being so handsome. She chose nursing, then him, and consequently the rest of us in the end, despite having a smorgasbord of talents.

* * *

I guess it's human nature to recall the unjust incidents in your childhood quicker than others, and I have never forgotten my second cousin Eugene copping more than he deserved one afternoon in that claustrophobic little schoolhouse while we all looked on in horror.

It had been a fairly miserable day all round. It was a Monday afternoon during a heatwave in February and we'd all just come back in from lunch. Sister Ridiculata wasn't in the best of moods. It had been tuck shop day that day and since we only ever had tuck shop on the first Monday of every month nearly every kid in the school would put in an order and our lunches would be delivered from the local bakery.

One by one we all started to gag on the pies and pasties, and the bravest among us started to complain.

'Sister, there's something wrong with my pie.'

'Mine too, Sister. It tastes terrible.'

'Nonsense, the pair of you! Think about all the starving children in Africa who've never even seen a pie.'

We battled on with our pies and pasties until one of the other nuns came running across from the convent to say the bakery had called to apologise because they'd accidentally used sugar instead of salt in that day's baking. Hot, bothered and hungry we all traipsed into school after our disappointing lunch and said the prayer of thanksgiving, sang 'Ava Maria' and got out our green catechisms.

'Righto then, who made the world? Richard?'

'God made the world, Sister.'

'Why? Eugene?'

'Coz he luvsus.'

As I said, Eugene was my second cousin, and he lived about ten miles away in Edithburgh with his eleven brothers and sisters in a massive old house across the road from the Edithburgh Jetty. Eugene's dad (another farmer) was also called Eugene, so as we did with all our relations we identified them by prefacing them with their dad's Christian name.

The Eugene Tahenys had even more spectacular freckles than the rest of us because of how much time they spent in the water and I was in awe of how tough they were. One of their older brothers had a huge scar on his leg where he'd jumped on top of a stingray on purpose and only that very morning we'd all gathered round while Eugene showed us a blister on his sunburnt back that was the size of a dinner plate.

'Have you seen Eugene's blister from the weekend?'

'It's the biggest blister in the world!'

'I don't think blisters can even get bigger than that one.'

'Wow, Eugene, that's a really good blister.'

Sister Ridiculata was forever on Eugene's case about him mumbling and would often gnash her teeth at him and say, 'Open your teeth and speak! Euge!' and then gnash a few more times right in his face to drive home her point.

Eugene must have really mumbled God's reason for making the world that afternoon because we all looked up sensing danger when Sister's voice raised another notch.

'Why did God make the world, Eugene? . . . Why? . . . Because he loves us! (gnash gnash gnash gnash gnash) Open your teeth and *speak*, Euge!'

And with that, her hand came down and slapped Eugene hard on the shoulder. The rest of us held our breaths and were frantic for the blister.

Bit by bit, what looked like a pint of water slowly spread across Eugene's shoulder and spilled through his school shirt and down his back. 'She burst his blister,' someone whispered, and for a minute I felt even sorrier for Sister than Eugene. He'd gone up another notch in the hero stakes, and she just looked at us all while we all looked back at her as if she was the devil himself.

* * *

I used to take things so literally when I was a kid. When I first found out about sex it was from a book Mum had given to Genevieve to pass on to me. It was fairly heavily laced with God and his holy plans and fairly light on details. At one point it said that sometimes mothers and fathers try to make a baby after the children go to bed. We always said goodnight to Mum and Dad while they were still watching Channel Two, and so for a year or more I thought that Mum and Dad did it in the lounge room. For a long time after that I sat on the floor in the lounge room and was very wary of the couch.

I believed in Father Christmas (whom we never called Santa for some reason) for longer than the average kid. Even the year he gave my cousin Felicity a brand new bike and gave my sister Cate Felicity's old bike I still believed in him but kept it to myself that I thought he was a bit of a bastard.

I think we all started to smell a rat, though, one year at the town hall after the annual Warooka Christmas pageant when we were standing in line waiting to sit on Father Christmas's lap. I wasn't alone in thinking that Father Christmas sounded a lot like the butcher Roy Stuart, and then he picked up my brother Richard and put him on his lap and said, 'Hello there, Richard, and what's your name?'

One Monday morning Sister announced that we all needed to be very careful with Damien Taheny that day because he'd been half killed on the weekend. Damien was Eugene's younger brother and every bit as tough. I think he'd had a concussion on Saturday playing footy but for weeks after that I agonised every time I saw Damien roughing it on the oval with the other boys.

As I said, I used to take the word of adults very literally, and one lunchtime Damien was underneath about six other boys tackling a ball on the grass and I flew into the middle of them all and begged them to stop. My brother was disgusted with me and told me to 'rack off and go and play with the girls' but I was beside myself by now and bawling my eyes out.

'Don't you remember what Sister said, Richard? Damien's already been half killed – he's only got another half left!'

The nuns at St Columba's were from the Josephite order and wore white habits in summer and chocolate brown in winter, and their convent was a building right next to the school. Except for piano lessons in the music room I only remember actually being inside the convent on a handful of occasions.

Once was when we all sat cross-legged in the passage with a television set up at one end to watch Neil Armstrong land on the moon and another time was on a Friday afternoon when I was taken over to the convent for a lie-down after having wet my pants.

The problem was, though, that I hadn't wet my pants at all but had sat on a bottle of Marveer furniture polish that we used to oil our desks with every Friday after lunch, and there was absolutely no convincing Sister of this fact.

My cousin Carmel was in the same grade as me and she said it served me right for laughing at her about the trombone (our word for pumpkin back then) when she was in hospital having her tonsils out. A very cranky nurse collecting her dinner tray had mistaken spilled roasted trombone for something far more sinister in Carmel's bed and carted her off for another bath that day.

I laughed myself inside-out hearing Carmel protesting all the way down the corridor, 'It's not poo! It's trombone!'

A few years ago my sister Genevieve and I were reminiscing about St Columba's and Genevieve gave me an insight into the nuns that went part way to explaining the behaviour of some of the crankier ones in particular. Some Sisters were actually battling cancer or other ghastly maladies at the same time as teaching and some actually never even had a vocation to teach at all. They had joined the convent to be nuns and were sometimes ordered to be teachers because that's where they were needed the most.

Genevieve is a teacher herself and has studied religion and theology for years. She's far more forgiving than I, and I rarely spend time with Genevieve without learning something from her. From that conversation it dawned on me that kids weren't the only ones lacking in power back then.

One of the best storytellers I've come across is Aunty Maureen, who was the mother of the Eugene Tahenys, not really an aunt of ours at all, but we tended to refer to a lot of our parents' cousins and their husbands and wives as Aunty and Uncle.

Aunty Maureen hailed from further north on the Yorke Peninsula and was a convert to Catholicism, as were a number of my relations. A friend of mine refers to converts as 'industrial-strength Catholics' and this wasn't far from the mark in

Maureen's case. She went from a small Methodist family to playing the organ at mass every Sunday and ended up being the mother of twelve.

She told me a story once about one of her kids coming home from St Columba's with an order from Sister to bring back the mission money. Just before the end of the school year the nuns would send mission envelopes home to all the families to be filled with some charitable bucks for the missionaries overseas.

It was a stinking hot day and Aunty Maureen was pregnant with her eleventh or twelfth baby, Uncle Euge was in the middle of harvest and Christmas was just around the corner. A possibly very hot and overworked Aunty Maureen was given this ultimatum by a six- or seven-year-old daughter with her hands on her hips: 'Mum! Sister sayed that if we don't bring the mission money back by Friday then all the mothers are going to jail.'

To which Maureen replied in a heartbeat, 'Well, Elizabeth, you can go back and tell Sister sayed that nothing would please your mother more. I'll have the baby on the government in an air-conditioned cell, not a child in sight and three meals a day brought to me on a tray!'

For nearly two decades Maureen Taheny was the heart of the mothers' club at St Columba's and a highlight was the 'mothers' item' at our annual school concert, held in the Yorketown Town Hall. Maureen would lead them all in a rendition of 'Blue Spanish Eyes' or 'I'll Take You Home Again, Kathleen', and I remember one year when Carmel South's mother was in the front row on stage wearing a mini-skirt. This would be the equivalent nowadays of a mum in hipster jeans and a midriff top, and I was mad with jealousy and hated Carmel that day.

Another exciting event in the St Columba's calendar was the Sports Day. We had three teams: St Joseph's, St Mary's and St Columba's. I can still remember the thrill of the smell of our freshly painted white sports shoes in the laundry, lined up in honour of the day.

I wasn't at all athletic but I loved any day that deviated from the ordinary and I absolutely adored the theatre of the 'march past', where we would line up on the asphalt court and march around to the rousing amplified music while our parents looked on through the wire mesh fence.

My family was always in St Joseph's team and though I never got to hold the banner myself I was immensely proud of my brothers one year when not only did Richard hold the banner but Justin had the very great honour of leading all three teams in the march-past beating the drum. I remember Dad telling him on the way home what a great job he had done and how he had been the only one marching in time.

Last but not least of our annual highlights was the St Columba's bazaar. A tradition that is carried on today by most schools, the bazaar was a fundraising effort in the form of a fete comprising food stalls, chocolate wheels, raffles, merry-go-rounds and the like.

The St Columba's bazaar was all of the above, with the exception of food stalls, chocolate wheels, raffles, merry-go-rounds and the like. Basically our yearly fundraiser was about nine families turning up with all the crap they had found in their sheds and selling it to each other. Although I'm sure I'm not romanticising the event with the memory of barbecued chops and sausages.

One year at the end of the bazaar we came home with two television sets: one that had no screen that Dad had donated and bought back himself and another one from the Detmars that had no sound. Dad knew full well that there was method to the madness if we put them on top of each other but Mum was less than impressed on the way home.

'I can't believe you paid twenty dollars for our own television, Denis.'

'Hmmm, funny isn't it . . . bazaar, almost.'

One of Dad's best lines was one night when we were driving home from Yorketown in the very wee hours of Christmas morning. There had been a lot of last-minute Christmas shopping, a visit to an aunt and uncle, midnight mass in the Yorketown church and then Mum and Dad had dropped in for quick drinks with their great buddies Sparks and Margaret Harris while we kids waited in the car. The quick drinks weren't quite as quick as we'd have liked, and the time was passed in agony while we resisted the temptation to turn around and check out the Christmas presents that were jammed into the back of the station wagon and covered with a blanket. By the time we finally hit the road most of us were asleep and blissfully unaware of the slight hitch that lay ahead of us. Just past the Peesey swamp and about two miles from Warooka we ran out of petrol.

Dad must have been inspired by the knowledge that there was little likelihood of any passing traffic and far too long a walk for him to our place to fill up a jerry can and bring it all the way back. So he got out of the car and opened the back door and shook my brother from his sleep. Richard was about fifteen at the time and woke up quite disoriented for a few seconds.

'Guess what, Richard? . . . You got a bike for Christmas!'

* * *

My class at St Columba's was made up of four: myself, my cousin Beth Taheny, my other cousin Carmel South, and Michael Patrick Kennedy. I had grown up with Michael Patrick, and his mother was one of my favourite people in the whole world. Mrs Kennedy loved a party, loved a laugh and taught me how to do the same. I've only realised in recent years, looking at old photos of Mum's, how physically beautiful Mrs Kennedy was. She had cheekbones and a smile that belonged to Hollywood and she was beyond generous to our family in a thousand ways. Not the least example was that she would stay on the piano for hours at parties to keep the night alive and kicking. One enduring memory is of her throwing her arms around me on countless occasions and saying, 'God love you! I wouldn't be dead for quids.'

I was in love with Michael Patrick for what seemed the entirety of my childhood and presumed that it would be reciprocated eventually and that I would grow up and marry him and run the pub with Mrs Kennedy.

One of the most distressing days of my life was the day we laid Alice Kennedy to rest. It wasn't that many years ago actually but she used to laugh and tell me they would never get her in a coffin no matter how old or dead she was: 'They'll get one leg down in the casket, Fifi, and I'll kick the other one up in the air and then they'll straighten that one out and I'll kick the other one up again and they'll never get the damn lid on. Ever.'

I stared at the lid of her coffin and was engulfed with sadness. No one I had ever known had spelt out their distaste for mortality as well or as often as Mrs Kennedy. She had scoffed and laughed at it so many times, and her wake was a testament to the joy she had given so many of us. But I found it near impossible to celebrate the life of Alice Kennedy that day. The one person I wanted to celebrate with was the one person who couldn't be there.

One recess time at St Columba's, it was announced that someone had spilled green paint in the art cupboard and if the culprit hadn't owned up by lunch then everyone was getting the strap. Lunch was pretty sombre that day and before we knew it Sister had rung the bell and we were all lined up with our hands held out.

'Where's Michael Patrick?'

'In the toilet, Sister.'

Someone covered for him for a while, but Michael Patrick had run away at lunchtime and had no intention of returning to the scene of a crime that wasn't his and taking part in its ridiculous repercussions. My hero Mrs Kennedy backed him up and from that day he relocated to the public school. To me he was also a hero, but I missed him – now it was just Beth, Carmel and me.

Carmel and I had a fascination for the convent where the nuns lived, and we would jump at any opportunity to be sent over there. One morning we knocked on the back door to collect the scrap bucket to take down the road to old Mrs Solomon for her chooks and saw Sister Eunice without her veil on, which was without a doubt the most amazing thing we'd seen since we had spotted Sister Margaret hanging out her bras and undies. Most kids hated taking the scrap bucket to Mrs Solomon's house because it was a pretty creepy excursion. But the cameras were rolling as ever in my head and Carmel and I were two young heroines who bravely crossed into Mrs Solomon's territory to find evidence of other kids who'd been before us and were slaughtered in her house. I can still remember the smell of rotting fruit as we came around the back of her house and began the weird daily ritual.

'Ding dong bell, pussy's in the well.'

For some reason known only to old Mrs Solomon we had to sing this greeting as we peered through her screen door into the blackness of her house.

'Who put him in?' she'd warble as her silhouette appeared.

'Little Tommy Finn,' we'd sing as we passed the scrap bucket to her liver-spotted hands and she'd exchange it for two peaches. I swear I haven't eaten a peach for forty years.

Carmel and I were puerile to say the least. Another all-time favourite was to visit Aunty Mon and our ailing Uncle Dick. The whole point was to be given some lollies to share with Uncle Dick and wait for Aunty Mon to say, 'Mind the sticky on you, Dicky.' Now that was funny.

Beth, my other classmate, was a quiet girl and for a long time she ran the tuck shop, which was actually only a few jars of Cobbers, Clinkers and Raspberries in the art cupboard.

Carmel and I were forever conning her into giving us two cents' worth and telling her we'd pay later and of course later never ever came. Beth had kept a record and before long we owed ninety-five cents between us and I was panic stricken. There was absolutely no way I could get my hands on ninety-five cents and Carmel was in the same boat as me. Eventually, after a few sleepless nights, I came up with a brilliant plan: tell it at confession on Friday. And that's how it worked for the next year or more. Carmel and I got our lollies and Beth kept a record and every time we hit the one-dollar mark, Beth shut up shop until we confessed.

We used to walk over to the church for confession every Friday, and I kind of loved and loathed confession. I enjoyed my spotless white soul as we headed back into class but I found it depressing that it would be full of black spots again by the end of the day.

I reckoned that if I didn't have any brothers and sisters my soul would have stayed white for a lot longer, but most of the time I hated my brothers and sisters and hating anyone was a sin and telling them you hated them was another sin and on and on it went until your soul was as black as thunder by Tuesday.

Most sins were venial sins, though, and pretty easy to get rid of. Mortal sins were the worst kind and if you died with one or more on your soul before a priest could get to you then unfortunately you would go straight to hell. I always thought that that gave an unfair advantage to people who died slowly as opposed to people who were hit by a bus or choked to death, but I didn't lose too much sleep over it, having never personally committed murder or adultery.

Having said that, I did freak out a bit once on a Wednesday when I told Genevieve that I wished she was dead.

'That's a mortal sin, Fiona.'

'No, it isn't.'

'I'm pretty sure it is.'

'You're a dickhead, it is not.'

I would have liked to have checked with a higher authority but it was nearly Friday and rather than owning up to someone that I had actually told Genevieve that I wished she was dead I just decided to take special care crossing the road and chewing my food for the next two days.

When I was about eight or nine a new girl came to the convent and I was insanely excited to find out that she was in the same grade as me. Mary-Anne Williams and I became inseparable from that day on. Her parents managed one of the pubs in Yorketown and I spent as many weekends at Mary-Anne's house as I could muster. Mary-Anne had two older brothers and one younger sister who we completely ignored. We locked ourselves in Mary-Anne's bedroom at every opportunity for the next five years or more. We went from paper dolls to the Bay City Rollers to ABBA from Grade 4 to Year 9 and pretty much excluded the rest of the world.

Mary-Anne's dad was called Sugar Williams and he was a big drinker with a big heart and a wicked wit. Mrs Williams worked from sun-up to sundown and I adored their house and every minute I spent there. All the Williamses were funny and irreverent and I guess that's why I loved them so much.

Before they came to Yorketown, Sugar and Mrs Williams used to run the pub in a tiny place called Appila in the mid-north of South Australia. I think the population of Appila was about twenty and on the odd occasion that someone rang the pub looking for accommodation Sugar used to tell them he'd have to run upstairs and check the diary. Having neither a second floor nor a booking diary he would then proceed to serve the two or three customers at the bar while the phone lay on the counter and eventually get back to them to say they were very lucky indeed, there was one room left.

One day someone from the health department stopped by for an impromptu inspection and informed Sugar that there were too many flies in the kitchen. Sugar responded to this with a question: 'How many am I allowed to have?'

There was no doubt the Williamses were battlers. I didn't notice it at the time but looking back they probably had less than most people I knew. They did have a colour television, though, that Sugar was immensely proud of. He used to call me Ferrina for some reason and would shoot me the same question from his lounge chair every time I walked through the door: 'Has colour TV made it to Warooka yet, Ferrina?'

'Not yet, Mr Williams,' I'd reply. And then he'd laugh his arse off.

He nearly coughed up a lung when he heard about the two TV sets from the St Columba's bazaar.

The day Mary-Anne arrived at St Columba's couldn't have come sooner as far as I was concerned. I'd had a punch-up with Carmel at recess, which was fairly common, and we'd pulled a hunk of each other's hair right out of our heads. The fight had started when I overheard one of the Grade 7s informing Maria Wigley that all mothers were on the pill and though I wasn't completely sure what the pill was, I had gathered from Father Tuit's sermon on Sunday that it was a wicked tablet indeed, and so I immediately butted in and insisted that my mother wasn't.

'Don't be an idiot. If mothers weren't on the pill they'd all have a hundred babies.'

I didn't really like being called an idiot but I also didn't have a confident argument so I changed the subject. 'Idiots don't come from Warooka; idiots only come from Yorketown.'

'Idiots *do so* come from Warooka, and stuck-up people come from there too.' Carmel South had taken the bait and we were away.

'Fight! Fight! Fight! Fight!'

In our best ever bout on record, Carmel and I went about three rounds of the asphalt court until Sister God-knows-who separated us and sent us to opposite ends of the school.

I was sitting in the lunch shed with a bleeding scalp when I spoke to Mary-Anne Williams for the first time. My heart sank when I found out that she was from Yorketown. She would probably hear what I'd said about Yorketown people and be Carmel's friend instead of mine. I was desperate for a new best friend and had set my sights on having Mary-Anne Williams all to myself, but there were four other girls in the South family and there was no way I could compete for friendship from the wrong side of the Peesey swamp.

And then a little bit of luck came my way in the form of my Aunty Frances South pulling up right in front of the schoolhouse in her Fairlane 500 and slamming out of the car with a wooden spoon in her hand.

'Where's Veronica Taheny?'

Mary-Anne and I enjoyed every bit of the drama that played out in front of us. Veronica was another one of the 'Eugene Tahenys' and had mastered the art of giving 'dead legs', which was a knuckle punch to the middle of the thigh. Being two years younger I had never had the pleasure of receiving one of Veronica's famous 'dead legs' but I'd seen the bruise she'd left on my brother Richard once. She had a spectacular technique.

Apparently that morning Aunty Frances had seen yet another of Veronica's calling cards on my cousin Caroline's leg and had come to school to deal with Veronica in person. I filled Mary-Anne in on all of this to my own advantage. 'That's Carmel's mum. I wouldn't hang around with the Souths much if I was you. Aunty Frances is mental.'

I learnt at an early age to dodge trouble wherever I possibly could, and I have to admit at times I was nothing short of a coward. I was also insanely disorganised and never knew where anything was. It was impossible to know because my desk and my school bag in particular were filled to the brim with my own chaos. One morning Sister asked us all to open our desks and put our hands behind our backs. 'There is a thief in this room and I'm about to find out who he or she is.'

I was thrilled to have the monotony of the morning broken and was all ears and eyes, as was everybody else, to discover who the thief might be.

Sister was at her wit's end over the amount of complaints she'd had from kids missing things, and she turned everyone's desks inside out as she walked up and down the two aisles in the room.

'Aha! Fiona Taheny.'

I was as shocked as anyone else and scared to boot. Sure enough, right there in my desk, shoved in with all my dog-eared catastrophes, was Denis Detmar's calculator, Thomas Luke's ruler, Jacquie Barnes's compass, and the list went on and horribly on. I was no thief but I was a terrible borrower, and have been my whole life. I somehow manage to absorb things that have no business being in my possession. Only yesterday I noticed a remote control in my handbag from a hotel I'd been staying at on the Gold Coast . . .

I don't remember what happened to me over that, but my heart nearly gave way that same afternoon when we were having an assembly outside and Sister Bernadine came over from the music room and announced that someone had the Grade 4 piano book and she needed it to be returned.

At this stage it wasn't a major offence to still have the piano book and the culprit could have handed it in pretty safely right there and then. This did prove problematic, though, as I was indeed the culprit and knew for a fact that the piano book was in my schoolbag in very bad shape, having lost an argument with a rotten banana.

My new pal Mary-Anne Williams knew about the book but not about the banana, and tried to whisper a reminder to me.

'Who's talking? Is that you, Mary-Anne Williams?' demanded Sister Bernadine.

'Yes, Sister.'

'Well?'

'Maybe Fiona's got the piano book, Sister.'

Sugar Williams couldn't have delivered the line better himself, and everyone but Sister started to laugh at Mary-Anne's wonderful joke. Only Mary-Anne and I knew that it wasn't a joke and neither of us was laughing when Mary-Anne was hauled up to the front of the assembly and strapped on the back of the legs in front of everyone for being such a smart alec.

Years later Mary-Anne and I were sitting through a tedious science lesson in Year 9 at the Yorketown Area School when our teacher was taking us through the periodic table. I had psychologically left the room and was staring into space when Mary-Anne nudged me and I became aware that Mr Haddow was talking to me.

'Fiona Taheny?'

'Yes?'

'Fe! What does Fe stand for?'

Mary-Anne whispered the answer to me. I was too grateful to even question it and repeated what she'd offered on the spot.

'A ferret!'

'A ferret?'

'Yes, sir, a ferret.'

'Get out!'

Next thing I knew I was standing outside the science lab wondering what the hell I'd done wrong. Not only did I not know what Fe stood for, I also wasn't completely sure what a ferret was.

Eventually everyone spilled out of class and I kicked Mary-Anne in the back of the leg.

'Thanks a lot, Mary-Anne.'

'You're welcome, Fiona. That was for the Grade 4 piano book, by the way.'

Mary-Anne Williams actually wrote in a history exam answer once that 'Harold Holt was either at the bottom of the Ocean in Portsea or possibly in Fiona Taheny's school desk at St Columba's Yorketown.'

The sad thing is I was never cured. Even as I'm writing this I'm looking at my bookcase at home and right there on the bottom shelf is the unreturned *Web of Life* from my matric year in 1979.

Sorry about that, Mrs Huxtable.

CHAPTER 4

BOARDING SCHOOL AND BEDPANS

At fifteen it was finally my turn to go to boarding school, and I was nearly out of my skin with excitement. For the last few years I'd been eaten up with envy hearing Genevieve and Richard telling hundreds of stories from school and at last my bags were packed and I was heading for Adelaide, surely one of the biggest cities in the world.

Driving into the grounds of Cabra Dominican College is like driving into a cliché of a majestic old-world boarding school, particularly in 1979 when the beautiful grounds were dotted with real live nuns in habits with rosary beads in tow.

The food was disgusting, the heating was nonexistent and the rules were unbending, and yet I've never enjoyed myself more.

Mum and Dad were with me in the front parlour as we waited for the head nun, Sister Paul, to collect me and take me upstairs. When she entered the room my nerves nearly won out over my excitement, as she was more than a dominant presence. A very tall lady, Sister Paul was referred to as 'Stretch' by generations of boarders.

The year I turned sixteen was about the time I gradually began to take my own place at that kitchen table. On weekends home from boarding school I began telling stories of my own. My impersonations of Stretch were a big hit at home. She spoke in a seriously creepy, soft voice and the angrier she was the quieter she became.

I saw Sister Paul only a month ago in Alice Springs and the weird phenomenon with nuns is how distorted they can become in your memory. She's still tall but not quite the seven foot seven I would have sworn by, and she appeared to be the same age that I would have pegged her at more than thirty years ago.

She walked me up the stairs on that first night at Cabra and noticed I was crying in the wake of saying goodbye to Mum and Dad. She put her hand on my shoulder and said, 'It's nice to see tears, dear. Tears mean you've left behind people you love.' A year later in the following months after Felicity died it was Sister Paul who would find me well after 'lights out' wandering around the corridors of Cabra in tears and it was Sister Paul who comforted me and made me cups of cocoa in the dead of night. I conveniently put aside the recollections of her kindness in the daylight hours and she became Stretch again.

The first two girls I laid eyes on at Cabra were Tessie Leahy and Rhani Sidhu. They were doing the rock'n'roll on the balcony and I've never heard Suzi Quatro's 'Stumbling In' again without seeing a picture of those two very pretty dark-haired dancing fifteen-year-olds.

Tessie and Rhani had both been boarders for a year before this, as had four or five other girls in the Year 11 dorm. It was fairly easy to distinguish the old boarders from the new. The ones laughing and calling out to each other were the old, and the ones sitting on the edge of their beds looking like they were about to be sick were the new. Either that or they had been exceedingly unpopular the year before.

The dormitory continued the cliché of everything you'd expect a boarding school to be: rows of beds down each side with a thin partition dividing pairs of beds into a cubicle which you shared with another girl.

I had been pretty uptight about meeting whoever I was sharing my cubicle with because I still knelt down to say my prayers at night and I was terrified of being made fun of.

I was more than relieved when Carmel Clarke came around the corner and asked if I was Fiona Taheny. One of the first things she told me was that she still knelt down to say her prayers at night and hoped I didn't think she was weird. For the rest of that year Carmel and I kept an eye out for the other one when we said our prayers and if someone was coming one of us would give the warning and the other one would say, 'Found it!' and hold up the shoe they were looking for under the bed.

I knew two girls who were starting at Cabra that year: Louise Noonan, who was from Jamestown and had been one of the Hornsdale Leprechauns, and my cousin Beth, who I'd been to school with my whole life.

The most popular girls in my year on first impression were Jane and Liza, and as it turned out I was dead on the money. Jane Mortimer and Liza Lyons had it all from where I was sitting. One dark and one blonde, both olive skinned, both leggy and both beautiful. They were Cabra's answer to Jaclyn Smith and Farrah Fawcett from *Charlie's Angels*. I was terribly shy around them for a while but over time we became great buddies and damn them both if they weren't clever and funny as well.

The first person I ever met from the Northern Territory was Jasmin Afianos. She was the daughter of an illegal immigrant from Greece who, Jasmin had us believe, was wanted for murder back in his home country. Jasmin has been one of my best friends and allies since our first night together at boarding school in 1978. She hailed from Tennant Creek and used to regale us with stories about her dad. It was hard to tell at first how much of Jasmin's stories were truth or fiction but I was fascinated by her and more than a little bit in awe. She had already been expelled from a boarding school in Queensland before coming to Cabra and seemed to be fearless of everyone and everything, particularly the nuns.

The first night in a boarding school after 'lights out' is a fairly surreal experience. It really is a stepping stone to leaving home forever and as much as I had been counting down the days I was actually preparing to join in on the collective sound of girls sniffling in their beds when I was distracted by something scarier than Stretch. It was pretty intimidating that first night as a new boarder. I remember identifying the 'cool' girls pretty quickly and I instinctively knew they were out of my league. Mum had taken it upon herself to rustle me up a new dress and a haircut for the occasion and I was dubbed 'wedge head' by the time I'd unpacked my suitcase. I hadn't really spoken to anyone by 'lights out' and then a terrifying Year 12 girl called Eliza Whitlaw took it upon herself to have a bit of fun at our expense.

All of a sudden the lights went on in the dormitory and Whitlaw made her entrance.

Eliza Whitlaw was a big domination of a girl, and reminded me very much of Bea Smith from *Prisoner*. 'So how many of you new girls are virgins?'

I pretended to be asleep immediately, but she went up and down the dormitory asking the same question. About three yeses and seven nos later she was at the foot of Jasmin's bed and I was next. The poor girl in the bed opposite me had responded with a 'half and half'!

'So what about you, Afianos? You a virgin?'

Jasmin gave it straight back to her: 'What are you? Desperate? Piss off, you fat pervert!'

Jasmin was fearless. She made it her business to taunt Whitlaw for the rest of our time at Cabra. Whitlaw scared me senseless, but she didn't scare Jasmin, and neither did the nuns.

It takes a lot to scare someone who had a dad in Tennant Creek who went crazy on booze and threatened to kill people on a very regular basis. Jasmin used to impersonate him in one of his rages; she'd put on the thick Greek accent of her drunken dad and we could never get enough of it.

Years later I apologised for trivialising what she'd been through and for how many times I'd said, 'Jasmin, do your dad!'

She told me it was nothing to be sorry about. She had learnt from her mum how to deflect his rage and how to never let him see fear. Jasmin still believes that's how her mother protected herself and her girls. He had potentially been a dangerous man, but he never actually laid a hand on any of them.

Later that night in the dormitory, I showed Jasmin my photo album and visually introduced her to my home town and my family. Afterwards she pulled out her album that only had pictures of one person.

'Did you know I've got a baby?' Jasmin has always talked big and to the point. As it turned out her baby was 'Floppy', an Aboriginal boy with cerebral palsy that Jasmin had unofficially adopted when she was eight. He was institutionalised in Tennant Creek and was only a few months old when Jasmin wandered in and claimed him as her own. Until she was sent to Cabra, Jasmin looked after Floppy, and was free to take him home whenever she could on weekends and after school.

Once again I underestimated the information she'd imparted, perhaps because she was so frank and without drama, or perhaps because I'd come from such a sheltered world that I couldn't get a handle on hers. It wasn't until years later that I realised that while I was in my boarding school bed sniffling with traditional homesickness, the girl in the next bed had lost her baby.

Jasmin moved back to Tennant Creek years ago, and since I live in Alice Springs we now reside in neighbouring towns five hundred kilometres apart, but that's the way it is in the Northern Territory. It was in Jasmin's pub that I performed my first paid stand-up gig, but that's another story. We've shared some extraordinary experiences over the years, not the least of which was the birth of her son. I was pregnant myself at the time with my fifth baby and hauled myself out of bed when the phone rang at 2 a.m. Her labour hadn't progressed and the Flying Doctor was airlifting her to Alice Springs, though she put it more like this: 'My baby's stuck, they're going to cut it out in Alice.'

I met her at the ambulance outside the hospital, and I have never seen anyone look so vulnerable. She was as white as a ghost and completely silent. Being a traditional screamer myself in the throes of labour, I was at a bit of a loss as we entered the lift for maternity, but Jasmin was enduring a near five-hour second-stage labour, practically unheard of in this day and age.

She was near catatonic, and for the first time in our friendship it was up to me to be the strong one. We were left alone waiting in a labour ward and after a while in came a midwife to prep her for surgery, armed with a catheter and razor blades. 'Well, well, well,' she said and I looked up, and to this day I still don't believe what I saw.

'Oh my God, Jasmin, it's Whitlaw!'

And it was.

* * *

'Forgetful Fi' was what they all called me, my whole childhood. I can't think why my mother encouraged me to become a nurse. I guess to be fair I hadn't left her with many options. I'd graduated from Cabra Dominican College with a C average at best, and university was out of the question. I'd been at boarding school for two years, having done nothing but laugh and laugh and laugh. It was without doubt one of the most joyful times of my life, at great expense to my parents.

Back then in 1980 all a girl needed was a fob watch to qualify as a nurse's aide, and so I began my career at a private nursing home in Adelaide the January after leaving school.

I remember my first day. I was working the afternoon shift, and after a brief chat with the matron I was introduced to my first patient, Mrs White. Mrs White had no speech as she had suffered a stroke, and my instructions were to organise her shower and get her ready for tea.

I made small talk as I collected Mrs White's nightie, slippers and toiletries and then wheeled her chair to a bathroom. I understand now how dim I must have seemed, but I really had no clue what my responsibilities actually were.

Matron passed me in the hall a couple of times and I must admit she looked at me rather strangely. On her third leg past me in the passage she turned back and asked me what on earth I was doing.

'Waiting for Mrs White to come out of the shower.'

'But I thought I told you to shower her.'

'Oh . . . I . . .'

'She can't shower herself. She's paralysed. You have to be in there with her.'

To my eternal shame I then actually said in a horrified whisper, 'But she'll be naked.'

As if that wasn't bad enough, that same night I saw a dead body for the first time in my life. Mrs Lim, and I'll never forget it. We were having a supper break at about nine o'clock and heard an almighty crash from one of the top rooms. Mrs Lim had been on her commode and suffered an ill-timed fatal heart attack. A big woman, her bum was actually wedged into her portable loo and when she went down, it went with her. I suppose nobody really has an expectation of what their first experience with death will be but a woman on her head with her bum in the air and a commode on top was certainly something I hadn't bargained on.

Probably the best way to sum up my nursing career is to say it was like being caught in a never-ending episode of Mr Bean without the laugh track. I was in a constant state of anxiety, and the more anxious I became the more mistakes I made.

My official nursing training happened in Yorketown about thirteen miles from Warooka. I remember being in Matron's office a lot during my training, and filling out more than my fair share of what were called incident reports. Incident reports were official hospital forms that documented accidents and misdemeanours by the nursing staff.

I'm pretty sure that the first incident report I filled in had to do with my inadvertent use of Mrs Barklay's expressed breast milk in Mr Bridge's hot Milo one night, and subsequent stuff-ups are just too numerable to recall. I do, however, remember one incident that I didn't own up to.

Aunty Dot was a long-term patient in the geriatric wing of the Yorketown Hospital. Even though everybody referred to her as Aunty Dot, she was actually my grandfather's sister. Aunty Dot was nearly ninety when I became one of her nurses, and while she hadn't completely lost her marbles she was, as one of my cousins used to say, a few streets off the main road.

Aunty Dot had never married and had lived all her life in the original homestead on my dad's farm. She was a pretty significant part of my childhood. At the start of every shift she and I would go through a fairly odd verbal ritual.

'Morning, Aunty Dot.'

'Who are you?'

'I'm Fiona. I'm one of Denis and Deirdre's girls.'

'Well, that can't be right.'

'Why's that?'

'Because they're fine-looking people.'

'So what am I then?'

'You? You're an ugly little beggar.'

Nice one, Aunty Dot. I didn't really mind. I remembered her in better days, and she was always kind to us when we were kids.

One night I was on drug trolley duty in the geriatric ward and I was dosing out the evening medication. Aunty Dot was on a fairly mild sleeping drug and after I watched her swallow it I poured up Mr Bridge's nightcap. Mr Bridge was pretty much off his rocker and was on a very heavy sedative. Damn! I turned my back for a second and Aunty Dot had downed his as well.

I was exhausted even at the thought of another incident report, more time in Matron's office and the possibility of having killed my great-aunt and everybody finding out. I proceeded to hatch a coward's plan that was completely driven by fear: say nothing and hope for the best.

Easier said than done. That night was the longest night of my life. I slept the sleep of Macduff, and by the time I made my way to work the next morning I was expecting the worst.

I listened intently during handover and pretended to be as surprised as everyone else when the night duty nurse gave us a rundown of the evening's events.

'Mr Bridge's had a shocking night and had to be given a shot of Valium at five o'clock this morning, and Aunty Dot seems to be in some sort of a coma and is on half-hourly observations for the next twenty-four hours.'

None of it was good news but it could have been worse. I clung to a fading hope and decided to keep my mouth shut for a while longer. Luck was on my side. Aunty Dot woke up at about two o'clock that afternoon and lived for another eight years.

* * *

After I finished at Cabra and while working as a nurse's aide in Adelaide I rented an assortment of flats with an assortment of girlfriends, until I stumbled across one of the best rental finds of my life.

Actually, it was my dad who found what we still refer to as 'Trevelyan Street' in an ad in the *Southern Cross* newspaper. At the time my sister Genevieve was also living in Adelaide, studying for a teaching degree, and we had decided to look for a house to rent with a few other mates to keep costs down. We found a house all right, but it did come at a bit of a cost, at least for poor Genevieve.

Dad had called me the night before, quite excited about how cheap the rent was and how large the house sounded and what a great location it was. A meeting was set up for the next day to have a look at the place and my father drove the two hundred or so kilometres to Adelaide to check it all out with me.

The house in Trevelyan Street was beautiful. It was a five-bedroom glory with a gorgeous attic, two bathrooms, a huge kitchen and a creek running through the block at the boundary of the property. To me it was a castle and I wanted it on the spot.

Mrs O'Riordan, the landlady, showed us through and then invited us into her own home, which was only a few doors up the road. Even though the house she was about to rent us was very run down and in serious need of a reno and paint job, the rent was inexplicably low – that is, until Mrs O'Riordan shared her master plan for Trevelyan Street over a cup of coffee with my dad and me.

You see, she was a little eccentric, and heavily involved with a very charismatic arm of the Catholic Church. She intended to gradually buy five or six adjoining properties and create some kind of Christian commune in the street. And she explained to us: 'In the meantime, I'll rent this at a very low cost, but I will require someone from the house to attend my weekly prayer groups and be involved in my larger plan for community Christian living.'

Dad shifted in his chair a bit and 'ahemed' a couple of times, and eventually I broke the silence brilliantly.

'Well, that's perfect. My sister Genevieve just loves prayer meetings.'

So that was that. Six of us moved in to Trevelyan Street and paid bugger-all rent. We were seven minutes from the city and had our very own creek and an attic! I guess the only down side was the sound of Genevieve slamming the front door every Tuesday night on her way to Mrs O'Riordan's.

'I could kill you, Fiona!'

Trevelyan Street became a famous house for parties, and it had about a four-year rotation of housemates. Everybody wanted to live at Trevelyan Street, and in time just about everyone we knew had at least crashed there for a time. In the beginning it was just one guy called Chappy and six girls: Genevieve, me, Mary-Anne Williams and two of her cousins, and my own cousin Marianne Moloney.

Chappy was hysterical fun, but more importantly had loads of handsome friends from Sacred Heart College. Back then we were interested in only two types of males: ex-Sacred Heart ones, or ex-Rostrevor ones. These were the two Catholic boys' boarding schools in Adelaide.

The early days at Trevelyan Street were intoxicating for me. I'd only ever known Warooka and then boarding school, and here I was, liberated at last, in a huge house with a weekly pay cheque and a constant stream of mates.

We had barbecues and dinner parties, and would invariably end up playing hide-and-seek or murder in the dark. Some Sunday afternoons we played 'war games' in the overgrown backyard.

I did host a book club on Saturday afternoons, but the only books on offer were by Harold Robbins and Jackie Collins, and we'd go straight to the raunchy stuff and read out sex passages as if they were literature and laugh until we couldn't breathe.

'Get out of bed, you whore!' is still a phrase that will make a couple of my oldest girlfriends explode. Lulu Cain was standing on a chair reading it out loud when Mrs O'Riordan walked into the living room on an ill-timed house check.

Genevieve kept a certain measure of civilisation to the place and brought in the odd vegetable, but in reality at that time the rest of us were caught between childhood and grown-up land. Except, I suppose, for Mary-Anne's cousins, who lived down one side of the house and pretty much kept to themselves. They had huge stuffed toys in their room and wore very slinky underwear and disco clothes that made the rest of us feel like country heifers. Because of their tiny bodies and penchant for teddy bears we used to refer to them as the 'little girls'. They also had real boyfriends with names like Rocco and Franko, who picked them up in hotted-up cars with mag wheels.

I remember Jasmin visiting Trevelyan Street once. She had by now left conservative Adelaide behind, and was working in a women's refuge in Sydney. Jasmin was staying for a couple of nights and as Mary-Anne had the only double bed in the house she asked if she could doss down there. Mary-Anne was a bit concerned and came out the back to find me.

'Did you know Jasmin wants to sleep in my bed?'

'Yeah, so what?'

'She works in a women's refuge, Fiona! She's probably a lesbian.'

Jasmin just happened to be in the bathroom at the time, and we were sitting right underneath the window.

'Mary-Anne, you fuckwit! If you had half a brain you'd know the difference between feminism and lesbianism. I happen not to be a lesbian, for your information, but if I was, you would be the last woman on earth I'd crack onto.'

At times Jasmin and I have suffered from poor judgement, particularly in our youth. I guess the best example would be the time we stole a car, but even now I prefer to recall it as 'borrowing' more than stealing. It was at Trevelyan Street, and Mary-Anne Williams had gone away for the weekend and left her car keys with Genevieve along with strict instructions not to let them anywhere near Jasmin and Fiona.

'Don't be stupid,' I said to a snoozing Genevieve on that fateful Saturday morning. 'We don't even have our licences, we just need to park it out in the street so Chappy can get into the driveway.'

And minutes later we were on our way. Roaring up King William Road with what we hoped would be a day of blissful independence.

Our first matter of business was to drive past Suzie Metcalf's place to see if Jim Bourke's car was parked outside, and thus be the first people we knew to have confirmation that they were indeed sleeping together. None of our business at all, of course, but more than interesting to two nineteen-year-olds.

Having determined that Suzie was very much the slut we suspected her to be, we then headed towards Goodwood to do a few laps around the front gardens of Cabra Boarding School and yell a collection of obscenities at some unsuspecting nuns or boarders as we hooned past. This second option was more Jasmin's idea than mine, as my sister Cate was still at Cabra and I was terrified of being spotted.

Nonetheless, I didn't object too valiantly as, after all, Jasmin was the driver and therefore the captain of our misdemeanour. I needn't have worried because we never did make it to Cabra. Less than thirty minutes after take-off we were hurtling back to Trevelyan Street and away from a crime.

'Fucking hell, Jasmin! You just hit a car.'

'Side-swiped, Fiona, and it was only a bull bar.'

We pulled up outside of Trevelyan Street and were horrified to see the massive dent on the front right mudguard of Mary-Anne's car.

'Oh my God, Jasmin, we're dead!'

'Just shut up and listen to me, I know what to do.'

About ten minutes later we were back on the road and heading towards a panelbeater near the Anzac Highway. I had snuck back into the house without questions and got exactly what Jasmin had instructed: a wig, dark sunglasses and the money from the rent tin.

I was getting into disguise while Jasmin laid out the plan.

'Okay, you have to act like you're crying, and tell the guy at the garage that your husband is on his way back from a business trip, and you need the car fixed in one hour or he'll kill you. Start crying, Fiona, we're nearly there.'

'I am crying, Jasmin . . . Genevieve's behind us.'

Genevieve and Chappy had been following us for some minutes and were waving frantically and tooting their horn for us to stop. No such luck. Jasmin and me, the bewigged housewife, sped off again and the chase continued, down about three or four back streets, across Anzac Highway and unfortunately back down a dead-end street. Trapped and forlorn, I peeked over the top of the shades and wound down the window to be faced with a surprisingly mild-tempered Genevieve.

'Fiona, you two need to come home straightaway. Jasmin's mother rang. Her father died this morning.' She turned to Jasmin. 'Sorry about your dad, Jasmin.'

'That's okay, Genevieve, you didn't kill him.'

It's been an unusual phenomenon but I have been with Jasmin at some of the most poignant moments of her life and believe me, there have been many.

Maybe it's in her blood to be unconventional, but for as long as I've known her, Jasmin has always done things Jasmin's way.

Poor old Stuart Littlemore, the unsuspecting host of *Media Watch*, actually looked a bit bewildered one night when Jasmin's newspaper, the *Tennant & District Times* found its way yet again on to his program.

'And back to the *Tennant & District Times* . . .'

I did laugh from my living room in Alice Springs. There had been a blackout at Tennant Creek that week, which was the most newsworthy item Jasmin had to run with. The heading simply read: 'BLACKOUT IN TENNANT CREEK', and the whole front page was empty and black.

After a while we all lost touch with Jasmin. She and I would end up together in the Territory, but for a couple of years she stayed in Sydney and worked in and out of refuges.

* * *

One of the most famous parties we ever had was the house-warming. Even my husband, who I didn't meet for another two years, remembers hearing about it on the night and in fact nearly turned up. We had over five hundred people come, and I was beyond excited. We all met for a drink in Chappy's room and waited for the first guests to arrive.

I had spent a hundred dollars on a black faux taffeta dress and arched myself dramatically against Chappy's bright red wardrobe for effect.

Right: My first communion day.

Below: Mum, Dad, Genevieve, Richard and me (the baby, albeit briefly) at Point Turton in 1964.

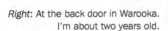

Right: At the back door in Warooka. I'm about two years old.

Right: Warooka (Mrs Hough's house in the distance).

Above: Genevieve, Richard and me in Warooka in 1965.

Right: My first day of school.

The whole of St Columba's primary school, Yorketown, 1973.

Our family portrait. Winter, 1971.

Top: My brothers and sisters and me at 'Cletta' about twenty years ago.

Bottom: Nana's eightieth birthday at the Irish Club in Adelaide.

My oldest girlfriends and me at Louise Noonan's twenty-first birthday at Hornsdale.
From left to right: Louise Noonan, me, Jane Mortimer, Liza Lyons, Tessie Leahy and
Mary-Anne Williams.

Jasmin and me at Tennant Creek in 1993.

Right: Dad, Michael Patrick Kennedy and Tessie Leahy at the O'Loughlins' before Chris left for Alice Springs.

Left: My grandmother 'Gammy' and me on my wedding day. Lorna Honner and Genevieve Honner in the background.

Right: Chris and me being congratulated by Jan and Michael Taheny.

Little Tess at Ilparpa, just south of Alice Springs, when she was about four.

Right: Biddy and me at 'Cletta' on Sarah's wedding day in 1994.

Two-year-old Albert (Bertie) on the farm at Warooka.

'What do you think of my dress, Chappy?'

'I think it's stuffed.'

'Why?'

'Because I just painted that wardrobe today.'

The beauty of faux taffeta, I discovered, was that it's pretty much made of plastic and fairly easily cleaned. I managed to have it restored in time for the party but I did smell pretty strongly of turpentine that night.

That party was so big it was quicker to access other rooms by climbing out of windows than negotiating the passage and it went well into the next day.

I was doing a radio interview about ten years ago to promote my first Adelaide Fringe Show on Mix FM and the morning host, Kev Mulcahy, introduced me like this: 'Our next guest is a woman I haven't seen for over fifteen years. Do you know, Fiona, the last time I saw you was after a huge party at Trevelyan Street and you were doing a Gidget impersonation. You were standing on top of an ironing board in the passage asking someone to squirt you with the hose.'

I hope Mrs O'Riordan wasn't listening.

* * *

After about a year I had to vacate Trevelyan Street and move back to the Yorke Peninsula. It was time to get serious about my nursing and get some formal training. I began an enrolled nurses course at the Southern Yorke Peninsula Hospital, not knowing that my experiences there would fuel some of my earliest stand-up routines.

My time in Warooka outside my nursing shifts was spent mostly partying with my brother and his friends. I lived in the nurses' quarters between late and early shifts but the rest of the time was spent at Mum and Dad's in Warooka. Richard's friends were all local blokes that I had known my whole life. They all had nicknames: Irish (Michael Patrick Kennedy – an Irish name), The Fox (Stuart Murdoch – slick as a fox), Scoobs (Ernie Coop – came across some girls skinny-dipping once and got so excited he made a sound like Scooby-Doo), Flange (Tony Lange – shortening of 'fucking Lange'), Gopha (no idea, never knew him by any other name) and Sleeping Bag (Roy Dick). I guess for a couple of years I was kind of an honorary part of the gang.

I also had two lifelong girlfriends, Julia Kennedy and Joanne Penberthy, in Warooka, and when I think back on those times, as clichéd as it sounds, they were nothing less than 'the good old days'. We partied in shearing sheds and footy clubs, and Cold Chisel was the soundtrack. We'd drive a hundred miles or more to cabarets in country town halls, and Led Zeppelin was the soundtrack. The boys went surfing at Pondalowie and Berry Bay while I looked out for sharks, and Men at Work was the soundtrack. We'd often end up at the Warooka pub well into the night and Michael Patrick (who I was still mildly besotted with) would man the bar and Richard would tell stories, and our collective guffaws were the soundtrack.

By now Richard and I had left our childhood bickering behind us and we were both up for as much fun as was on offer. He lived in the original farmhouse that my great-grandfather had built and it played host to many parties. In fact at that time the house was known either as 'Headquarters' or 'Dick's till Six'.

After one party at 'Headquarters' I was driving to Yorketown at 5 a.m. to clock in for an early shift at the hospital. It was in the dead of winter and always a pretty creepy thirteen-mile drive in the black of night. At about the halfway mark from Warooka to Yorketown is the aforementioned Peesey swamp, a couple of miles of salt lakes that I reckon would make a great location for a horror movie.

I was listening to Sting's 'Every Breath You Take' and singing along to the tail end of it. 'I'll be watching you, I'll be watching you, I'll be watching you, I'll be . . .'

Never have I had a more massive fright in my life. There was a pair of eyes staring straight at me in the rear-view mirror. I don't know how I didn't run the car off the road. But it was nowhere near as sinister a circumstance as it looked. A drunk surfie from Richard's party had stumbled into my unlocked car and passed out.

We befriended a lot of surfies in those days, mostly boys from the city who came for long weekends and holidays. We partied with them a lot and were led astray by them more than once, and they by us. I remember a surfie tooting the horn for me outside of Mum and Dad's one evening. I had a few days off and was catching a lift back with him to Adelaide. Mum was very unimpressed with the horn honking.

'All the way to Adelaide with someone we've never even met? Bring him inside and introduce him or you're not going anywhere.'

It was raining and I went outside and tapped on his window. 'Sorry, but I have to introduce you to my parents.'

I couldn't have been more mortified and I certainly didn't make it to Adelaide that night. There stood my new friend in our living room, dripping wet, in a dirty old duffle coat with a black kitten peeking out from under his collar.

'Um, Mum and Dad . . . this is Fruit Bat.'

My first exposure to dope was at Warooka. I always found it easy to say no to it because Richard was one of the non-smokers in our gang. He had an amazingly strong character, and I took his lead, I guess out of respect for my big brother.

We were at a party across from the pub at the old Jehovah Witnesses' house which was by now a very run-down rental and there were bongs and joints flying along with the beer.

'Hey, Fiona! Why don't you have a go?'

'No thanks, I don't smoke.'

A few more people egged me on and before I knew it the whole kitchen was chanting at me.

'Suck it in! Suck it in!'

I've often deflected awkward occasions by making a massive arse of myself. I saw a bowl of green stuff on the table and grabbed a big spoon.

'I told you I don't smoke . . . but I love eating it!'

I had no clue that ingesting the stuff was pretty much the same as smoking it. Honestly, I was as green as the grass I'd just swallowed, and Richard just stood there shaking his head and then dragged me home.

Only hours later was the familiar 'Oi, oi, oi' from Dad, which was the regular Sunday morning wake-up call for mass. I was off my coconut that morning. I found the shower confusing, the drive to the church utterly fascinating, and the sermon so incredibly hilarious that I could barely keep it together. My stoned brain was imagining the Corinthians at their letter box, getting another letter from Saint Paul.

'Richard, do you think the Corinthians ever wrote back to Saint Paul?'

'Shut up, Fiona.'

'I think the Corinthians are very rude.'

'I swear to God.'

'What are Corinthians exactly?'

A lot of people married as young as I was often note that they missed out on a lot of their youth. I'm pretty sure I crammed ten years of partying into four before I turned twenty-two. I didn't actually drink until the day I turned eighteen but I recall taking quite a shine to it when I did.

CHAPTER 5

GROWING UP . . .

I met my husband-to-be Christopher in 1981. I was still nursing in Yorketown and on one of my frequent visits to Adelaide. Genevieve was still living at Trevelyan Street and had organised a dinner party with a friend of hers, Peter O'Loughlin. She had recently been invited by Peter to his brother's twenty-first and the two of them thought it would be fun to get some of the Tahenys and O'Loughlins together.

I remember so many details of that night. I particularly recall behaving appallingly, showing off and talking too much and making fun of Genevieve's cooking. What also happened that night was that I fell in love with Christopher the minute he walked in the door.

Cate had had a lot more experience with falling in love than me. I loved kissing boys and partying with them and flirting but I could never understand how a boy could rip your heart out. I'd heard Cate crying into her pillow over a bloke on a few occasions and thought she was bonkers for caring so much. I had always heartily subscribed to the plenty of fish in the sea theory.

Tim, Peter, Judith and Chris O'Loughlin walked into the kitchen at Trevelyan Street and the first thing that struck me was what a handsome lot they were. I started blabbing first.

'So, which one of you had the twenty-first last week?'

'Er, that was me.'

Chris was definitely the quietest of the four. I had actually spotted him a few months earlier at the South Adelaide Football Club. Cate came up to me and said, 'See that guy over there in the green jumper? I think that's one of Peter O'Loughlin's brothers. You know, Genevieve's friend?'

I thought he was gorgeous, and asked Cate to keep an eye on him while I got us a couple of drinks. Cate kept an eye on him and watched him leaving while I was at the bar. I'd only seen him from a distance, and I was seriously disappointed when I found out.

'Damn, I was going to introduce myself. He's a spunk.'

The O'Loughlins and we discovered that we shared a lot of common ground at that first dinner party. We knew loads of the same people, and coincidentally they also had a sister called Genevieve and a brother Justin. Genevieve O'Loughlin was great mates with the older Kennedy girls from the Warooka pub, another connection that has entwined our families to this day. Years before that dinner party I had spied on Brigid and Maryanne Kennedy through a crack in the kitchen door of the pub when they had some groovy grown-up friends from

Adelaide to stay. One of their friends was standing at the bar wearing a pair of blue jeans and a grey cap, and I reckon I'd never seen a more beautiful face in all my life. I found out at that dinner party that that had been Genevieve O'Loughlin.

We waved them off in the early hours, and I made a mental note to ring up the guy I was currently going out with and break it off with him first thing in the morning. As the O'Loughlins disappeared down the street I said out loud to no one in particular: 'I'm going to marry Chris O'Loughlin.'

Genevieve wanted to slap me I think, and she tuned to me with a reply.

'You're a very selfish girl, Fiona.'

However, procuring the affections of Christopher O'Loughlin proved to be a fairly exhausting project. He hadn't quite come away from our first encounter head over heels. In fact I think he described me to Tim later that night as 'Good fun . . . but a bit much.'

I set about running into him again accidentally, and it was taking forever. I begged a good friend of mine, Louise Noonan, to help me out.

'I *know* he drinks at the South Adelaide Footy Club. Can you just come and sit with me and wait until he turns up? I'm going to marry him one day and I *promise* you can be my bridesmaid.'

This went on for six weeks or more. I got as much information as I could from Genevieve via Peter as to Chris's itinerary, and was nearly giving up hope one Friday night at the Queen's Head Hotel in North Adelaide. I'd heard on good authority that he often came to the Queen's Head, and every time the front door opened I had my heart in my throat. Mary-Anne Williams was my co-conspirator that night, and I was actually sitting on the toilet when she came running in with the news.

'Fiona! He's here! He's here! He just walked in.'

I just about flew off the toilet but was harpooned by the flush button. There actually was no button and I had to stick my finger right into the hole where it should have been, and believe it or not my finger was stuck. I was frantic.

'Oh shit, Mary-Anne, my finger's stuck in the toilet.'

Mary-Anne didn't answer me because she wasn't there anymore, so I waited for someone to come into the ladies' while my future with Chris hung in the balance.

My finger wouldn't budge, and the cubicle was too long for me to reach the door. Finally Mary-Anne came back.

'What are you doing, Fiona? He's in the front bar right now!'

'My finger's stuck in the flush button.'

I've always found that my girlfriends, when in cahoots in chasing boys, took the job very seriously. Mary-Anne didn't laugh about my finger being stuck or even act like it was an unusual predicament. She grabbed some soap, scaled the toilet door and rescued my finger like it was an everyday act of goodwill.

'Thanks, Mary-Anne. I promise you can be my bridesmaid.'

That night Chris and I had our first proper one-on-one chat at the Queen's Head Hotel. I told him that I had been at his mother's and sister's funeral and he told me later how much he appreciated my bringing it up openly. (The worst of it was that not only did the O'Loughlins lose their mum and precious baby sister, but they had to suffer the agony of them being officially missing for twenty-four hours or more.) But by then I knew enough about grief to know that it's okay to say stuff out loud.

They must have taken their cue from their dad to keep going because even though their heartache was only two years old when I met them, they struck me as a happy mob.

My first date with Christopher took a long time coming. I had started my nursing training in Yorketown and I was in and out of Adelaide either on days off or for study block at the Royal Adelaide Hospital. One weekend we Taheny girls were invited to the O'Loughlins for a Sunday barbecue for Peter's twenty-fifth birthday.

At about three o'clock in the afternoon Chris made his move, and what a smooth move it was.

'Hey Fiona, do you want to go for a bike ride?'

He had a Suzuki TS250 that he used to cruise around the Adelaide Hills on. I actually loathed motorbikes but didn't think this would be the time to let on.

'Yeah, I'd love to.'

'I'll just go and get you some gear then.'

I had no idea what the 'gear' entailed, and my heart kind of sank when I found out. I'd gone to a lot of trouble deciding what to wear that morning and was feeling more than pleased with myself, having managed to squeeze into a new pair of size 8 prototype jeans. Chris handed me a pair of plastic yellow daks with a matching jacket and I came back out of the laundry feeling as wide as I was tall and somewhat humiliated as I straddled the back of his motorbike in full view of everyone and we headed off down the street in the wake of hysterical laughing from our collective brothers and sisters.

Once we were out of sight and after the fear of being on the back of a motorbike subsided, I began to be more thrilled by the second. I had the most enormous crush on this guy and here I was with my arms wrapped around him as tight as I wanted for as long as the ride lasted. It was bliss. He pointed things out every now and then, and I'd nod my helmeted head as if I was interested. The higher up Mount Lofty we went the happier I was because I could hang on even tighter, and then about five minutes before we reached the summit, my right shoe fell off and went flying down the mountain. They were brand new shoes too, bought the day before in honour of the prototypes and the barbecue invite, but I couldn't have cared less.

Eventually we were at the top of Mount Lofty, and Chris took off his helmet and gestured to the view as if he'd designed it himself. I was struggling with my helmet and hobbled over to him.

'Where's your other shoe?'

'Oh, don't worry about it, it doesn't matter.'

'Where is it?'

'It fell off a few miles back.'

'Why didn't you tell me to stop?'

'Oh . . . I didn't want to bother you.'

He looked at me like I was a bit of a dickhead and we headed back down and back to the party.

I went back to Trevelyan Street that night terrified that that was the end of Chris and me before anything had begun. And then the phone rang.

'Hi, it's Chris, um, I wondered if you wanted to go for another bike ride on Saturday?'

'I'd love to.'

So that was that. I was now officially off my scone with happiness.

Saturday came around and he picked me up and we headed for the Adelaide Hills again. I was wearing leather boots this time and started feeling like an old hand as pillion passenger. I was still too scared to open my eyes and look at much but I thought the terror was more than compensated for by the lengthy inadvertent hug with the man of my dreams.

After a while I could feel a sharp pain in my right ankle and looked down to notice that one of my boots was on fire. This time I decided it was worth telling Chris to stop.

'You must have had your leg too close to the exhaust.'

'You're costing me a fortune in shoes.'

The bike rides continued for a month or more. We used to stop at little coffee shops and have Devonshire teas in Hahndorf, or go to the Norton Summit pub and drink beer.

Chris made a speech at my fortieth birthday and recalled those bike rides. 'That's when I fell in love with Fiona. She told me so many stories and made me laugh over beers and cups of tea in the Adelaide Hills.'

Very frustratingly, though, he would drop me back at Trevelyan Street and leave straightaway every time.

'He hasn't kissed me yet,' I'd moan to anyone in the house who'd listen.

'He will.'

Cate was very optimistic on my behalf.

Finally, after yet another bike ride one Saturday afternoon, he took his helmet off and said, 'Would you like to go for something to eat?'

'Yeah, I'm starving.'

'No, I meant for dinner . . . tonight.'

'I'd love to.'

I guess that was our first real date. We went to the Talbot Hotel in the city and came back to Trevelyan Street for a rather awkward coffee. Some of the others were still up, and as Chris got up to leave and said goodnight to everyone I think Cate kicked me under the table.

'I think I left something in your car.'

I followed him out and the others waited in the kitchen with bated breath. Half an hour later I came back inside victorious. Not only had I kissed him but I had also told him I detested motorbikes.

* * *

Happy, happy days were the months that followed. I came within a hair's breadth of failing nursing because I couldn't concentrate on anything but Christopher O'Loughlin and when I would see him again.

I started spending less and less time at Trevelyan Street and more and more time at the O'Loughlins' at 21 Johnstone Street. I felt so at home in the O'Loughlins' house and was tickled pink by a piece of art that dominated their dining room. It was a massive oil painting by none other than Jenny Huff, the artist who had grown up in the house across the road from me.

To fall in love with someone is wonderful enough, but to fall in love with their family has got to be an added bonus. The O'Loughlins were and are the most eclectic bunch of people you can meet from one family.

There was Justin the dentist from Alice Springs, who appeared to be a very quiet guy but was an extraordinary channeller of humour. For some reason I've always felt funnier around Justin than just about anyone. Then there was Genevieve the journalist, who terrified me out of my wits when we first met, and made me wonder how on earth a person could be so beautiful and so smart at the same time. Next came scientist Peter, who I have had some of the biggest gut-aching laughs with in my life. And then there were the twins: handsome Tim, funnier than Seinfeld, and beautiful Jude, who looked like a young Meryl Streep and was playing the guitar singing a Randy Newman song the first time I laid eyes on her in Johnstone Street.

What struck me most about these guys was not so much how they must have missed their mother but how much she must have missed them.

I fell in love with the O'Loughlins for a thousand reasons. I loved the house, unremarkable suburban home in Glengowrie that it is. It is filled with books and so much of their art, particularly of Tim and Jude, who are both now teaching artists. The house hung heavy with happy ghosts, not just of Geraldine and Libby, but of who this family must have been in more carefree days.

Mr O'Loughlin was fascinating to me. He had an almighty bark to him, but he spent his bark on trivial things. If you loaded the dishwasher wrong or used the wrong cycle on the washing machine he'd roar like a bear with a sore foot, but it was Ivan at the dinner table that I loved the most. I was a bit bewildered at first by the O'Loughlin dinner table. Their conversation could turn instantaneously into the fiercest arguments I'd ever heard. Politics, art, religion; they're programmed to be devil's advocate to each other and then in a split second someone, usually Tim, would say something hysterical and they'd collapse with laughter. Ivan was as informed as the rest of them and joined in as heartily on any subject from greenhouse gases to the authenticity of Tutankhamen, and while he never really raised his own voice in the heralding hurricanes he definitely added energy to them.

'Ivanovitch, double agent, triple star' – as Tim and Jude used to laughingly refer to Ivan as – is a gentlemen and the most beloved grandfather I could ever hope to have had for my kids. I remember looking at him one night in those early days and realising what made this dinner table so different to my own. This was an uncensored home. Just about any subject was up for grabs and language was as free flowing as the wine. I've rarely known Ivan to pass judgement on any of the choices his kids have made or the opinions they've held. He'd disagree from a distance and with respect if they stopped going to mass, and yet he'd rip your head off if you parked on his lawn. Maybe he wasn't as liberal before their lives were flipped upside down, but there he was, the father of six young adults who'd had their hearts broken, and I wondered if this was his way of helping them through and keeping them close and hoping never to lose anyone again.

On the flip side I think it was equally enjoyable for Chris to meld into my family. I think he loved our table every bit as much as I loved his, but ours was a kitchen table and a seriously cramped one at that. We were more inclined to talk about the footy and impersonate the drunkest bloke in the pub last night. Mum and Dad's place was an enormously happy place to be and had become a real hub in town after the pub shut.

Christopher met and connected with heaps of the locals that I had grown up with and made friends for life with Stewie Murdoch, Wayne Hayes, Ian Hills and others.

He fell in love with the coast especially, and now instead of me hankering for Adelaide every chance I got, it was Christopher hell bent on heading for the Yorke Peninsula every weekend.

To paraphrase the words of John Lennon, they were great days indeed.

CHAPTER 6

ALICE SPRINGS

Chris left for Alice Springs on the 3rd of July 1983. Most of his family and a lot of his extended family gathered at the Adelaide airport to send him off. It must have been a weird day for the O'Loughlins. It was three years to the very day that Geraldine and Libby hadn't returned from Alice Springs. Chris would be the third member of his family to live in the Red Centre, but I doubt if he had any idea that day that he was heading to Alice Springs for more than twenty-five years so far.

He started working for the Northern Territory Government in a dental laboratory pretty much straightaway, and moved into a house in O'Grady Crescent with his sister Genevieve and his cousin Julie Egar. Julie was a particularly special cousin to the O'Loughlins, as her father Paul Egar was the pilot of the plane that had taken their mother and sister to Alice Springs, and he also had lost his life.

Julie worked for a bank, and Genevieve worked as a journalist for the *Alice Springs Star*.

It was only three weeks after Chris left Adelaide that I decided to surprise him for a visit. He'd mentioned over the phone that auditions were being held for a community performance of *Godspell*. This production was to be the official opening of the Araluen Arts Centre. I decided that since my nursing training was finished I had nothing to lose with a brief sojourn in the Northern Territory. I also decided that if I scored a part in *Godspell* I would stay on in Alice Springs indefinitely.

I resigned from the Yorketown Hospital and booked the last seat available on the Ghan. The last seat just happened to be a first-class one, so I really did have my first Alice Springs encounter in style. However, leaving South Australia didn't happen without an incident that could have been disastrous. Ever since I was a kid I have had a pathological propensity to lose things. I was the kid who literally didn't know what day it was, and I lived with the constant stress of not knowing where I'd left my lunchbox, my library books or my school blazer. It's a condition that has followed me into adulthood. I've lost everything from passports to diamond rings. Even a child, once . . .

I was all set to catch the bus from Warooka to Adelaide, where I would have a last overnight at Trevelyan Street and then head to Alice Springs the next day. I had all my worldly goods in two suitcases, and Dad walked into the kitchen and nearly had a fit to see me counting out $1,500 in cash at the table.

'What the hell are you doing with all that money?'

'It's all of my savings and holiday pay.'

'Why isn't it in the bank?'

'Because I wanted to touch it, Dad. I've never even seen this much money before.'

I headed off the next day with two suitcases and fifteen hundred bucks in my wallet. Dad made me promise that I'd put the money in the bank as soon as I got to Adelaide.

Sadly, as soon as I arrived in the city the first thing I did was leave a suitcase in the middle of Franklin Street. Sometimes my air-head knows no bounds. I must have hailed a taxi and carried one suitcase across the road and forgotten about the other one by the time I was inside the cab. Also, in my defence, I was about as excited as a girl could be. Heading off into the middle of Australia to find adventure, and my boyfriend.

I was having lunch with one of my best mates, Simon O'Leary, in a pub in the Rundle Mall and it wasn't until after we'd ordered that I realised I was one suitcase short.

'Shit, Simon. I think I left a suitcase in the middle of Franklin Street. Can you order me a beer while I find a phone?'

I headed out into the Mall and found a phone box and rang the bus terminal. All was good. Someone had found my suitcase and they said they'd hold onto it for me for as long as I needed. I headed back to the pub where Simon and I caught up, laughed, and had too many beers as usual. It wasn't until it was time to pay the bill that my heart stopped. 'Simon, my wallet's gone. I think I left it in the phone box.'

Sure enough, I had, and while I know that I am one of the most forgetful people on the planet, I also reckon I'm one of the luckiest. I raced out into the Rundle Mall and there was my wallet sitting on top of the pay phone where I'd left it, all by itself, for over an hour, in the middle of a capital city, with my life savings inside.

* * *

Seeing Alice Springs for the first time really is remarkable. I think the first thing that smacks you in the face is the colour of the sky. And it's not just that a winter sky in Alice Springs is cloudless and blue. It's the intensity of the blue and all the other colours of the landscape. Alice is a winter wonderland without the snow, and everything seems to be more defined. Introducing your eyes to the Red Centre is like finally putting on those reading glasses that you've needed for a while.

True, Alice Springs has few buildings that boast the grander heritage of architecture that so many southern towns and cities enjoy; it is young, after all.

In live performances I have gone more for the gag than the truth of what it's really like to live in a town full of ockers, intellectuals, artists, Americans, traditional land owners, tourists and itinerant Aborigines. Alice Springs is beautiful, racist, hot as hell, ugly, magical and set smack in the middle of Yeperenye Dreamtime. It has helped me and hindered me, and only ever tenuously felt like home.

Without a doubt, Alice Springs can be a dusty and oppressive place in the middle of the day in the middle of the summer. But all this aside, the centre hosts a sunrise every morning that will forgive it every swallowed fly and sunburnt shoulder. And for a long-term visitor like me the sunsets, especially those projected against the mighty Macdonnell Ranges, will make up for every pang of homesickness.

* * *

Christopher was without doubt very surprised to see me standing at the window of the dental laboratory and, as happy as he was, I'd hazard a guess that he might have also been a tad annoyed that I'd literally moved in on his new territory in such brazen style.

We had a great weekend though, and within a week I had scored myself a part in *Godspell* and found accommodation sharing a flat with a guy called Tex, who I've never come across again.

There's an old saying in Alice Springs that if you live here long enough, you don't need to travel the world because eventually the world will come to you. And I guess there's a fair bit of truth in it. Central Australia has played host to a fair share of international movie stars: Jessica Lange, Meryl Streep, Tom Selleck, Max von Sydow and William Hurt, to name a few.

One day when I was working for the *Alice Springs Star* newspaper we got a call from someone to tell us that there had been a possible sighting of Rod Stewart at Marron's Newsagency. Marron's is in the main street and I was up and running for the door in seconds. The editor, Dave Nason, yelled after me, 'Where do you think you're going?'

'Rod Stewart's at Marron's Newsagency.'

'And you sell advertising space, so get back to work.'

* * *

I really am pathetic when it comes to celebrities, and I always have been. When I was about ten years old I was swimming with my cousins in a public pool in the Barossa Valley and believe it or not there was Jacki Weaver sitting on the edge of the pool with her legs dangling in the same water!

I couldn't take my eyes off her and gradually swam nearer and nearer. Eventually I was right underneath her and for some reason was hugging both of her legs as I stared up at the famous face.

'You're Jacki Weaver.'

'Yes, I am.'

I couldn't believe it was really her and that she actually spoke to me. I wanted the moment to last forever. Apparently it nearly did. The last thing Jacki Weaver said to me was, 'You need to let go of my legs now.'

I have rarely come into contact with a celebrity without making a first-class dickhead out of myself. Another pearler involved the Camel Cup and Linda Evans. The Camel Cup is a famous camel race held in Alice Springs every year and Linda Evans is the actress who played Krystle in the 1980s television show *Dynasty*. Linda was in Alice Springs in 1986 making a telemovie with Jack Thompson, and the Camel Cup was being incorporated into some scenes in the movie. Very heady stuff indeed, and I was missing none of the excitement.

I was married to Chris by now and pregnant with Henry at the time, and feeling more than a bit glamorous in brand new hot-pink overalls and matching earrings. I'd never seen a film being made before and spent the day following the crew and the actors around and watching them do their stuff.

I remember overhearing the director asking someone where the twenty extras were and I listened carefully to the answer: 'Behind the stables, waiting for go.'

I headed straight for the stables and reasoned that the director would hardly notice if there were twenty or twenty-one extras in the scene. So there I was, standing with twenty strangers, about to get my first walk-on role in a movie.

'And . . . action!'

Just like the movies. Off we headed, me and my twenty new colleagues, mastering a fairly simple manoeuvre. I was busy trying to be one of the extras walking the closest to Linda to maximise my chances of staying off the cutting room floor when I realised that the director was yelling 'Cut!' and something else: 'Who's the pregnant extra not in costume?'

In slow-motion horror I looked around me and realised that all the other extras were dressed as jackeroos or jillaroos. I don't know why I hadn't noticed before. I guess I was just too caught up in my mission. God knows what I looked like, standing there with my bright pink dangly earrings in my fluorescent maternity overalls and sunglasses staring back at about forty pissed-off actors and film crew.

And I can't believe what I did next. I ran away. I knew I was caught out so I simply bolted. Back to the crowd and the Camel Cup and my husband, with a story that I had no intention of telling him.

This leads me to the most famous visitor ever to come to The Alice; Pope John Paul II. He arrived for a brief visit in 1986 and was here to deliver a particular message to the Aboriginal community in the Arrernte language. The RM Williams shop in town sold out of moleskins and western shirts as literally thousands of people spilled into town from Aboriginal communities all over the Territory and Western

Australia. Non-indigenous folks were not encouraged to join the massive crowd at Blatherskite Park due to the almost unmanageable numbers so we happily set up camp beside the Stuart Highway and waited for the Pope to drive past.

'That's him.'

'Here he comes.'

It was almost like being at a Christmas pageant, and surreal to see the Pope in a bulletproof vehicle driving past us in downtown Alice Springs. Except technically he didn't drive past us. No kidding, his Popemobile broke down directly in front of where we were standing.

I was holding Henry, who was about six weeks old at the time, and Chris and I stood there and watched as the mafia-like minders muttered into walkie-talkies, and tried to persuade His Holiness to stay inside the vehicle until the problem was fixed.

The Pope was having none of it, and stepped out of the truck to acknowledge the crowd. As he came nearer to us I held Henry up higher and Pope John Paul II actually made the sign of the cross in his direction. Christopher, meanwhile, had a bigger plan and grabbed Henry and held him much further forward, to which the Pope responded by walking over to us and cradling Henry's head in his hands and kissing his face.

I know I'm a drama queen, but I outdid myself this time. I actually started to cry and began speaking with an Italian accent.

'He kissda my baby! He kissda my baby!'

I was beside myself, and it was a Jesuit priest standing about five people up from us who snapped me out of it. He leant across the crowd and tapped me on the shoulder.

'Knock it off,' he said. 'He's Polish!'

* * *

For flatmates, Tex and I didn't cross paths often. On the day I moved in I was greeted by a cockroach in the bathroom the size of a guinea pig, and from then on I managed to spend as little time as possible in my new rental. I pretty much lived at Chris's place.

The *Godspell* auditions were held in the Totem Theatre, which is basically a corrugated iron shed on the edge of the Todd River. The director was Cate Jones and I couldn't work out whether she was a genius or a nutter. She used terms like 'organic' and 'self-realisation', and she may as well have been speaking Spanish for all I understood. She was so riveted by the project and so passionate that she might well have been directing *King Lear*.

I was extremely unworldly, and this became so evident to me in that first nine months or so in Alice Springs. While I had had a fun and full existence up until now, I had never really been exposed to much of anything outside of a Catholic, politically right-wing world. Good Lord, I'd only been in Alice Springs a week and I'd met a homosexual Aborigine *and* a heroin addict!

Alice Springs was my New York. I loved every minute of it and have always maintained that my political and social education began in the middle of Australia. That's not to say that Alice Springs is a bargain basement of left-wing extroverts, but it has always had a disproportionately strong arts scene and that was the scene I was drawn to.

So there I was backstage at the Totem Theatre about to audition for a musical I'd never seen or heard before, waiting for a beautiful German girl called Uli to finish her time on stage before my name was called.

'Fiona Taheny!'

'Yes?'

I stood on the stage and had no clue what was expected of me.

'Fiona, I want you to go behind the curtain and come back out again . . . backwards . . . as a pig on heat.'

Honestly, I do not remember what happened next. Suffice to say I scored a part, and my new life in Alice Springs had begun. *Godspell*, for all its hype at the time, was nonetheless an amateur production, so my next objective was to get a job.

I noticed an interesting thing about Alice Springs in those early days. Up here people aren't as readily defined by their work as we tend to be down south. A plumber is just as likely to be best buddies with a doctor as he is with anyone else. There's an osmosis between socio-economic groups in Alice Springs that has always delighted me, probably because I have a distinct lack of letters after my name.

I've often wondered if this phenomenon has anything to do with the weather and traffic. Our lifestyle in the Territory affords us plenty of sunshine and an average working commute of about five minutes. We're left with a lot more time on our hands to be more than an accountant or a hairdresser. One thing I know for a fact: despite our lack of pompousness regarding job descriptions, and despite an ongoing image of The Alice being chock-a-block full of beer-swilling ockers, Alice Springs has the highest per capita population of university graduates in the country. I remember when I first arrived being gobsmacked at meeting an anthropologist. (I'd never met one before, and that was hot on the heels of the gay Aborigine and the heroin addict.)

A couple of years ago I was at a backyard barbie, and it went a bit like this:

'Hi Jack, I'm Fiona. What do you do?'

'Hello, Fiona. I'm an anthropologist.'

'Yeah? . . . Who isn't?'

I kid you not; there are seven in my street.

So in 1983 I suddenly found myself job hunting in Alice Springs. I tried a few money earners in that first year. I worked as an assistant in a camera shop first and then had a terrible month or so working at the Alice Springs Hospital. I was what was known as a ward clerk, and the ward sister took an instant dislike to me. She refused to call me by my name and mostly spoke about me as if I wasn't there. 'You nurses go and take your lunch break now and then ward clerk can go when you're finished.'

On my twentieth birthday a florist walked into the ward with a bunch of roses from Chris and the ward sister told me to get rid of them before they gave her hay fever. I walked out that afternoon and never came back.

My next job was working on commission selling advertising space for the *Alice Springs Star*. I earned very little money but the memories are more than worth it. The *Star* was a left-wing paper and one of only two local rags in town. The other paper in Alice Springs (which is alive and well still) was the *Centralian Advocate*, a Murdoch publication, and we were barely a thorn in their side in the revenue stakes.

Heady days indeed, and how I loved stepping into the office every morning. The *Star* was just a one-roomed shop in a small shopping plaza. Genevieve O'Loughlin was the head journalist, and I used to be in awe of her confidence and articulateness as I eavesdropped as she barked down the phone at politicians and members of council. She was always in and out of the office, heading out bush or to the law courts. It's hard to believe, looking back, that she was only in her mid-twenties.

The editor of the *Star* was a guy called Warwick Sinclair, and he was all of nineteen. It was a room full of child prodigies, including Colin Wicking, the cartoonist, who was the grand age of twenty-one. I was gobsmacked by the excitement of it all and couldn't wait to get there every morning to see what would happen next.

Debbie and Helen were cousins and two single girls who were living it up in the way young people can only do in their early days in Alice Springs. Debbie was the office secretary and Helen, my boss, was head of advertising. They seemed to spend most of their time in the office reliving the weekend just gone or making plans for the weekend ahead. Helen was hilariously dry and Debbie was equally blunt.

'Helen?'

'Yes, Debbie?'

'You know that gravel rash you got on your shoulder last Saturday having it off with that bloke at Ayers Rock?'

'Yes, Debbie.'

'I pashed him at the Stuart Arms last night and he doesn't remember a thing about you.'

'Thank you, Debbie.'

Colin Wicking insisted on being referred to at all times as Mr Wicking. A very eccentric and gifted young bloke, he rarely joined in on much nonsense or bothered with small talk. However, one morning he was kind enough to notice that I wasn't quite myself.

'Good morning, Mr Wicking.'

'Good morning, Fiona. Have you been crying?'

'Yes, as a matter of fact, I have. Christopher and I just had a huge fight in the car on the way in.'

'Go on, then.'

'I sat on a pair of dentures on the front seat of his car and ruined them.'

That was the first time I heard Mr Wicking laugh out loud.

I spent most of my time on the phone being told to bugger off by local businesses or traipsing around town knocking on doors and being thrown out of car yards, offices and hotels. I soon learnt that not many people were interested in advertising in the *Star*.

One afternoon we all listened in on an interview that Genevieve was conducting in the back of the office with a couple who were about to launch a new school in town. ACE schooling system was an acronym for Accelerated Christian Education, and its two representatives in the office that day looked like a pair of odd bods to say the least. It was socks, sandals, greasy hair and cardigans all round. There was only a thin partition separating the office into two rooms, and we all leaned up against it for an easy eavesdrop. Genevieve was asking the questions and somehow keeping a straight face.

Genevieve:	So, what is it exactly about the ACE schooling system that separates it from other curriculums?
Mr Christian:	Well, for a start, we incorporate corporal punishment into our education system.
Genevieve:	Really?
Mr Christian:	Yes.
Genevieve:	In what way?
Mr Christian:	Well, we use bats.
Genevieve:	Bats? Exactly what kind of bats?
Mr Christian:	Well, they're a bit like a ping-pong bat.
Mrs Christian:	Only bigger, dear.
Mr Christian:	Yes, slightly bigger than a ping-pong bat.

The next edition of the *Star* ran with the front page headline: ACE SCHOOLING SYSTEM OUT TO BAT!

This was followed by a Mr Wicking cartoon, which was Colin at his finest: a kid sitting at his desk being thwacked across the back of the head with a ping-pong bat and yelling in indignation at the top of his lungs, 'Jesus Christ!'

I plodded along, trying to sell enough ads to live off, and then hit the jackpot one afternoon after indiscriminately dialling businesses and coming across a building company called Sitzler Brothers.

'Hello, my name is Fiona and I'm calling from the *Alice Springs Star*.'

'Yes, what can I do for you?'

'Well, I was wondering if you would be interested in taking one of the five-by-two-centimetre ads on the TV lift-out thingy that runs down the side of the page right next to the programming, and we're doing a deal this month for a two for one.'

'No, that doesn't really sound like something we'd be interested in.'

'Okay then. Thanks for your time.'

I was over being offended or embarrassed by now.

But then the man on the other end of the phone continued, 'It's just that we're coming up for our twenty-fifth year in the business and I think we'd be looking for something bigger.'

'Bigger than a two-by-five?'

'Yes. How about a full page?'

I nearly fainted.

'A full . . . you mean an ad taking up a whole page?'

'Yes.'

'Wow!'

'So what would the cost be for that?'

'A lot! . . . Sorry, I'll just find out . . . Um, are you there? Yes, that will be three hundred dollars.'

'Great. Well, Fiona, if you'd like to come by the office and work out the copy with me I'll see you sometime this afternoon.'

I bought Chinese take-away that night. A full-page ad meant about sixty bucks for me.

'Chris, I sold a full-page ad to the Sitzler Brothers today and I designed it myself, it's going to say "SITZLER BROTHERS: BUILDING THE TERRITORY FOR 25 YEARS".'

I couldn't wait for the next edition of the *Star* to come out. Not just because I'd sold the ad and scored a commission, but I really felt like I'd done something creative as well. And indeed I had. Wednesday mornings were when the papers came back from the printers in Queensland and I tore the paper open to bask in the glory of my own handiwork. A few people in the office were sniggering when I walked in and Mr Wicking asked me how well I'd done in history at school. And then I saw my mistake.

SITZLER BROTHERS
BUILDING THE TERRITORY
FOR 75
YEARS!

No wonder people in advertising jump off tall buildings. I not only lost my commission but was docked sixty bucks the next week for having to rerun the ad.

CHAPTER 7

MATCHES AND HATCHES

By the time Chris and I became engaged, I still had an awful lot of growing up to do. We had been apart for about eight months with me back down south and him in Alice Springs. While not technically 'broken up' we had both decided to spread our wings a little and had had the odd date with other people. Our telephone calls became increasingly ridden with arguments as I think we were both way more anxious about our new arrangement than we cared to let on to each other, let alone ourselves.

One Wednesday night at Trevelyan Street we had reached a stalemate on the phone and a very long silence ensued that was finally broken from Christopher's end of the line.

'Fiona, we really need to work this out. I'm going to fly down this weekend. I really reckon it's decision time.'

'Okay.'

Decision time! I could barely wait to get him off the phone. The excitement was all too much. I had to tell someone. Surely I couldn't be expected to keep this all to myself? And so, without even the slightest concern that I might be jumping the gun, I raced out to the backyard to find my oldest friend in the world.

'Mary-Anne! You'll never guess what.'

'What?'

'Chris and I are getting engaged.'

Mary-Anne and I celebrated with a joint that she had nicked from one of her brothers. I think it was only the second joint I'd ever had in my life and it did the trick as we giggled and guffawed well into the night, trying to wrap our heads around the whole delicious idea.

I practised signing my name Fiona O'Loughlin for the next couple of days, incessantly daydreaming and then every few hours or more succumbing to the temptation to share my news yet again.

'Louise, you can't tell anyone! This is the biggest secret I'm ever going to tell you but you'll never guess what . . .'

'Jane? I have got the biggest secret, but you have to promise that you won't say a word to anyone . . .'

By the time Saturday morning and Christopher O'Loughlin arrived I was just about out of my skin with anticipation. I was a little bit surprised that he hadn't popped the question at the airport but I wasn't at all concerned as we had the whole day ahead of us and no one but myself and about twenty of my closest confidantes even knew that Chris was in town.

'Well, what shall we do today?'

Chris seemed to have made no firm plans at all. Either that or he was just stringing me along. I couldn't have cared less. This was going to be one of the best days of my entire life.

'I don't mind. Where do you want to go?'

'Well, I thought I might pop in and see Robert Fox before I do anything else.'

'Oh, Robert Fox? Um, why would you want to see Robert Fox . . . today?'

'Because he's my best friend and I'm only here till Tuesday. What's wrong with that?'

'Nothing. It's just that he works in a service station and service stations are depressing and I really don't feel like stopping at a service station or going inside a service station today.'

We spent a good hour at the service station chatting to Robert Fox and just as the faintest hint of fear started to grab hold of me my spirits soared again after we headed off and Chris suggested we take a drive around the Adelaide Hills and then stop at the Norton Summit pub for lunch.

The Adelaide Hills and the Norton Summit pub had featured heavily on our very first date and I sat back in the passenger's seat utterly thrilled with the turn our day had taken, and began to rehearse my acceptance speech in my head.

I think it was after the second beer at the Norton Summit pub that my heart started to sink. Chris had downed his drink and reached for the car keys.

'We'd better get going. Do you want to come with me to go visit Dad?'

'Yeah, sure. Can you wait for me for a minute? I need to make a phone call.'

Disappointment had started to turn to blind panic as I rang Trevelyan Street and nobody answered. I had given everyone the all-clear to announce my news after six o'clock and it was nearing five-thirty and not a proposal in sight. In desperation I rang the Cabra Boarding House and left a cryptic message with my bewildered sixteen-year-old sister Sarah.

'Sarah, this is really important. You need to keep ringing Trevelyan Street until somebody answers. Give whoever answers this message, they'll know what it means. "Fiona rang. He didn't ask me." Got it? Tell them to tell that to everyone.'

My mood was black and in hindsight I can see that maybe a girl who is more disappointed in having to lose face with her friends than having appeared to have lost a marriage proposal is quite possibly too immature to be considering marriage in the first place. Dear me, I made life very complicated that day and evening.

Having driven down from the Adelaide Hills and now on our way to Mr O'Loughlin's house, Chris swung the car towards North Adelaide and suggested we have one last drink by ourselves at the Queen's Head Hotel. The Queen's Head Hotel was where Chris and I really first hooked up and for the third or fourth time that day my hopes began to rise.

We were in the beer garden and the bells of St Peter's started to ring at six o'clock.

'Fiona, will you marry me?'

'Yes, yes, yes, yes, yes, of course I will!'

'Where are you going?'

'I'll be back in a minute. I just have to make a couple of quick phone calls!'

Saved by the bell quite literally, I don't think Chris will know the full extent of my engagement subterfuge until he reads this book but my cover was nearly blown the very next day.

We were in the Rundle Mall shopping for an engagement ring when we ran into my cousin Maurice.

'Hey you guys! Congratulations. Yeah, I've been checking the paper for days for the engagement notice.'

'Well, Maurice, you're a bloody psychic. He only asked me last night. C'mon Chris, the shops will be shut in half an hour.'

* * *

I was married at twenty-two and moved back to Alice Springs a week after my wedding. I guess I was one of many brides that invested most of my energy in the wedding day and barely stopped to consider the consequence of marriage.

The third of seven children from a very traditional Catholic culture, I was marrying Christopher O'Loughlin, who was also one of seven and it was the first wedding for both families. It was a big day for everyone.

Joined in holy matrimony by an uncle each (both were priests) at 11 a.m. in Yorketown, we then filed into the pub up the road and partied long and hard with two hundred of our nearest and dearest.

* * *

There's no doubt looking back we made a fine couple, even if I do say so myself. I was a pretty bride and Chris O'Loughlin was drop-dead handsome. With his hair already prematurely greying at the sides, he was athletic and only an inch or so shy of being the quintessential tall, dark and handsome . . .

Leaving the reception was when the enormity of what I'd done first hit me. The two of us embarked on our married life in a borrowed Ford station wagon at two o'clock in the morning. The groom was contentedly looking forward to our wedding night, which was to be in a motel thirteen miles up the road, and the decidedly drunk and dishevelled bride wanted to quite literally jump out of the window.

We were heading for the coastal town of Stansbury and I think I started to cry at the halfway mark.

'What's the matter? Why are you crying?'

Because I hardly even know you and I've made a terrible mistake. We haven't even lived together and it was so much fun getting the wedding organised and having six bridesmaids that I didn't even have time to think about what I was really doing, and it was such a good party and my family are still at the pub singing around the piano and I want to be with them but instead I'm in a car with a stranger and I've left home forever and now I have to go and live in Alice Springs for the rest of my life.

'We don't have any toothpaste.' Thank God I'd left my honeymoon bag behind with all my girlie bridey things in it. It sort of gave me something to cry about without having to let on what I was really crying about.

As we neared Stansbury I'd graduated to heaving sobs and poor Chris was frantic.

'Fiona, if you can just stop crying, I promise as soon as we get there I'll get you some toothpaste.'

By now I really was crying about the toothpaste. My wedding night was ruined. I didn't have my gorgeous new things, no change of clothes or underwear or make-up.

What a terrible omen, everything's ruined.

True to his word, as soon as we drove into that sleepy little town Chris pulled up out the front of a house and knocked on the door.

I must admit I did start to love him again as he stood before a gruff old man who'd been woken up at two-thirty by a guy in a morning suit.

'Um, sorry to bother you but it's my wedding night tonight and my wife really needs some toothpaste. That's her in the car . . . she's crying.'

Maybe the old man had never been in love or maybe he was telling the truth when he said his teeth were false and he couldn't help us. In any case he slammed the door in my new husband's face and we set off again.

Chris was undeterred and approached a man in the street who'd obviously had a big night out and was staggering home.

I was still in the car but I knew we were in luck. They actually hugged for a second and then we followed him home and were given a half-used tube of Colgate.

All to no avail, sadly. I simply couldn't pull myself together and spent an hour in the motel bathroom wallowing on the floor. Hope was fading fast for Chris as he waited in the bedroom.

I've got nothing to change into and I'm not going out there naked. I want my beautiful new nightie.

I emerged eventually, having showered and washed my hair. I looked like a drowned rat in four hundred metres of tulle, still wearing my wedding dress. I don't remember the rest.

* * *

So here we were. Married and living in Newland Street, Alice Springs. It was not much bigger than a flat on a block of land, really, with one bathroom, three bedrooms and one shared kitchen, living and dining space. I can't begin to tell you how ugly that little house was. Green net curtains, red kitchen cupboards, beige walls, burnt orange shagpile carpet, mission-brown doors and architraves, aluminium windows with horrible fly screens, a very nasty dark green lino, and monstrous heavy curtains in the living room covered in a palm tree print.

I didn't really know where to begin but nor was I particularly fazed. I was happy to be at the beginning and instinctively knew that it would only ever get better than this.

I was just so thrilled to be a married lady I didn't care much about anything else.

We had one wooden table that Justin O'Loughlin had given us from his dental surgery with four matching chairs and they were my most prized possessions.

In the early days at Newland Street I used to cling to that little table as it honestly was the only aesthetically pleasing thing in the house. It used to fold down to a half circle and I would rearrange what was on it every day. Flowers or fruit bowls or crockery. I was playing house, I guess, but it didn't take me long as that table was really the only thing I had to work with at first.

Only a few months ago I came home from overseas to find that little bric-a-brac table ruined in the backyard after it had been left out in the rain and I grieved for it big time.

* * *

The Monday after Chris and I were married we set off on a five-day fly/drive to Tasmania. Chris has since told me that on the first night in Launceston he went for a walk and was overcome with a sense of responsibility and panic. Poor bugger. Little did he know that within two months we'd have a baby on the way and plenty more where that came from. It's strange because I was going through some similar anxieties myself but neither of us thought to let on to the other. If the truth be known, we were actually still a bit shy.

On about the first Saturday after our honeymoon we went shopping at the Coles complex in Alice Springs and had our first married fight.

We were in the newsagency and I spotted a set of white salt and pepper shakers with little pink flowers painted on them. They were $7 each.

'Chris, we have to get these. They'll look great on our table.'

Did I mention I was a complete dickhead at the time? 'Fiona, we can't just buy things every time we feel like it. We're paying off a house now and we can't afford to waste money.'

Well, that was that as far as I was concerned. The honeymoon was over. In fact, I went home that afternoon and wrote a letter to my dad telling him how sorry I was but the whole marriage thing had been a terrible mistake. I was interrupted halfway through by a knock on the door, and there was Chris with a bunch of flowers and the salt and pepper shakers. Awww shucks!

One afternoon I couldn't resist a fabulous belly laugh at my new husband's expense. He was sweeping the front verandah and some guys from his footy team came past on a jog and stopped to chat. From inside the house I overheard one of them ask where the new missus was and then I realised they'd probably stopped for a gawk at Chris O'Loughlin's new bride. His mates were facing the front of the house and Chris had his back to me standing there chatting to them with a broom in his hand. It was all too perfect. I flung the front door open and screamed at him like a fishwife.

'And when you've finished with the front yard you can bloody well get round and do the bloody back!'

Bit by bit I started feeling lonely for my girlfriends and sisters and used to moan my case from the couch to Chris. The couch was a white vinyl cast-off from TAA housing. It had brown woollen cushions and was propped up at one end by three bricks that stood in for a missing leg.

'It's not fair! You've been living here for ages and you've got all your footy mates and people from work and I haven't got anyone. I need a girlfriend.'

One Sunday there was a knock on the door and when I opened it there was Chris, believe it or not, dressed as a woman.

'Hello.'

'Hello, I'm Doreen. I heard that you're new to town and wondered if you'd like some company?'

'Really, Doreen? Well, why don't you come in and I'll put the kettle on.'

Doreen was wearing my purple Country Road 'going away' dress and she had on a yellow wig.

As I was making the coffee I couldn't help wondering why blokes thought girls were actually called names like Doreen.

'So where's your husband?'

'I'm not sure, Doreen. I think he's gone somewhere.'

'Oh, men, they're always off doing one thing or another, aren't they, Fiona?'

Again, I wondered why blokes thought girls actually talked like this.

I was about to wind things up with Doreen anyway when a couple of Chris's mates started knocking on the front door, but she bolted down the passage at the sound of them and I never saw her again.

* * *

Being married at a young age I reckon is tough wherever you live but I remember after I'd had my third baby I truly felt the walls were closing in on me in Alice Springs. It was a seriously male-dominated environment. The Northern Territory in the 1980s was akin to the rest of Australia in the sixties and women had a pretty defined role. We were housewives who supported our blokes while they carved a living mostly out of small businesses or government positions. Much backslapping and Friday arvo drinks was the norm and if you'll allow my melodrama, I actually felt like I was drowning.

Not surprisingly it was at about this time that I began performing and writing a weekly column in the *Centralian Advocate*. My column was hardly controversial stuff – more my take on the minutiae of my domestic world – but nonetheless one Friday afternoon over a cold beer, a bloke sitting at the bar next to my husband turned around and said to him, 'You ought to smack your missus in the mouth, mate.'

My husband is regarded these days by other blokes as a serious new-ager, what with having a wife that he *allows* to leave home and tour for much of the year, but I remember being seriously pissed off one lunchtime when my father-in-law was visiting.

Maybe I was paranoid but I had a gut feeling that Chris had upped the macho stakes out of some weird deference to his father's patriarchal sensibilities. Basically, he asked me to make them lunch.

I did, but not before finding an old shawl and fashioning it over my head, face and shoulders. The funny thing was that as I served them lunch my father-in-law didn't notice a thing and Chris followed me out to the laundry pretty pissed off himself.

'What's with the headgear?'

I was still wearing it and had started doing some ironing, not because I actually ever do any ironing but because I'm nothing if not committed to a sight gag.

'Well, if you're not prepared to treat me like a Westerner, then I'm not prepared to dress like one.'

I might have a lot to say about marriage, but I still believe that when Chris asked me to marry him one of the smartest things I've ever done was say yes, and even smarter was to add: 'But I don't do windows.'

* * *

At times I just had to grin and bear it and I remember going along with a wifely duty one fair weekend in 1986 when I was heavy with child. It was Christopher's cricket grand final and as I loathe all sports and love Saturday sleep-ins I'd managed to avoid having to suffer through spectatorship until now.

'Fiona, it's the Grand Final, all the other wives are coming and we're supposed to bring a plate.'

He set off without me and I grudgingly followed an hour or so later with a plate of scones, jam and cream and found myself sitting in the sun for an eternity, watching him field and watching the grass grow beneath me with precisely the same amount of interest.

No one said hello and I literally sat there for three hours watching my red-capped husband far in the distance not giving me the slightest bit of attention.

Finally it was over and I headed to the car to retrieve my scones as all the blokes headed off the field. My scones were a disgrace, having baked in the car for the better part of a Saturday afternoon.

The jam had turned to jelly beans and the cream had turned to butter and I turned to my returning red-capped husband to notice something that became more curious by the second.

It wasn't him! Wrong cricket game, wrong oval.

* * *

Christopher's cousin Michael O'Leary lived about three doors down in the same street with two other guys, Lachie McKerrow and Gerry Mabberack. All three had been to our wedding and

bit by bit they became my buddies as much as Christopher's.
Especially Gerry.

I needed to get a job pretty quickly after the wedding and
Gerry helped me land one, as his assistant in a medical lab. So
a month after Chris and I were married I added lab assistant to
my eclectic resumé and started working at Peveril's Pathology.

The building was very expansive for the twelve or so
employees who occupied the space and Gerry and I spent our
days in a lab at the back. My job was to plate out samples of
ghastly bodily fluids on agar dishes for Gerry to examine under
the microscope.

Specimens were delivered to the lab twice a day from the
surgeries and medical centres around town and since everyone
at Peveril's had very specific jobs, we really didn't interact with
each other much outside of smoko and lunch breaks. Except
for Gerry and me, who spent any free time playing practical
jokes on each other and anyone else we could think of.

Frank was the boss and when I saw the UK comedy *The
Office* for the first time I rang Gerry in Perth and told him
that Frank had his own TV show: Frank was a lot nicer than
David Brent but he did enjoy regaling us with his personal
philosophies and insights. In fact, if you egged him on enough,
some of our lunch breaks could go for ninety minutes or more.

One afternoon Gerry was at his bench waiting for some
work to come in and he picked up the phone and put it on
speaker and dialled the number of Peveril's.

The call went through to the front desk.

'Good afternoon, Peveril's Pathology, Sharon speaking.'

'Goodarfunoon Pevril's Poligy, Tharon thpeaking.'

'Hello.'

(Heavy breathing.)

'Okay, I'm hanging up.'

God knows why we thought that was so funny but it kept us amused for a week or more whenever we had some time on our hands. And we were all ears at smoko getting the latest rundown on the crank caller from the girls in the front office.

One other afternoon while Gerry was in the middle of another crank call I noticed someone in the doorway. It was Frank and a policeman standing behind him.

They'd been tracing the calls and had found out they were coming from an internal line. There was poor Frank trying to look like he had control of his ship in front of the cop and poor Gerry trying his best not to laugh while Frank handed down his sentence.

'I'm sorry to say this Gerry, but the cost of the trace will be coming out of your pay cheque.'

We waited till they left and then exploded again.

I don't know why that place made me laugh so much. Maybe because my job tasks were so dull and repetitive. It reminded me of afternoons at high school when I just couldn't hold it together. Or maybe it was hormones, I found out I was pregnant soon after I started working at the lab and from then on I was laughing on the other side of my face. Morning sickness is bad enough without the first job of the day being opening samples of poo, wee, sputum and worse.

* * *

Outside of my puerile behaviour at the pathology lab I was getting on with being a grown-up married person and even went so far as to throw a few dinner parties.

The first couple we had over for a meal were Cathy and Barry Skipsey. Barry sang in a local folk band called Bloodwood and we had met them during the course of *Godspell* and the Araluen opening.

Everything was going swimmingly this night despite my limited expertise in the kitchen. I was cooking fillet steaks with a mushroom sauce and decided to add a last bit of garlic to the pan before I served it up. I reached up for the garlic salt and knocked a tin of Milo out of the cupboard. The whole tin upended into the pan of steaks and mushrooms and I was left with two options: either serve up chocolate steak and mushrooms or rinse the steak under the tap.

I chose the latter and I must say no one really went wild about their dinner that night. But Cathy Skipsey did comment on what lovely salt and pepper shakers we had.

The other disaster I had in my kitchen that year was on Christmas Day. It was only three months after the wedding and since we couldn't afford to head south we decided to put on Christmas lunch at our house and invited Rebecca Murdoch, who was a girl from Warooka living in Alice at the time, and my cousins Aaron, Simon, and Kent Honner who were up here on holiday.

I rang my mum and asked her how long it took to defrost a turkey and she said about two days. I rang her again and asked her what she put in the stuffing and she said breadcrumbs, egg, thyme, salt, pepper and onion.

I rang Mum again and asked her if white onions were as good as brown onions and I think she hung up.

I learnt two important lessons that Christmas. I learnt that leaving home and setting up house at the age of twenty-two can be irresponsible and dangerous; and I also learnt that when your mother tells you that a turkey takes about two days to defrost she presumes that it's in your refrigerator and not sitting on top of the washing machine in the laundry in 42 degree heat.

I was nauseous, homesick and extremely pissed off that a stiff drink was out of bounds due to being pregnant. My cooking skills must have been as lacking as my mathematical ability because for some reason I didn't take the turkey out of its plastic packaging ready for the oven until we had all finished our prawn cocktails. And to be honest they were more seafood filler cocktails, as real prawns were about as out of reach geographically as economically back then.

The smell of that turkey was so astonishingly foul that I ran to the bathroom, abandoning my guests, and threw up from my very soul. On and on I heaved, and then cried the desperate tears of a Yorke Peninsula girl who wanted her mother.

Meanwhile the rest of the house was struggling not to heave themselves and Chris had to actually drive the damn bird out of town to the dump while Rebecca managed to save the day by carving up a small ham that she had brought along. Eventually, after I pulled myself together, we enjoyed an albeit very late, very light Christmas lunch.

Simon Honner declared magnanimously at the end of that Christmas that if there was anything you could live without on your Christmas dinner plate, it would definitely be the turkey and the stuffing and the gravy.

* * *

I was incredibly lonely in the first few years of being married, and I missed my brothers and sisters more than anything else. It's not that I didn't have friends in Alice Springs back then. I did, but I didn't have a history with anyone and I was terrified of being forgotten by my old life and everyone in it. I began a daily battle with the telephone very early on.

Chris comes from a family every bit as close as mine, but they are way more independent of each other emotionally and always have been, and he has never understood my need for such heavy contact with my siblings.

Back in the late eighties, Chris and I lived on one income, paying off a house, with three babies in the space of three years, and we certainly didn't have money to burn, which is probably why I would look longingly at the phone like an alcoholic at a bottle of scotch every time I walked past it.

Phone calls were more expensive back then, and I reckon I played a significant part in Telecom profits. I never intended to talk for long but I couldn't resist a quick chat with my sister Cate every morning. More often than not a quick chat turned into forty minutes or more. Every argument I ever had with Chris was repeated and dissected and analysed until I hung up satisfied that he was a complete bastard for taking me away from my family in the first place, and that I was well within my rights to make an occasional phone call. Then I would ring Mum to find out everything I needed to know about what all the others were up to and fill her in on which baby had said what funny thing and which one was eating solids and who was toilet trained and blah, blah, blah, blah.

Chris came home from work one afternoon with a face like thunder and said, 'We got the phone bill today,' and didn't say another word to me for the rest of the night. The next morning he actually unplugged the phone and went off to work with it tucked under his arm. His parting shot was, 'Why can't you just write letters like your grandmother would have had to do.'

I wrote my sister a letter that afternoon, and I must say I was bloody pleased with myself. It was a complete piss-take of a letter from a bygone era, and I sent it off to her and kept a copy for myself.

My Dear Sister Cate

What a thrill it was to hear all your news via the Telecom Cable Network, but alas my dear, our correspondence must be contained to Australia Post from here on as Mr O'Loughlin has threatened to deem our marriage null and void if there is ever a repeat of last month's account.

This outcry, I regret to tell, was accompanied with some unsavoury language that I shan't repeat for fear of this letter falling into the hands of infants. Speaking of which, how are your offspring? You were troubled with lactating complications when last we spoke and, while I am hesitant to write of such personal details, allow me to suggest the oil of the paw paw, a wonderful healing property (for cracks).

I have endured an exhausting day commencing with a most vexing visit to the Woolworths Corporation, upon where the youngest of my brood was accused of pilfering a sweet by a controller of the checkout. I refused to compensate with coin for the alleged misdemeanour, confident in my defence that sweets placed so enticingly low to the sight and grasp of an infant was a dishonest ploy by the store to coerce a mother into paying for sweets that were deviously intended to be stolen in the first instance.

I must sign off for now, dear sister, as there is much to do in these hectic days. I am most grateful to Mr O'Loughlin and the Telecom Company for awakening me to the frivolous error of my ways and have resolved to achieve a higher standard of frugality not just in communication but in all areas of domesticity. So with little malice in my heart but rather a new economic wisdom I shall commence at once with the preparation of a highly unpalatable ox testicle for our evening meal.

Yours as always in vengeance and sarcasm,

Fiona

* * *

One of the things that surprised me most about becoming a mother was how confident I felt. I was only twenty-three when Henry was born, and an instinctive force took over from the moment he arrived. I just knew we were made for each other.

Henry had had a shaky beginning. Before I knew I was pregnant I woke up one morning with a really sharp pain in my side and made an appointment to see a doctor that day. After she examined me she asked me a couple of questions.

'What type of contraception are you using?'

'Um, er, I'm using natural contraception.'

The truth was I was more than happy for babies to arrive as soon as I was married, and I actually had no clue what natural contraception involved.

'I see, so when did you last ovulate?'

'Oh, I wouldn't know.'

And then she looked at me the way some people look at simpletons and she said, 'You're pregnant.' And as the first wave of excitement rose up inside me, she added, 'But you're not going to have a baby. You have an ectopic pregnancy and you need to be admitted to hospital immediately.'

I remember ringing Chris from a public phone box in Todd Street to tell him, and then shortly after that we were waiting outside the specialists' rooms at the Alice Springs Hospital.

'Dr Bloomer will be ready for you shortly.'

I wish I could say that I was beside myself with worry sitting in that waiting room but all I remember thinking was what a pity the specialist didn't have an 's' on the end of his surname. You see, we already had a Doctor Cutter in Alice Springs back then and a surgeon called Doctor Butcher and I reckoned that a gynaecologist called Doctor Bloomers would have rounded things off nicely.

'Mrs O'Loughlin.'

I was led into his rooms and something fairly extraordinary happened. He didn't examine me; he just looked into my eyes for an uncomfortably long moment.

'So, some people think your baby's in your fallopian tube and that you need an operation to remove it. What do you think?'

'I don't know.'

'Well, do you know what I think? I think your baby is exactly where it's supposed to be.'

He was quite right, Dr Bloomer, and he proved it not long after with an ultrasound. So there we were, Chris and I, twenty-four and twenty-two, married six weeks, and a baby on the way.

I believe morning sickness is one of the most dastardly blows that Mother Nature has on offer, and what infuriates me most is the nonchalant acceptance of it by men and even some women. More than once I have encountered blokes, doctors, relatives and others who have had the gall to insinuate that morning sickness is all in the imagination or can be rectified by ginger tablets, massage, aromatherapy or other magic remedies. I'm here to tell you this is all utter nonsense.

Why it strikes some and not all expecting mothers I don't know, but I would love to say this out loud to the world.

Morning sickness is a ghastly, mostly fourteen- to sixteen-week, incarceration of twenty-four-hour nausea. It is not in the imagination; it is in the upper half of the torso, and only ever goes away when the sufferer is asleep. One other brief respite can be enjoyed after a bout of vigorous vomiting, but the relief will last for less than ten minutes. The actual act of throwing up is not proof of the existence of morning sickness as the inability to vomit is as hideous, if not worse, than throwing up itself.

The taste of copper in the mouth is as constant as the nausea, and will only go away while one is eating. The tiredness is overwhelming, and from personal experience can lead a woman to nod off while waiting at a checkout. A woman with morning sickness will attempt to shallow breathe for its duration, and can smell a cigarette a kilometre away.

Raw meat and coffee will become the devil himself.

Apart from the chronic cases that require hospitalisation, a woman with all this to contend with is usually either still in the workplace or at home caring for other kids, and she is not treated as an unwell person because it is not a life-threatening illness, nor does it have any long-term ill effects.

But she is unwell and she is trapped in this physical horror for at least three months.

If you are a woman who never experienced morning sickness, be thankful rather than suspicious of its reality, and if you're a bloke who just doesn't understand it, then shut the hell up and hang out some washing.

My sister Sarah is of the chronic variety that has nine months of morning sickness, and often ends up in hospital on a drip to rehydrate her, and my other sister Cate shares the associated sickness phenomena with us.

Associated morning sickness is when you experience something at the height of your sickness and you associate it with nausea for a very long time. To give you an example, Cate was at the height of her morning sickness at about nine weeks pregnant with her second baby, and at this time she chose some fabric for new curtains and a lounge suite covering. The material was imported and she didn't lay eyes on it again until well into her pregnancy. On the day that the curtains and re-covered lounge suite arrived Cate was reasonably excited about putting together her 'new look' living room. That is, until she came face to face with the fabric and started retching uncontrollably even though she was by now well out of morning sickness territory. I don't think she managed to hang those curtains for a year or more.

I've always said I'd rather have a caesarean every second Thursday than morning sickness and *I'm* no stranger to associated sickness either. When I was pregnant with Mary-Agnes, the kids and I had been counting down the days till the first McDonald's restaurant opened in Alice Springs. Finally it was McHappy day for the O'Loughlins, and we were all sitting at a table with our burgers in front of us and I was just about to chow down on a fillet of fish. Out of the corner of my eye I noticed a guy two seats across having a bit of a coughing fit, and then very unfortunately a piece of his masticated Big Mac flew out of his mouth and into the air and landed on my finger.

Morning sickness is a weird phenomenon. I bolted to the ladies' and vomited from my boots, and for a good three years just the sight of the M sign would make me dry retch.

As soon as my morning sickness with Henry was over I started to really love being pregnant. I ate myself into oblivion and poor Chris stood by and watched his 50-kilogram bride morph into a 75-kilogram monster with three double chins.

I was obsessed with a French patisserie on the other side of town and managed to find my way there as often as I could. I think I ate a Mars bar every day and downed soft drink like it was water.

I wasn't at all self-conscious about it until Chris came home from work unexpectedly one day to find me watching a video and hoeing into a delivered pizza with the lot at three in the afternoon. Even I was embarrassed for a second, and there was a kind of awkward moment.

'You know, I think I'm half bulimic.'

'Half?'

'Yeah, I've got the bingeing down pat, now I just need to work on the purging.'

Henry was born after an extremely long and awful labour, and there's no doubt about it, I'm not a star patient.

I really don't want to sound like a nut case, but I reckon the dominance of men in the obstetric world is illogical, hypocritical and a tad gross. Surely its women's business? And yes, I understand that males have dominated all professions for hundreds of years, so it's no surprise that this remains the case with obstetric science. But, and maybe I am a nut case, couldn't we now say thanks a bunch for all your help, fellas, and show them the door?

And who's marrying these guys? Who's waving her man off in his three-piece suit, in his Lamborghini, heading off to his plush rooms in the city to faff about with other people's vaginas all day? It really has always struck me as odd, and it always will.

Seriously, though, I'm not saying we should dispense with male obstetricians. I think if a doctor is needed for a complicated birth, then a doctor is needed, be they male or female.

And I'm a great believer in hospital births. In fact I'm always puzzled at the home birth option. My first thought has always been: 'Why would anyone want to ruin their own carpet?'

I think births should be in hospitals with midwives and midwives only, with doctors at the ready if the birth becomes a medical matter. With a straightforward delivery, though, there's nothing medical about giving birth.

So there.

I went into Henry's birth as ill-informed as was possible. I was too naive to even question an induction at thirty-nine weeks, and didn't comprehend that that induction would seal the fate of a caesarean birth. I didn't have high blood pressure. My baby wasn't breech or distressed.

It was a year to the very day that my beloved Uncle Maurice had had his stroke, the 15th of August, the Feast of the Assumption.

I wasn't due and my baby wasn't ripe. Anyway, I won't bore you with the details, but it went on and on and on, and I was a terrible patient.

I did an awful lot of yelling, much to the dismay of my mother and husband.

'I'm dying! I'm having a horse!'

'You're not having a horse, but you are scaring all the other women in the ward.'

'Your mum's right, Fiona. Why don't you breathe normally? The lady in the next bed isn't breathing like that.'

'Well why don't you go down to Kmart and buy a basketball and shove it up your arse, and we'll see how well you breathe?'

The pain was frightening and overwhelming and eventually I was being wheeled into the lifts of the Alice Springs Hospital to be taken upstairs for an emergency caesarean. They told me to say goodbye to Chris. I desperately whispered to him, and I believed every word I said: 'Chris, I'm dying, and none of them believe me.'

'I know.'

By this time I wanted the caesarean yesterday, and I hollered all the way into theatre.

Dr Bloomer was on hand, and I grabbed him by his tie and pulled him to within centimetres of my face.

'I will not have one more contraction, not one more! Are you listening to me?'

'Yes, Fiona, now just count back from ten.'

'Ten . . .'

Waking up from any anaesthetic is a weird experience. At first you don't know who *you* are, let alone anybody else. Then slowly, bit by bit, your life comes back to you. 'I'm Fiona, Fiona O'Loughlin, married to Chris, I'm having a . . . Oh my God, I had the baby.'

And there he was, the most beautiful baby I ever saw.

At my Uncle Maurice's funeral, my Great-Uncle John remarked during his eulogy, 'Maurice was called home on the 15th of August, the Feast of the Assumption . . . but in typical Maurice style he chose not to answer that call until the 16th.'

So a year to the day later, his great-nephew was here, called to earth on the 15th of August by a Syntocinon drip, but just like his uncle, little Henry Maurice chose not to answer that call until the 16th.

I'd never known happiness like I experienced that night. I kept waking up and remembering that I'd had him, and the joy that went through me was an actual physical surge. I kept Henry in my room with me and rarely left him in the nursery. I'd seen some of the babies in there and, quite frankly, I thought they were downright ugly. I felt so sorry for all the other mothers who didn't have a beautiful baby like mine. That's why I decided not to leave him in the nursery. It just wouldn't be fair to rub everybody's nose in it.

* * *

The most traumatic birth I had was Biddy's. I didn't have her in Alice Springs. I wanted to be nearer to my mother and sisters, and so I booked into Calvary Hospital in North Adelaide. I was desperate to give birth naturally this time. I had always been told that three caesareans were the limit, and since I wanted six kids I consequently felt that three future babies were at stake. I was staying with my father-in-law Ivan on the night I went into labour.

I had been to a movie with my sister Sarah and we were having a coffee on Jetty Road when I was hit with overwhelming anxiety. The baby wasn't due for two more weeks and Chris was still in Alice Springs. I went home to Ivan's house and put myself to bed. I was only staying with Ivan for one night and very much hoped this wouldn't be the night the baby came. As much as I love Ivan, he has never struck me as a natural midwife.

Sure enough, at 2 a.m. I was woken up by familiar cramping and realised the baby was coming regardless of what suited me. Poor Ivan, he must have thought these moments were behind him.

'Ivan! Ivan! I think I'm in labour.'

The pair of us sat up for an hour or so having a cup of tea. I felt like an idiot for waking him up so soon and knew that not much was happening and that it was way too early to head for the hospital. But going back to bed was out of the question. I decided to ring my friend Jane Mortimer, who was on standby as my support person in case the baby came before Chris left Alice Springs.

I told Jane that I was in labour and needed her to pick me up and drive me to the hospital.

She rang back about twenty minutes later.

'Why aren't you on your way over here?'

'Noni (her nickname for me since school), are you sure it isn't just wind?'

Unbeknown to me, Jane had had a sudden attack of cold feet after I called and had to be almost physically dragged out of the house by her mother.

She seemed okay when she turned up at Ivan's and minutes later we were roaring up Anzac Highway in a red Triumph Stag. Then we started laughing like hyenas. Jane was impersonating Prissy from *Gone with the Wind*.

'But Miss Scarlett . . . I don't know nothin' 'bout birthin' no babies.'

Jane's mother had told her to remember to wipe my brow. We thought this was hysterically old-fashioned.

I had chosen Jane as my support person because she was not particularly interested in babies. This way I was sure she would have way more time for me during the course of things. My plan worked spectacularly, especially at about the ten-hour mark.

'How are you now, Noni?'

'Wipe my brow.'

By now I didn't think it was funny anymore. Why I took so long to have babies is beyond me. I remember an airline steward being more than a bit concerned about me being on a plane from Alice to Adelaide at eight months pregnant. I tried to put her at ease. 'Trust me, I could go into labour and board a return flight from Adelaide to London and be back in time for transition.'

Poor Jane. She waited until she was thirty-nine to have her first baby, and I've often wondered if I had something to do with it.

Things started to go downhill at about the twenty-hour mark. My obstetrician came to examine me.

'Fiona, I'm going to examine you and I promise if you are anywhere near eight centimetres dilated we'll get this baby out naturally.'

We didn't make it naturally, little Biddy and I, and I know in the big scheme of things that a caesarean birth is a small price I paid for a safe outcome, but too often people can be too quick to point out the obvious.

'Just be grateful that your baby is healthy.'

It's like telling someone who just stubbed their toe to think about all the people who don't have legs. If someone stubs their toe they don't want to hear how lucky they are to have a toe in the first place; now's not the time because they JUST STUBBED THEIR GODDAMNED TOE!!! It's going to hurt for a bit.

* * *

Tess's birth was, by contrast to Biddy's and Henry's, a far less complicated experience, and I had the most wonderful obstetrician in the whole wide world. I knew I'd hit the jackpot with

Dr Michael McEvoy when I asked him whether he thought I should have a general anaesthetic or brave an epidural.

'Oh, I can't make decisions like that for you, Fiona. I don't know how you women do any of it in the first place!' By now it was considered unsafe for me to attempt a natural delivery again, so she was born via an elective caesarean. She was beautiful and placid from the second they gave her to me. Tess was a very uncomplicated baby and made my life relatively easy for a mother of three under three.

By the time Tess came along, my sister Cate had married Phil Taylor, a lovely bloke from Adelaide, and they were expecting their first baby. Cate and Phil have nine kids now and Cate and I have possibly spent a year on the phone counselling each other through a thousand milestones. The phone calls were usually in the morning over a coffee after the school drop-offs and before we start on the morning mess.

'Hi Cate, what page are you up to?'

'Hi, I'm up to the page where I shoot my husband and drown four kids. What about you?'

'They all hate me. I forgot it was casual day and they all turned up in their uniforms.'

'Bummer, I've gotta go. The neighbours just found Leo on the road again.'

* * *

As I've said before, I've never taken a photo in my life worth framing, but I have an enormous album in my head. When something really strikes me as moving, funny or beautiful I concentrate hard for a second and tell myself to 'make a memory'. I've been doing this for as long as I can remember. For some reason photo albums have always depressed me, as do home videos. I know it's a bit mad but I can't bear to watch videos of my kids when they were babies, six parts melancholy and six parts nostalgia, revisiting the sounds of their voices and the pudge of their bodies. I always just end up grieving and wanting those babies back.

A number of years ago when I was driving the kids home from school we were crossing the dry bed of the Todd River as we do every day and, out of the corner of my eye, I spotted what could have been trouble further up the Todd between some schoolkids and some Aboriginal men. I followed the bank of the river for a hundred or so yards and got out of the car.

St Philip's College is probably the closest thing we have in Alice Springs to a posh private school. At least it's the only school in town where the kids wear blazers and ties. I recognised the uniform as I got nearer. There were two St Philip's students, a boy and a girl who looked to be about sixteen, standing with two old Aboriginal blokes. I was a bit concerned as I got closer and saw that the boy had hold of one of the men and both appeared to be bleeding.

'What's going on?'

The girl had just finished talking to someone on her mobile phone. 'It's okay,' she said. 'He's cut his arm pretty badly but an ambulance is on its way.'

The situation was pretty simple. These kids were on their way home from school and had come across a man who had fallen over and cut himself.

Everything was under control and they certainly didn't need me, but before I headed back I made a memory.

The boy stood next to the man holding his arm up high above his head to slow the bleeding. The boy was wearing his private school blue and white striped shirt, his clothes representing everything it is to be middle class and white in Alice Springs. The man was filthy and had been wearing his clothes for months. He represented everything it is to be down and out and Aboriginal in Alice Springs. Help was coming and they waited, with one arm each suspended and joined together by the boy's hand around the man's wrist, and the man's blood poured not only down his own arm but down the boy's arm as well, dripping off his elbow and onto the sand of the Todd. Neither spoke and neither seemed to mind.

That's one of my favourite pictures in my head. Beautiful.

As you cross the Todd River, Aborigines are in full view always, sometimes drinking, sometimes fighting but mostly just sitting. I think it would be fair to say that it is usually in the car when you're crossing the river that urban Alice Springs kids, black or white, will ask their parents for the first time about the Aborigines in the river.

'Why do those people sit in the river all the time?'

To my mind it is a crucial question that requires a crucial answer, and it can go either way.

'Because they're drunks.'

'Because they're bludgers.'

'Because they're no-hopers.'

I guess, as is often the case, racism comes as much from ignorance as malice, but right at that moment you can either pass on intolerance or not, and it's such a heavy load to hand on to a little kid. A kid that may well spend his or her life in Central Australia has been given with authority a very heavy sack full of fat, pompous, pious prejudice.

'Why do those people sit in the river all the time?'

'I don't know, maybe they're waiting.'

'Waiting for what?'

'Waiting for better days, I think.'

Simple.

I had a phone call from a girlfriend years ago who lived on the other side of town. She was an educated specialist nurse, but I guess idiots are just idiots all the same.

'Hi, Fiona, it's me. Isn't it exciting! Nelson Mandela was released from prison today. I was going to invite you over for a bottle of champers but there's a heap of Abos hanging around the street. Can I come over there instead?'

I don't imagine that Alice Springs is host to more racists than anywhere else in the country, quite probably less, but because of our evident social problems I guess we are identified sooner for our persuasions. Many times I've been in a social situation when my heart's in my throat, as a conversation has turned to land rights or other Indigenous issues.

'The trouble with blackfellas is . . .'

Please don't say it.

'They need to assimilate . . .'

Please stop talking.

'The most primitive race of people . . .'

Fuck it, now we can't be friends anymore.

Racists scare me, quite probably because I used to be one, not actively, but passively. I used to share and listen to racist jokes with my friends. It was never seen as a bad thing in my childhood. I had one great-aunt who, up until her death in the 1990s, openly referred to Aboriginal people as niggers.

I remember an uncle years ago telling us kids that if we were good he'd take us for a drive later and show us a blackfella with red hair. That was on the Yorke Peninsula where I grew up, and I guess part of the reason we had such little understanding of Indigenous people was because we simply never crossed paths with them. There was only one Aboriginal community on the whole of the peninsula, a mission not far from Maitland. My understanding was that Point Pearce was a dirty place full of bad people who would come in to Maitland at night and steal from white people.

We used to have a beautiful fat white cat called Lugsy when we were kids. Lugsy had kittens one Friday night in the bottom of mum's wardrobe and I remember walking into the kitchen about a week later to find my dad and my uncle taping up a cardboard box with all the kittens inside.

'What are you doing?'

'We're sending them to the poor Aboriginal kids in Point Pearce who have never even seen a kitten.'

God knows what really happened to those kittens, but it dawned on me years later that they probably never made it to Point Pearce.

Before the arrival of European pastoralists the Yorke Peninsula was the home of the Narungga people and by 1880 there were less than one hundred souls of full Narungga descent on the whole of the peninsula. They were wiped out at the hands of the white man, and I'm sad to say that in my entire childhood I never heard a word about them.

* * *

When Henry was about three years old he came into the living room one rainy night where Chris and I were watching telly. 'There's a lady at the door.'

And so there was, and that was the night we met Wendy.

Wendy stood in the rain with a small dot painting with the paint not yet dry, and asked us how much we would pay her for it. I think we gave her about ten bucks and Henry was thrilled to have the painting in his room, and that was the first of many visits from Wendy.

'Hello, Peeona.'

She'd call from the front door whenever she was back in town. I'd since discovered that Wendy was from Hermannsburg, a dry mission, and came into town every few weeks or so on an alcoholic bender.

'No money, Wendy,' I'd say to her, 'but you can have some food.'

Wendy was indeed a cheeky drunk. After a while she didn't bother with knocking and I'd hear her greeting from inside the fridge.

'Hello, Peeona, just getting some dinner. You got any meat today?'

One day she turned up with about six other women.

'Hello, Peeona,' and then to her friends, 'I come here and teach Peeona Arrernte and she give me food, hey Peeona?'

Of course Wendy and I had no such arrangement but I didn't blow her story. Next thing, in front of them all, she squashed my nose flat with her finger. 'What's this called, Peeona?'

'Umm . . .'

'Oh, very bad, Peeona. You not practising. Got any meat?'

In an effort to cut back her visits I said to her one day, 'Hey, Wendy, if you ever see the red car in the driveway, don't come in whatever you do. My husband's a big grumpy bastard and you don't want to run into him.'

I came out of the shower one morning and screamed out loud as I smacked straight into a black man sitting in the passage.

'Oh that's just Henry, Peeona. He's cold, eh? You got a jumper?'

'Jesus, Wendy, that scared the crap out of me.'

Winter in Alice Springs is cold but brief, and at the time Chris only had two jumpers. I gave Henry the older of the two and reminded Wendy not to come by if the red car was in the driveway. A couple of Saturdays later Chris was in the front yard gardening and I heard Wendy's calling card.

'Hello, Peeona.'

I came out of the house and there she was, standing across the road with her mate Henry still wearing the jumper.

'Better not come in, eh? That the grumpy bastard? Seeya, Peeona!'

Chris couldn't believe it.

'I've been looking for that jumper everywhere . . . and I'm the bastard.'

About a month ago I was coming out of a supermarket in town fairly late one night and an elderly Aboriginal woman came up to the car. 'Scuse me, missus, you got two dollar please?'

It was Wendy. I hadn't seen her for thirteen years. She didn't look well, and certainly seemed not to remember me. I scrounged around my wallet and handed her some coins.

'Seeya, Wendy.'

'Seeya, Peeona.'

* * *

A few years ago I was making a Thai chicken curry very late in the afternoon. We had old friends from the Yorke Peninsula who were on their way to Darwin calling in for dinner that night. I realised I didn't have any coconut milk and grabbed my car keys to duck up to the shop. I didn't tell anyone I was leaving, as the corner shop is literally two minutes away.

On the way home I turned into our street and out of the corner of my eye I saw an old woman stagger and fall down on the footpath about half a block away. People stagger and fall down at a rate of knots in Alice Springs, so I continued on and pulled into my driveway.

I turned off the ignition but didn't get out of the car. It suddenly hit me what had just happened. I had just seen an old woman keel over in my street and I hadn't batted an eyelid, and I knew why. She was black. True story.

I sat in the car for a bit longer and mulled this over in my head. I was trying to think of the word that summed up this situation, and after a short time it came to me. Desensitised, that's what it's called. I'd read about this happening to people. You can see crap so many times that if you're not careful it doesn't look like crap anymore.

Be buggered, I thought to myself. I'm not an arsehole who sees an old lady fall over and drives right past.

What about the Thai chicken curry? said the lesser me.

I headed back down the street and the old lady was still lying there. As I got closer I realised she was bloody old, no kidding, in her nineties at least. She was wearing a nightie and she spoke very little English. When I asked her where she lived it sounded like she said Perderon. There were some Aboriginal kids, or I should say teenagers, standing near enough for me to call out to them.

'Do you know this lady?'

I didn't get an answer from any of them and then I suddenly remembered a nursing home in the next street. I helped the woman into the front seat of my car and as I drove around the block it looked like we were in luck. Out the front of the home was a nurse who seemed to be looking for someone up the street.

'Have you lost a patient?'

'Yes.'

She seemed relieved and headed over to my car, but when she peered through the window she groaned. 'Damn, it's not him.' She turned to cross the road.

'Do you know who this lady is?'

'Take her to the cop shop. They'll find out for you.'

Well, I thought that was a bit rich, taking a woman who's nearly a hundred to the police for falling over, so I headed back to the kids on the corner.

'You guys, I've got a really old lady in the car and I was wondering . . .'

'Yeah, we know her, eh,' one of them said.

'Really? What's her name? Can you show me where she lives?'

'Her name's Elsie, eh? We'll show you.'

So off we headed, Elsie and me in the front, and five teenage boys in the back.

'Which way?'

'She lib purder on [live further on], eh,' and he pointed down the road.

Purder on, purder on, and purder on we went. We live on the very outskirts of Alice Springs and you can be in the bush in minutes. They'd pointed me out of town so that's where we headed. We drove east for a while, Elsie staring straight ahead and the five boys mucking around and laughing in the back.

'Where to now?'

We were at the end of the bitumen about ten kilometres out of town and one of the boys pointed to a dirt track heading to the right. Off we went again and by now the sun was setting and just before a slight panic set in I noticed a fire from an Aboriginal camp up in the distance. I slowed down just on the outskirts of the camp. A couple of adults looked up at our arrival and a few dogs sniffed around the car. Apart from that we were barely noticed.

I turned around to the back seat just as all five of my adolescent passengers jumped out. I called out after them.

'Hey! What about Elsie?'

'She lib purder on, eh!'

And one of them pointed deeper into the bush.

Elsie and I headed off again. Elsie hadn't said a word since we left town and didn't really respond to anything from me.

I followed the dirt track as long as it lasted. Eventually it just stopped and the bush took over; there was nowhere to go but back. By now I was seriously worried. I wasn't sure where I was and it was minutes away from darkness. I turned the car around and found my way back to the camp.

Suddenly everything seemed surreal. It was like I'd stepped out of my suburban world of visitors and Thai chicken curry and gotten caught up in another place without even noticing the line that separated them. I wanted to go home.

'You tell me where Elsie lives.'

I had spotted one of the boys by the fire and headed over towards him. I heard laughing behind me and turned around to see the other boys.

'She lib back in town, eh? Thanks for the lift!'

It was pitch black on the way home. Elsie stared straight ahead and I was pretty pissed off. We drove in awkward silence for a while and then for some reason I got the giggles. I don't know what was funny in particular, but before long Elsie had been contaminated by me and we were both roaring laughing.

I felt bad as I pulled up out the front of the police station. I left Elsie in the car and walked up to the front desk to find out if they could help.

It really was that simple. Within minutes a police officer had identified that she lived in Hidden Valley and we were off again. Hidden Valley is a typical town camp in Alice Springs. It is incredible that these camps are so near the main roads but hardly visible from your vehicle. Driving into a town camp for the first time really is quite literally like driving into a third world. The houses are without windows and doors. There's litter everywhere, mangy looking camp dogs and near-naked babies and toddlers.

Elsie's family were sitting around a campfire when I turned up, and I realise now that what I experienced that night was a fundamental difference in our cultures.

'I've got Elsie over here. Is she your mother?' I asked one of the men as I walked towards them. He pointed to another bloke who nodded and stood up and headed towards the car.

Elsie plonked herself down by the fire with the rest of her family and I was barely given a passing glance by any of them as I reversed my car and headed for home.

If I'm honest I'd have to say that I was seriously miffed that I wasn't showered with gratitude by Elsie's family. But I understand now that that's my white man mentality.

'Thanks for bringing Mum home.'

'Oh, not at all, it was a pleasure.'

'I hope it wasn't too far out of your way.'

'I'm happy to help, really. Goodbye.'

'Safe driving then, and thanks again!'

Culturally that's the way we are, I guess, extravagantly polite and extravagantly insincere at the same time. We expect to be acknowledged for fits of generosity because that's the way our society operates. I can't help but think that the Aboriginal way is somehow more graceful.

* * *

From what I can see, government, legal, social and health professionals work around the clock for answers and solutions. I've known people, Aboriginal and non-Aboriginal, who've spent lifetime careers in Alice Springs as nurses, social workers, doctors or lawyers specifically working towards better days. And there have been some better days and there has to be more to come.

In the meantime we will still see hungry babies, torn-up toddlers, homeless kids and drunk, dishevelled, destitute men and women who are trapped in the here and now.

And to my mind, anyone who drives past this reality in a river bed, in a comfortable sedan, and passes judgement on their fellow human beings in front of their own children simply isn't helping anyone!

CHAPTER 8

LIFE AT THE TOP

Long before I became a comedian the stage beckoned relentlessly, and more times than not the consequences were pretty disastrous.

When I was about nineteen and nursing in Yorketown, I joined a local band as the token chick and rehearsed with them for a couple of months. The band was called 'No Lines Marked' and they had regular gigs in various pubs in the district. I used to do about three numbers with them: a couple of Blondie covers and the Divinyls hit 'All the Boys in Town'.

My first gig with the band was on a Saturday night at the Melville Hotel in Yorketown. I was working a 'late' at the hospital, which was from about three o'clock in the afternoon till eleven, and I had my gear to change into as soon as the shift finished. I could barely contain myself during the shift and at about 10 p.m. the charge sister let me go early. I put my make-up on in the toilets, blue eyeliner and hot pink lips, and I squeezed into a new pair of jeans and headed down the street to the Melville Hotel feeling every inch the rock star.

By the time I got to the pub some of the excitement had turned to blind fear. The place was packed and the band were about to get back on stage after the break. Mickey Allen, the lead singer, came over to me. 'We'll do "Stairway to Heaven" and then bring you straight on.'

I headed to the bar and started feeling desperate when I heard 'Stairway to Heaven' start. I really wanted a beer to calm my nerves but there was only one barmaid to about fifty punters. My heart was pounding and it took forever to get served. Finally it was my turn.

'Can I have a schooner of West End?'

No sooner had she poured my beer than I heard Mickey's voice over the PA.

'Put your hands together for Fiona Taheny.'

I skolled the beer on the spot, and then raced onto the stage. By the time I had hold of the microphone I was raring to go, and waited for the end of the opening drum set to start singing. I looked out at a sea of people already getting into the song and I took a big breath, and unfortunately one enormous long beer burp that came from my boots went straight through the microphone and right round the room.

This was hideously embarrassing to say the least, and second only to a performance in a piano bar about a year later.

* * *

One of the many jobs I took on in the year I temporarily moved to Alice Springs was to sing in a piano bar. Two nights of the week my dulcet tones would entertain the crowds in the cocktail bar of the Old Riverside Hotel. Except, to be honest, there weren't really ever any crowds. I think the biggest night we had would have been about sixteen people, and that included me and the piano player.

Most nights I guess there were about six or seven in total. There was one regular, an old bloke who sat at the bar and every now and then popped a shot of Drambuie on top of the piano for me. I think he did this when I was singing a particularly difficult number.

I sat up high on a stool to the right of a yellow baby grand piano and my repertoire was appalling. I chose random songs from a book called *101 Hits For Buskers*, and belted out anything that I recognised. There was no rhyme or reason to my sets and I could go from 'Que Sera, Sera' to 'The Streets of London' to 'Click Go the Shears' with absolutely no apologies.

I think it was the night of my seventh gig when things took a serious nosedive. My old mate at the bar had just delivered a third Drambuie as I was about halfway through 'Danny Boy'. Now, anyone who has ever sung 'Danny Boy' knows that there's a pretty high note at about the halfway mark. I must have thrown my head backwards a bit to facilitate that high note and then I realised that the stool and I had parted company. In fact I was airborne. It all seemed to happen in slow motion, and the next thing I remember I was flat on my back, staring at the ceiling, with the microphone cord wrapped around my legs.

Even worse than the fall was the silence that followed. I actually lay there longer than I needed to, having no clue how I was supposed to get up off the floor and leave the bar with eight people just staring at me in stunned silence. Somehow I must have managed it, and I don't think I even flinched when I collected my pay from the manager a while later. He said as he handed me the fifty bucks, 'We're going to have to let you go.'

Que sera, sera.

* * *

By 1994 I was writing and recording a weekly piece for ABC radio. They were three-minute vignettes of 'the world according to me' and were being syndicated nationally. I had just been asked to commit to the ABC for another year and was worried that I might have said all that there was to say from the perspective of a housewife in the middle of nowhere. I had been very autobiographical in my weekly on-air blabfests, and between that and my weekly column in the *Centralian Advocate* I was actually starting to get a little tired of the sound of my own voice.

At around the same time I heard about a comedian who had moved to town and was married to Kieran Rickhard, a friend of mine from the Araluen/*Godspell* era. We all ran into each other at a community cabaret at the Totem Theatre and I recognised Scott Casley from the comedy trio The Found Objects, who performed fairly regularly on the ABC television show *The Big Gig*.

For some reason within a week of meeting Scott I knew that I had solved my ABC problem. I pitched them the idea of my bringing a husband into the series and then rang Scott and asked him to 'marry' me. *Scott and Fiona* was born. Scott was a stay-at-home dad at the time to two little boys, and I was pregnant with Bert. Once a week we would meet at either of our homes and come up with a new scenario for our alter egos who bore the same Christian names.

Scott and Fiona was a three-minute weekly segment of a couple in their thirties who argued incessantly about anything from homebirths to wheelie bins, and I found a creative satisfaction from them that I had never come across in stand-up. The difference, I guess, was being able to choose how much of my actual self I was prepared to expose.

Stand-up is so naked. As my mate comedian Paul McCarthy puts it, it's the exotic dancing of the soul. With *Scott and Fiona* I was still writing from my own well of truth but the added ingredients of make-believe shrouded the line that divided fact from fiction. I ended up telling more and exposing less. I also realised how much I loved writing dialogue.

Scott Casley was a funny, funny man, a great writer and a generous collaborator. He had had a fairly big lick of the showbiz spoon and had decided that it was a scene that no longer interested him, so in a way we were on different roads. He was heading out of town and I was heading in.

Scott and Fiona served different purposes for us both. For Scott I doubt that it was much more than a creative outlet at a time in his life that was mostly dedicated to parenting, and for me it was to become a project that spanned more than a decade and would nearly bring me to my comedic knees.

After Scott Casley left town, I remember filing away the twenty or so *Scott and Fiona* scripts and being very depressed indeed. I missed Scott and Kieran as friends but I missed Scott's alter ego immensely. He was the other half of the fictitious couple that we had created and I believed that *Scott and Fiona* had barely gotten started. We had also had a few successes: ABC radio had syndicated the radio sketches nationally, and apparently we had been a small hit with ABC listeners in Tasmania, who were privy to the minutiae of Scott and Fiona's domestic dramas on Saturday mornings.

Thrilled to the back teeth was I when years later after a gig in Launceston I was approached by a woman about my age. She told me she remembered *Scott and Fiona*, and that she and her husband had listened to every single episode. Their favourite was 'the wedding video'. I nearly kicked a hole in the telly one night watching *Everybody Loves Raymond* when Ray Romano and his wife Debra had one of their biggest fights after Debra discovered that Ray had taped a football game over their wedding video. Scott Fennergan had done exactly the same thing, you see. Ten years ago!

I don't recall exactly how, why or when, but after a time I fished out the *Scott and Fiona* scripts from the rusted black filing cabinet housed outside to the left of the laundry door and started a monumental rewrite. All of a sudden I was convinced that *Scott and Fiona* was the next big Australian sitcom, and what motivated me more than anything else was my absolute conviction that Australia would be worse off for not meeting the Fennergans.

An American friend of mine living in Alice Springs had actually written a *Wonder Years* episode and lent me a number of scripts and set me up on the computer with a template for writing in TV language.

Once I got started I barely came up for air for six months. Dinner and bedtime had never been so vigilantly overseen by me, because that was when the real fun began. Every night I would hit the computer and retreat into the world of the Fennergans while the O'Loughlins slept. Chris would poke his nose in the door around midnight with a fairly half-hearted 'Will you be long?'

I usually kept at it until 2 or 3 a.m. and then I'd lie in bed hatching grand plans of somehow bringing it to the attention of a network. I decided at about this time that my best course of action was to keep going with my stand-up and get a career and a high enough profile to get my script noticed.

It started to fascinate me that behind every story that ever makes it to a stage or a screen lies a writer with a germ of an idea that grows and sweats and writhes and agonises while the writer is sustained by nothing but hope, and in my case, cigarettes and coffee.

To say I was a little obsessed with *Scott and Fiona* would be a mild understatement, but I was focused and happy, and sure in my world of writing in a way that I never have been on stage.

I eventually started humbugging ABC Television and secured myself an interview with the head of comedy to pitch *Scott and Fiona*. Two years had passed since those late-night typing marathons and I had by now performed my first Melbourne Comedy Festival show and started to harvest a small but steady live audience. By no means a heavyweight stand-up, I nervously stood on the steps outside the Melbourne ABC offices and introduced myself through the intercom.

'Fiona O'Loughlin for Mr Friedman please.'

Bzzzz.

I was in.

My friend Marty Lappin, who was a Melbourne comic, had lent his eye to the script a number of times and he not only picked me up from the airport but accompanied me to my first ever network 'pitch'.

There we sat, in reception outside the Comedy Department, and whispered words of encouragement to each other while we tried not to be overawed by the sight of Roy and HG wandering in and wandering out.

'Fiona O'Loughlin?'

After being shown in to Mr Friedman's office, Marty and I both sat on a couch and after some initial pleasantries Mr Friedman swivelled in his chair and we were down to business.

I've taken longer to eat a sandwich than my first meeting at the ABC took.

'So, Fiona, tell me about your idea.'

'Well, I've written a script about a couple who move from Sydney to Darwin and she hates it and he loves it, uhmmm, because, you know . . . Well, Darwin's really hot! and . . . anyway, they're called the Fennergans . . . You know . . . like the antihistamine?'

I shot a desperate look at Marty who magnanimously ventured in with: 'It's basically autobiographical, based on Fi's own experience in the Northern Territory, and like she says in her stand-up, the thing about . . .'

'Can I just stop you there?'

Mr Friedman had clearly heard enough.

'I'm interested in the drama. Every comedy is built on drama. I'm not interested in jokes at this stage. I need to take a phone call right now and I'd like you to just think about what I've said and give me a direct summary of the drama in one sentence when I get back.'

And with that Mr Friedman left the room.

'Jesus, Marty! This is so embarrassing. What does he mean he's not interested in jokes?'

'That must have been what he was thinking when he commissioned *One Size Fits All*.'

One Size Fits All was a fairly ordinary all-girls ABC comedy on at the time. I started laughing and then kind of mock wailing and slid onto the floor with my head in my hands and between my legs.

'Rightio then.'

Mr Friedman appeared not at all concerned to find me in a rudimentary yoga position on the floor of his office, and I tried to rearrange myself as delicately back onto the couch as I could to respond to his request for the 'drama' of my script to be outlined in one sentence. The game was well and truly up, and I gave it a half-hearted go, to say the least.

'Well, they don't fit in . . . and you know . . . it really is very hot in Darwin, well, more humid than anything, especially in the build-up.'

About five minutes later Marty and I sat on the steps of the ABC, smoking cigarettes and reliving every horrible moment of our meeting.

'Jesus, Fi, you may as well have just given him the number of the Darwin Bureau of Meteorology.'

'He didn't give me a chance. Not interested in the jokes? What sort of a Jewish bloke in charge of a television comedy department isn't interested in jokes?'

I soldiered on with *Scott and Fiona* despite my disastrous early pitch. I even got a call from Mr Friedman a week later to say that he very much liked the script. Of course it 'wasn't anything the ABC were interested in at the moment' but he thought it was funny and well written. That gave me an enormous boost of encouragement.

Stand-up was by now my day job, so to speak, and I was performing at festivals here and overseas for three to four months of the year and getting steady work as a corporate speaker interstate and every so often a television appearance thrown in. I never missed an opportunity to talk about *Scott and Fiona* to television people and continued retouching the script whenever I got the chance.

I became more confident in 'pitching' my sitcom and at one stage it was inches away from a development deal with a production company. Even though the ultimate answer was no I still came away with my optimism intact after a producer told me she had been reading it on a flight from Melbourne to Sydney and as she was disembarking the guy she'd been sitting next to admitted he'd been reading over her shoulder and said, 'That's a very funny script.'

I guess my confidence in *Scott and Fiona* grew the more I worked on it and the more I researched my product. Australia was being very short-changed at the time by a gaping hole in home-grown comedy narratives and I'd decided I wasn't going to be left out by the time networks finally came around to understanding why *Kath and Kim* had been such a phenomenal success.

It still annoys me that we are drip-fed a relentless amount of American product. Dare I say 'in my day', but the truth is we were offered so much more local and culturally relevant television comedy in the 1980s than what's on offer now and the reason is basic maths. Networks can buy the likes of *Two and a Half Men* and *How I Met Your Mother* at a fraction of the cost of producing something home-grown. In my opinion this will all come at an even greater cost to our cultural identity while we continue to turn our backs on our own Australian originality by offering next to no reflection of what's going on in our own backyard through the medium of comedy.

And that, to my mind, is ultimately what narrative comedy is all about. Holding up a mirror to our own society and dissecting and examining it under a veil of laughs. God bless Gina Riley and Jane Turner and Chris Lilley. God bless Paul Hogan and the creators of *Mother and Son*. God bless *Kingswood Country* for that matter, if only for succinctly pointing out what a racist, intolerant bunch of dickheads we were at the time.

I never really believed *Scott and Fiona* wouldn't eventually see the light of day and as every year went by I simply aged the central characters. Scott and Fiona were no longer a young couple relocating to the Northern Territory but rather now a more mature duo embarking on a sea change of sorts. The essence of the story was still the same, and Darwin wasn't going anywhere in a hurry. It had been ten years since the dawn of the Fennergans and I was as committed to their survival as ever.

At last. The phone rang. My manager was on the other end.

'Hey, Fi, Channel Seven are looking for ideas for sitcoms. I've organised a meeting with a guy called Michael Horrocks next week when you're in Sydney. Don't get your hopes up. They're basically chatting to every comic in the country with a script.'

My pitch to Channel Seven was almost as excruciating as that first time at the ABC. For the first time I started to doubt myself and my story. All of a sudden in the middle of the interview I started to feel weary. For once the network door had opened and invited me in, as opposed to me knocking persistently on the other side. Like a marathon runner that pegs out in the last one hundred metres I started to falter, and while I really liked Michael Horrocks I sensed that I was wasting his time and mine.

'Lovely to meet with you, Fiona and hey, in the meantime, why don't you leave the script with us and . . .'

I don't remember how we finished up but I vividly recall clutching my script tight in my hand and being very reluctant to hand it over. I'd been fuelled on hope for over a decade now and I didn't want to play the final card. *Scott and Fiona* would be safer under my bed where they'd always been. I had a strong sense that this was their final chance and didn't know if I had the energy to listen to the phone not ringing yet again.

Two days later Andrew rang me again.

'They love it, Fi. I think they're going to make it.'

'Really?'

'Yep, you need to come back down to Sydney and meet with a script editor they've got lined up and . . .'

'Sorry, Andrew, I'll call you right back. Someone's at the door.'

Of course no one was at the door but I needed to jump and scream for joy, and I needed to do it right there and then. I ran through the house like a madwoman, jumped on about five beds, screamed with happiness and danced with the cat. I've always told my kids that, in its simplest form, life is just a series of good days and bad days. This was a good day and I savoured every millisecond of it.

The news got better and better. It was still very early days in the big scheme of an eventual actual sitcom making it on to the telly, but every step in the process was taking the Fennergans closer and closer to the light of day.

The initial meeting with the producers and the script editor in Sydney was an absolute thrill for me. Sitting at a boardroom table having people talk about *Scott and Fiona* out loud was probably the greatest highlight to date. While they loved the script, it had to be completely overhauled for a myriad of reasons, but mostly because of my inexperience in writing for television. I was more than happy to finally let go of the reins and hand the whole caboodle over to the experts.

Doug McLeod was on board as the script editor and, as he had edited *Kath and Kim* and other successful Australian comedies, I knew that my project was in very safe hands. Another producer besides Michael Horrocks was Ben Swaffer. He was a writer and producer behind *Stella Street* in the UK, and *Scott and Fiona* was his first project since moving his family from London to Sydney.

It was all too good to be true. I adored Doug and Ben and they seemed as committed to *Scott and Fiona* as I was. The first hurdle was to complete a rewrite and have a polished enough script for a development deal with Channel Seven to go ahead.

From memory it was only a matter of weeks after the initial meeting that I signed my dream project over to Channel Seven. *Scott and Fiona* was no longer mine, but co-owned by myself and Seven. The next year was the happiest year of my life professionally. Back to living and breathing *Scott and Fiona*, outside of stand-up commitments I spent my days writing and rewriting the first three episodes, with emails sailing back and forth between Doug McLeod, Ben Swaffer and myself.

Every second Monday I would fly from Alice Springs to Sydney and check into a hotel and spend two full days working side by side at Channel Seven with Michael, Doug and Ben.

What's the old saying? Find something you love doing and you never have to work again? I'd found it all right, and not once that year did I cross the Sydney Harbour Bridge in those taxis without fully appreciating what a golden time it was and how grateful I was for just simply being lucky me.

The script was getting stronger and stronger ,and the characters more and more defined, and we were heading to another crucial stage of the sitcom process. The time was coming for Scott's character to be cast and a 'read through' to happen.

Ideally, I wanted Scott Casely, the original Scott, to read for the part, but he was in New Zealand now and not inclined to come back into the world of performance. Carl Barron was asked and kindly came into Channel Seven for the first ever read of *Scott and Fiona*.

I was a bit shy about having such a well-known name as Carl reading for a part in my yet to be commissioned sitcom, and I remember trying hard to swallow my salt and pepper squid at lunch that day, just after Carl arrived, when something suddenly dawned on me. I had to excuse myself and find the ladies' for an unexpected but very serious panic attack. Twelve years of writing and working towards this sitcom, and not once, not even for one split second, had I ever actually considered the possibility that I might be a truly awful actor.

Somehow I got through it. Carl was magnanimous enough to give his all to the read, but I knew instinctively that the role of goofy Scott Fennergan was not something that was really up his alley. But the dialogue came off the page easily and convincingly. Ah, the joy, the joy. We were inching closer still.

The next step was a full 'read through' with a full cast in front of the big bosses of Channel Seven, a truly crucial stage, as it would be on the strength of this that we would be commissioned for a pilot episode to be made or not. Chris flew down with me for the read through and it was a nerve-racking but memorable time.

Darren Casey, my favourite comedian in the whole wide world, had been cast as Scott, and two of my best comedy friends, Andrea Powell and Damian Callinan, had joined up for the two main characters outside of the Fennergans. My real sister Emily was on board to play my on-screen sister and I think Michael Horrocks may have filled in for the yet to be cast teenage actor in the role of Ned, Scott and Fiona's son.

We all gathered upstairs in a Balmain pub on a winter Tuesday morning for a quick run-through and then bit by bit a small audience of Network Seven executives arrived, the camera rolled and a very jerking, stilted portrayal of the first episode of *Scott and Fiona* ensued. It felt awkward pretending to be in Darwin while actually being in an upstairs bar in a city hotel, and we had no set other than two parts of a modular lounge suite that had to pass as everything from a Greyhound bus to a bed to a front bar in the course of the half-hour narrative. It actually felt very similar to putting on a play for your mum and dad in the living room as a kid, and I felt incredibly self-conscious and responsible for everybody else's discomfort as well as my own.

Finally it was over and we all headed downstairs for a pub lunch. I remember briefly meeting with a couple of the Channel Seven heavyweights and I found it impossible to gauge what they made of the whole thing. One thing I did know is that the dialogue had worked. The cameraman had had a hard time not laughing out loud, and that gave me a quiet confidence that I hugged to myself for the next week or more.

I think out of everybody that day Chris had the best time. Doug McLeod mistook him for Hugh Jackman, and to this day I haven't heard the end of it.

As with most things, it's the waiting that's the worst part. For the next week or so I actually took the phone off the hook at least a dozen times for an hour or more so that I didn't have to listen to it not ring.

The phone did ring, though, and it was Michael Horrocks to say that we had been 'green lit' for a pilot. Every dog has his day, and it seemed that this was mine. We were actually going to Darwin to make a pilot and *Scott and Fiona* was actually going to see the light of day. I flew to Sydney for the last time before filming started for two days of rehearsal with the full cast.

Walking into Channel Seven was beyond surreal. A whole floor had been taken up by thirty or more people all working on *Life at the Top*, which was by now the working title. People were actually getting up and parking their cars and coming to work for the day on a project that had started in my little spare room on a typewriter more than thirteen years ago. Wardrobe girls, cameramen, continuity, assistant directors, make-up artist, location scouts. There was absolutely no way I could take all of this in my stride. I had a ridiculous grin on my face for every waking hour of the day and it was all I could do not to kiss everyone I came into contact with fairly smack on the lips. I wanted to skip instead of walk and sing instead of talk but I managed, I hope, to appear normal.

William McInnes had by now been offered and accepted the part of Scott, and that was the only black cloud hanging over me in the midst of all the excitement. I had desperately wanted a fellow comedian to play the part of my character's husband. I had never really acted before outside of a couple of television commercials and I knew well enough that I would be excruciatingly intimidated by a real actor, especially one with a pedigree as fine as William's. Having signed a lot of my rights away with the initial contract, though, I had no final say on this and other matters, so I had to take a deep breath and finally meet with the award-winning star.

He was, of course, exceptional. I have encountered more than my fair share of funny human beings through the course of my career and William McInnes is one of the most hilarious people I have ever had the pleasure to know. At the first rehearsal he portrayed Scott Fennergan so closely to the character I had long conjured up that I actually ducked out for a cigarette to hide my emotion. I had nothing to worry about acting alongside William McInnes, because from the moment he picked up the script William McInnes was nowhere in sight. I could only see Scott Fennergan, Fiona Fennergan's husband: a nice bloke, a bit of a dickhead, a pool pump salesman, a great dad, and as comfortable as an old shoe.

Before we get to Darwin I need to tell you what my absolute passion for *Scott and Fiona* was all about.

Scott and Fiona were a long-time married couple who had made some questionable financial choices and somehow found themselves on the back foot and relocating from Sydney to Darwin with their only son in an attempt to secure themselves financially and in some ways emotionally as well.

I guess in many ways I was trying to make sense of my own life through escaping to a fictitious family. I was answering a lot of my own questions about living life in an obscure Australian location and using just about every past humiliation I had endured as fodder for the story.

I once went to dinner at the home of a local pharmacist in Alice Springs. It was back in our very modest monetary days, and Chris and I were thrilled to be included in such a savvy social circle. A lot of handwringing had gone on about what I was going to wear and in my weekly stint as a volunteer clothes sorter for St Vincent de Paul I came across a more than suitable 'grown-up' matching skirt and blouse that I made my own for the cost of three bucks and fifty cents. Our hosts lived in the flashiest house in town and we were very chuffed with ourselves as we pulled into their driveway with a bottle of Mateus Rose and some after-dinner mints in anticipation of a splendid evening ahead.

The night with our new pharmacist friends went well except for one small hitch that fortunately I remained blissfully unaware of until some days later. Sadly, I was wearing . . . take a deep breath, dear reader . . . the chemist shop uniform.

This little drama was re-enacted in the pilot episode of *Life at the Top*, along with some equally horrifying episodes from my past life as a nurse. Fiona Fennergan was a nurse as well in the sitcom, and I walked a dangerous line between truth and fiction in just about every scene I wrote.

It was liberating and cathartic to expose some of my most traumatic moments and transform them into what I hoped would be entertaining television, but I wasn't just hell-bent on entertaining. My pride in the Northern Territory was also a big motivation in *Life at the Top* and I wanted to showcase Darwin for what it is and what it is rarely perceived to be by the rest of Australia. I desperately wanted to draw a line in the sand and distance myself from the bushwacking, boot-scooting, cowboy, crocodile country profile that the Northern Territory is often packaged as.

Now was my chance. Before I knew it we were all in Darwin and filming was starting the next morning. The whole crew and cast were staying at the same hotel and since half of the cast were some of my dearest buddies from the comedy world, there was almost a school camp atmosphere surrounding us. I couldn't wait for the show to begin.

Happy, happy, days ensued. Every scene was shot on location and I experienced deja vu with every location, bar none. The house was precisely as it had been in my imagination: a weatherboard construction up on stilts surrounded by tropical trees and even a real baby crocodile in the garden.

Darwin sunsets, Scott and Fiona slanging matches, Ned Fennergan's first day of school, Fiona Fennergan's first shift at a nursing home and Scott's first day selling pool pumps, all finally transported from a script to a reality. I have never been so happy. In the words of my cryptic grandmother whenever she was feeling entirely satisfied in the moment: 'This and better will do me.'

'It's a wrap!' I'm sure Dana the director used the old cliché for my benefit, but it was Friday night at eight o'clock and indeed it was a wrap. We were done. It was over. *Life at the Top* was in the can.

I wouldn't have been at all surprised to find myself a bit let down at the end of filming, but I had no room for anything but satisfaction and optimism. Only that week I'd read a newspaper article quoting a Channel Seven executive who stated that every television pilot they made had an eighty per cent chance of being commissioned.

Everything that could be done had been done and now it was in the hands of editors and later would be delivered to the hands of the 'suits' at Network Seven for a final decision on whether a full series of *Life at the Top* would go ahead.

'They can't NOT make it, surely?'

'This has to get up.'

'It's a winner.'

'Hilarious.'

Everyone from the lighting technician to the girl in charge of props had an opinion over drinks back at the hotel, and every opinion was favourable. I don't think anyone was more quietly confident than me. I've rarely come off stage after a live performance without a swag of self-criticisms. Why didn't I say that? I shouldn't have said that! Damn, I stuffed up that bit. But this time was different. We'd done all we could. I had just had the best working week of my entire life, and I was a bouncer in my own brain. Nothing but positive was allowed in.

I think I flew the plane home myself the next morning, not literally, but I was flying high still, and it took me days to settle back into my real life. No sooner had I started to resemble Fiona O'Loughlin, Alice Springs housewife and mother, than it was time to fly to Sydney and watch the pilot for the first time. I loved it. We all did. About twenty of the cast and crew had gathered at Ben Swaffer's home in Sydney for the viewing, and we celebrated well into the night with pats on the back all round.

I resumed my former life back in Alice Springs and the waiting for that final phone call began. It was mid-November and two weeks since seeing the pilot at Ben's place. Nothing to worry about at all, no news is good news, we'll know before the end of the television year, any day now, they have to decide soon if we're going to start filming in the new year. The phone still didn't ring. It was early December. Any day now, eighty per cent of pilots made go on to be commissioned, nothing to worry about, why don't they ring? These things take time. Surely if the answer was no, I'd know by now? Any day now.

I started to feel anxious by mid-December, and by the time we packed the car and headed to the Yorke Peninsula for Christmas I was feeling devastated. Deep down I knew that *Life at the Top* had been passed on. I'd read in the Green Guide of the *Age* that Network Seven had bought a new show from America: *Desperate Housewives*. Also *Dancing with the Stars* and *Sunrise* had been commissioned; no mention at all of a possible new sitcom based in the Northern Territory.

Christmas was at 'Cletta', my brother Richard's house, the original homestead that my great-grandfather had built about four miles south-east of Warooka. All of the Tahenys were there and it should have been a magic time. I tried hard to fill the 'life of the party' role that I'd been playing since what felt like the dawn of time, but my heart wasn't in it. I was so sad, and feeling guilty. I made a picture in my head of my Uncle Joseph Honner sitting across from me and laughing at something Richard had made a quip about as he raised his red wine to his lips and nudged his wife, my Aunty Genevieve. Uncle Joseph had just been diagnosed with terminal bowel cancer a few weeks before. How could I be so self-absorbed and tormented with disappointment about a TV show when Uncle Joseph was braving his own mortality? I tried to soldier on and find the 'craic', as the Irish say.

* * *

By the time Christmas was done and dusted, and as every day of the new year dawned, I finally came to the understanding that *Life at the Top* was over. It was well and truly time to move on but not before I had cried myself stupid in nearly every room of that glorious farmhouse. It seemed extremely self-indulgent at first to be so heartbroken over an intangible project particularly in the wake of the very recent Boxing Day tsunami that had destroyed the lives of so many souls, but nonetheless I was grieving and I made the most of my rare solitude to do it in spectacular style.

I woke up crying and fell asleep crying for a good ten days or more. It actually felt like someone had killed my family (albeit my fictitious one) and I honoured each Fennergan with my own personal wake. Channel Seven may as well have taken Scott, Fiona and Ned out into the parking lot and shot them all in the head in cold blood. I was so sad. And why not be sad? Even big burly farmers cry if they lose a crop, and I've seen footy players cry after losing a grand final. I'd lost a dream that had been more than fifteen years in the making and untold hours of work and creating, and this was one time I had no interest in maintaining a stiff upper lip.

I'm sure I must have puzzled a lot of friends and family that summer, as I'm usually in the thick of socialising on the Yorke Peninsula in January, and yet I rarely returned a phone call or ventured outside of 'Cletta' except for the odd dinner at Mum and Dad's or another dash to the Point Turton Deli for more tissues and chocolate. This was only my second bite from the black dog of depression, and from experience the only way through it is to feel it and wait for it to let go.

My son Henry once explained to me what you should do if you ever get caught in a current or 'rip' in the ocean. 'You just let it take you, Mum. Don't fight it and go with it along the shoreline until it eventually lets go.'

I think the same advice should apply to anyone caught in a severe 'rip' of melancholy. Take the time to go with it and for God's sake don't fight it. Fighting it is how most people drown.

After a while I started almost enjoying my solitude and began paying attention to 'Cletta' in a way that I never had before.

Built in the late 1800s, 'Cletta' is one of the finest old farmhouses on the Southern Yorke Peninsula and has been beautifully restored in recent years by my brother Richard. All my life whenever I read historical fiction I set the plot in and around it, downsizing it if the central dwelling in the story is modest and adding staircases and other wings if the main house in the novel is grander. Nastassja Kinski is nearly always my leading lady and the late John Hargreaves my leading man, but always 'Cletta' is the house or castle. *Wuthering Heights*, *The Mayor of Casterbridge* and even *Seven Little Australians* all happened at 'Cletta', is I can easily relocate to different countries by simply adding mountains in the background or generally rearranging the landscape as I and the novel see fit.

'Cletta' sits not more than half a mile from the ocean but my great-grandfather Francis Taheny was an Irishman and thus had no interest in locating his home imperially towards the sea as he held the sea in very little regard.

Francis built his sandstone house with a view of his land, and lots and lots of it. Much of our family farm has long been sold off over the generations but once upon a time my great-grandfather was one of those Grass Castle Kings. My favourite room is the dining room. The dining room table, shipped over from Europe, still commands the room, and has two enormous sleeves that can be pulled out from the centre transforming it from a table that comfortably seats fourteen to an impressive twenty-two. One far wall is three-quarters made of timber panels that used to slide apart and open into an outside bedroom, allowing for the room to host a modest ball.

The kitchen is an equally monstrous size, with an adjoining scullery and gorgeous sash windows that look out onto a little mini sandstone 'Cletta', where they once smoked their meat. The interior of the house has two main bedrooms and a nursery coming off one passage and another much larger hallway that leads you to an enormous formal sitting room and the front door, where Catherine Earnshaw nearly lost her mind in my imagination three hundred years ago.

Attached to the house but only accessible from the three separate verandahs are the remaining three bedrooms. Add to this another entrance hall and two bathrooms and my tour of the farmhouse is now complete.

I spent a great deal of time wandering around 'Cletta' after my near nervous breakdown, and bit by bit I think that old house wrapped its arms around me and started to bring me back to the land of the living, strangely enough by allowing me to trawl thoughtfully through the past.

At first it wasn't my own past that captured my attention, but my long-gone relatives. It's an incredible thing to lie on a bed and stare at the same ceiling that your great-grandmother must have pondered a hundred years ago. Don't get me wrong. I'm sure Frank Taheny was a fine lover, but I found myself wondering about her and what her life must have been like.

What did she make of this windy, stubbled place? When did she see her first brown snake? Did she scream blue murder? Where did she have her nine babies? Did she scream blue murder? Who did she turn to when she had her first fight with Francis? Did she scream blue murder?

I don't know much about Margaret Sweeny, but I remember my own grandmother, her daughter-in-law, telling me how sad she was when she died.

'I felt like I'd lost my only ally.'

'Hmm. Methinks the ladies weren't exactly kicking up their heels at "Cletta" in 1929.'

I put the question to my great-grandmother's portrait in the dining room. She didn't answer me. She wasn't even looking at me. I got no answers from Margaret at all that day. Except having studied her face long and hard I now understood why Genevieve, Emily and I have such very economical top lips.

There was a blowfly buzzing interminably against one of the dining room windows, and for a moment I was a young Aunty Mag sitting at that same table on a laborious afternoon eighty years ago. She hated blowflies and their depressing sound, especially when she was already depressed, as she was that afternoon. She was in love with Friday Detmar, and he her, but Dot had just given him the strong tip: 'For goodness sakes, Friday! You're a worker. You most certainly will not marry Mag. No sister of mine will ever be married to a worker!'

I made up the bit about the blowfly, by the way, but the rest is true. Nana had told me about it years ago. She loved Aunty Mag; so did I, what little I remember of her. Funnily enough she actually looked a bit like a magpie. She wasn't a snob like a lot of my great-aunts, and she did end up marrying Uncle Friday. They were one of the happiest couples I knew.

Bit by bit my memories surrounding 'Cletta' got happier and funnier. One aunt of mine was visiting 'Cletta' when she was very young and before she had married into the family. She wasn't Catholic and Aunty Mon was highly unimpressed with this young Methodist hanging off her nephew. She read an announcement from the local paper loudly and pointedly: '"Miss Maureen O'Leary is engaged to be married to Mr Brian Dermody",' and then added for everyone in the kitchen to hear, 'Wonderful news, as Miss O'Leary is reputed to be an excellent Catholic!'

She came off a motorbike a while later and twisted her ankle so badly she had to stay the night. I remember her telling Mum about it years later.

'Oh Deirdre, I'd grown up hearing horror stories of how mad Catholics were, and there on the wall staring at me was the shroud of Jesus' face and, lo and behold, I turn over and there's the sacred heart of Jesus on the other wall! Jesus! Pulling his chest open and there's his bleeding heart with a crown of thorns wrapped around it. I didn't get a wink of sleep.'

These days 'Cletta' is a quiet place, but it must have been a hive of activity way back when eleven people lived there along with workmen and sheep and chooks and milking cows. Genevieve even remembers Mr Kluck, who lived and worked there until he died in his nineties.

Mr Kluck was a German prisoner of war escapee who had found his way to the peninsula all the way from Melbourne as a young man, and apparently until his dying day Aunty

Dot used to call him 'Mr Kluck' as if she was calling him 'Mr flea-ridden rabid dog with some cow shit on top'.

I don't believe Mr Kluck ever lived inside 'Cletta', but despite everything he and Francis Taheny had a lot of time for each other. In the early 1940s another local farmer once asked my great-grandfather why he still had 'that bloody Kraut' on his property. To which my great-grandfather replied, 'Well, I look at it this way. If we win the war, I've still got a very good worker, and if we lose the war then I'll be working for a bloody decent boss.'

* * *

I don't think Dad ever once went to the farm without calling in on his aunts. They referred to each other as 'Madam' and 'Girl'. I particularly liked 'Girl', Aunty Eileen. She had the biggest laugh I have ever heard and the only thing bigger than her laugh was her boobs. They were absolute mountains to my child's eye, and I used to be fascinated at how they heaved up and down with a life of their own when she broke into another guffaw, which she did on a very regular basis. She had a great face and a monstrous smile, and she and Madam immediately set about feeding us homemade rock buns or scones and jam whenever we set foot in their kitchen.

Bit by bit, by the time I was in my late teens Aunty Dot had started to become more and more forgetful as dementia gradually took hold of her. One day my brother Richard called in to visit the aunts with his best mate Michael Patrick and the dining room table was set for eight people or more and a leg of lamb was roasting in the oven.

'Are you expecting visitors, Aunty Dot?'

'No, dear, it's just that Dad and the boys will be back from the scrub any minute and they're going to be wanting lunch.'

She was referring to her father and her brothers, who had all been dead for decades, and Richard recalls being amused and sad at the same time. 'Cletta' must have really revolved around 'Dad and the boys' in its heyday. I remember when I was nursing Aunty Dot a few years later at the Yorketown hospital she very uncharacteristically burst into fits of laughter as I was walking her back into the sunroom from a trip to the bathroom. My dad's sister, Aunty Frances, who was also working at the hospital at the time, was standing nearby, and she and I both joined in on Aunty Dot's rare outburst of mirth.

'Aunty Dot! What's so hilarious?'

'Well, dear, I just think it's funny, don't you? What on earth are Dad and the boys going to think when they get home tonight wanting their dinner only to find out that we're all the way over here on Kangaroo Island?'

Dementia is a strange beast. Looking after 'Dad and the boys' had obviously been a large part of Aunty Dot's history, but Dad informed me later that night that as far as he knew Aunty Dot had never set foot on Kangaroo Island.

Aunty Dot's initial spell at the Yorketown Hospital, before being admitted on a permanent basis, was the result of a broken hip after a calamitous incident at 'Cletta'. 'Girl' accidentally backed over 'Madam' one Saturday morning, reversing out of the car shed.

'Oh for heaven's sake, Madam, what were you doing there in the first place?'

Aunty Eileen never appeared to lose much sleep over the whole unfortunate business, and went on driving until she herself went into a nursing home in her very late nineties. Her sister Aunty Mon lived in the town of Warooka, and also drove her own car until she was at least ninety-two.

All in all they were extraordinarily tough old birds, and in another defiance of old age Aunty Eileen continued to play the organ at mass every Sunday until she was ninety-eight.

* * *

I'll never forget one Sunday at 11 a.m. mass when every one of my ageing relatives seemed to be decidedly 'off the air', and basically all hell broke loose. To begin with, my beloved grandmother Gammy was visiting and had only very recently begun having 'spells' of confusion. Believe it or not, she actually lit up a cigarette in the front pew during Father John's sermon.

It wasn't long before she abruptly stubbed it out in her little compact ashtray and our concern shifted to my great-uncle. Father John had not been at all well and after stumbling through his sermon skipped a whole section of the mass, which led Aunty Eileen into a premature organ rendition of the hymn that preceded the offertory procession.

This was all too much for Aunty Mon, who always sat directly behind the 'Denis Tahenys' and knew the order of the mass like the back of her hand. She started to speak very loudly, and none of us knew where to look.

'He's come in too soon! Denis, he's come in too soon! He's come in too soon!'

Dad didn't know quite what to do, but by then Aunty Mon had risen to her feet and was yelling at her sister from across one side of the church to the other. 'Stop playing, Madam! Stop it, Madam! Stop it at once! He's come in too soon! Please somebody stop her! Somebody stop her!'

* * *

'Last one out turn the lights off' is an Alice Springs saying I've heard a few times, and it refers to the mass exodus at Christmas time of locals packing up and heading 'home' for the summer holidays.

We have packed the car and headed 'down south' on the sixteen-hour drive to Adelaide or the Yorke Peninsula over fifty times as a family, mostly for Christmas but with a fair whack of weddings, milestone birthdays and funerals thrown in. Chris estimates that the O'Loughlins have clocked up a conservative 97,500 kilometres on the open road since Henry was born.

I prefer to think of it as having driven to London and back at least eight times, or having made it nearly one quarter of the way to the moon.

Having just unloaded the car from our latest marathon from Warooka to Alice Springs I'm finding myself sitting here reflecting on our many, many confinements in the car.

Not just one car of course. There have been three in total, and never having been 'car' people, we all refer to our cars by their colour.

I don't think the 'yellow car' ever ventured down the Stuart Highway, as we were a very small family back then and were able to hitch a ride with Justin and Bernie O'Loughlin when we only had one kid in tow, but by the time we had graduated to two children and the 'red car' we were officially masters of our own ship and our own South Road.

I have loved and loathed aspects of every trip, but would not trade a second of the discomfort that we've suffered at times for the memories and the rituals and the – corny as it sounds – 'togetherness' of our encapsulated family riding the adventure of either inching mile by mile to South Australia or inching mile by mile back to Alice Springs.

Nowadays, I fly from Alice Springs to a capital city at least once a fortnight, and consequently what I really appreciate about the drive is having the actual remoteness of Alice Springs reiterated in my brain. We really do live a long way away from anywhere.

Watching the landscape change is another aspect that I have found more intriguing the older and wiser I get. Everyone has a landscape that is theirs for the keeping, and Central Australia does not belong to me, nor I to it. I live here, but I am a visitor. My landscape is the Yorke Peninsula. Being the backdrop to my childhood, it will always be my true home. My kids, on the other hand, do belong here. This is their landscape and their true home. Leaving here and retreating from this environment and then gradually entering back into my own origins is a cathartic experience that can never really be appreciated through the window of a plane.

Experiencing the trip through Henry's eyes when he was little was fascinating and, thanks to Henry, very funny on his first trip at two and a half years old in the 'red car'.

Henry is a man of few words and this was particularly the case when he was a kid. In fact, he was born looking so wise and serious it was all I could do not to give him a newspaper and a pipe instead of a bottle. His very first word was in the car, going over a huge bump in the road.

'Fuck,' said he.

This has gotten even funnier now because Henry has never been a fan of the F word. We all swear like sailors and he hates it. Every now and then I've had to pull him down a peg or two by reminding him of the first time he spoke out loud. Mothering is tough sometimes.

Anyway, back to the South Road. Kids from Central Australia obviously experience seeing the sea for the first time in a much more remarkable way than most, and Henry was the perfect age. He had actually been to the beach as a little baby but he had no memory of it, and was just old enough to articulate the experience in his own inimitable way. Standing on a cliff with his little glasses perched on his nose, his eyes were as round as saucers as he pointed to the ocean. He had a very deep voice and, as I said, a very economic vocabulary.

'Dad! Big bath!'

Earlier that day just outside of Port Augusta he'd had another first when we had screeched to a halt in front of an emu on the highway. Henry was in his car seat and he and the emu almost seemed to take a moment and look each other in the eye through the window of the car. His little mind ticked over and he looked at the emu, at Chris, and then back to the emu. Thinking he may have solved the problem but not completely sure, he looked back at Chris.

'Chook?'

Chris traditionally did most of the driving when the kids were babies. I would stay up all night until the 4 or 5 a.m. departure time, packing, making sandwiches, preparing baby bottles and wrapping Christmas presents. I could sleep standing on my head if I had to, so I had no trouble at all slipping into a coma in the front seat shortly after we pulled out of our driveway and remaining that way until the first kangaroo tried to join us via the windscreen or the first fight broke out in the back seat.

Chris and the kids particularly enjoyed the very beginning of the trip, and would ritually play the Enya song 'Orinoco Flow', which the older girls particularly loved, as we drove through the gap in the Macdonnell Ranges and turned right just after the big red rock that reads 'Thank you for visiting Alice Springs' and the arrowed sign that reads 'Adelaide 1533 km'.

Although happy to take requests, Chris has always been the DJ on our trips. He reckons whoever drives gets to choose the music, and his early favourites are always Bob Dylan, Cat Stevens and Van Morrison. Anyone having a quick gawk at Christopher O'Loughlin's music collection would swear he fought in the Vietnam War.

'Dad, can you play some Uncle Bob?'

'Dad, can you play Uncle Van?'

Until they were at least nine years old every one of our kids believed that Bob Dylan and Van Morrison were their actual uncles.

The bloody red car ate my ABBA tape.

Obviously, some trips have been more harmonious than others. Biddy and the erythema multiforme was far from pleasant.

About two days before we left, Henry had been discharged from hospital, where he'd been in traction for three weeks with a broken femur.

I must digress quickly and fill you in on how all of this came about.

About seven or eight girlfriends and I used to host playgroup every Tuesday at one of our homes. There was nothing very structured about it, and basically the kids fended for themselves while the girls drank coffee and yakked for a couple of hours.

One Monday night in early December when Henry was four, Chris and I had been invited for drinks to welcome a new bank branch manager and his wife to Alice Springs.

I remember making small talk with the wife and after finding out she had small kids I asked her in front of her husband if she liked drinking champagne and, if so, would she like to come to my place the next morning for playgroup. They both looked at me like I was some sad drunkard, but I hadn't really posed the invite that well. I'd made it sound like we all got boozed every playgroup, but the fact was that it was a special 'Christmas playgroup' and that's why the champagne.

Sure enough, Mrs Bank Manager turned up and about ten minutes after we'd popped the first cork, Henry had somehow found himself under a mattress in the spare room with twenty kids on top of him and his thigh bone broken in two.

His first visitors in hospital the next day were Mr and Mrs Bank Manager, and I could have sworn Mr Bank Manager gave me a look that said, 'Disgraceful women who drink champagne in the middle of the day deserve everything they get', but I can't be absolutely sure.

After waiting and hoping it would all happen in time for Christmas, Henry's leg had started to 'knit' well enough that they let him go home, and we were able to continue with our plans for the road trip 'down south'.

The day before we left there was another small hiccup with Biddy coming out in the brightest, roundest red spots that I have ever seen. Nothing like measles or chicken pox, just perfectly symmetrical bright red spots all over her body. I headed to the hospital with my peculiarly afflicted child and waited the interminable wait in outpatients until I was called for the paperwork part of the process. By this time, having had a kid in hospital for the better part of the past month, I was exhausted and not really very clear-headed.

The girl behind the desk asked for her name.

'Brigid O'Loughlin.'

'Date of birth?'

She nearly had me there . . .

'Fourteenth of the second . . . ummmm . . . 1988.'

The girl behind the desk wasn't having any luck at all finding Biddy's file.

'Does she have a middle name?'

'Yes.'

I knew the answer to the first part of the question and then my mind went completely blank. Then, of course, I started to panic, and because of the panic Biddy's middle name slipped even further out of my head.

'Sorry, it's on the tip of my tongue.'

I could have died with shame until the spotted three-year-old saved the day.

'Sarah . . . It's Brigid Sarah.'

All I needed now was Mr or Mrs Bank Manager to walk past and social services would surely be involved.

Eventually we were seen by a doctor and he was absolutely thrilled with us.

'This is erythema multiforme. Wow, I've read about it but I've never seen it before.' Next thing we knew every trainee doctor in the hospital came by to have a look at my now infamous daughter and her remarkable spots. Photos were taken, and lots of oohs and ahhhs later we were out of there.

As rare as it was, apparently it was neither dangerous nor infectious and would disappear in a week or two, and we were free to go and given the all-clear to drive down south.

The next morning we were in the car with Henry reclined as far back as the seat would go in his plaster cast in the front with me in the back between the baby in her capsule and the spotted one in the car seat. I woke up just outside of Coober Pedy. This is generally the part of the trip where everyone but Chris is asleep and he plays some of his more obscure favourites like George Winston, Kila, Little Feat or Beth Orton.

Tess was screaming for her bottle and wouldn't drink it unheated, so I was relieved to see the mounds of earth from the opal mines that start dotting the landscape when Coober Pedy is getting close.

We had a very quick stop at a service station, and while Chris filled up the car I ran into the servo and asked the guy behind the counter to heat the bottle in the microwave on high for forty-five seconds please.

He just looked at me and shook his head, and I asked him if he didn't have a microwave – and could not believe my ears at his answer.

'If you're not buying food, lady, you're not using my microwave. I'm sick of heating bottles for free and I'm not doing it anymore.'

This demented man must have been waiting for a fight all day, and I can't remember what I said, but for some reason I started blubbering like an idiot and strung some expletives together with an argument about hungry babies and weary travellers and banged my way out the door.

I nearly asked Chris to go back in and have a go at him but there was something not quite right about the bloke and he was dangerously big, so we let it go and drove to the next truck stop to get the bottle heated and forgot all about it.

Well . . . not quite.

Three weeks later to the day we were back at that service station on our trip home, and again Chris filled up the car while I headed into the servo with the baby bottle. I stood at the counter until it was my turn to be served.

'Hello, could I have four hamburgers with the lot, five dollars worth of chips, two spring rolls and four chocolate milkshakes please? And would you mind heating this bottle on high in the microwave for forty-five seconds?'

He put the bottle in the microwave straightaway and returned with it forty-five seconds later.

'Thank you very much for that, and oh, by the way, we're not feeling very hungry after all. Do you mind if I cancel that order? Thanks.'

I don't know why I actually turned and ran out of the servo, but my instincts were spot on. The demented one started running around the counter and chased me out into the street.

Chris must have been at least a bit startled by the sight of me screaming towards the car with a giant demented arsehole chasing after me, and to his credit he had the car started and we roared out of there and down the main street like Starsky and Hutch.

It had actually scared the shit out of me and I didn't start laughing until the getaway was good, and turned around to see Mr Demented standing in the middle of the road writing down our number plates.

* * *

By the time Tess was about six months old my hankering for performing was getting stronger by the day, and for the next few years I satisfied myself by emceeing local cabarets at the Araluen Centre and even starring in a few of them.

Araluen was the hub back then for performing artists in Alice Springs, and every couple of weeks there would be some kind of themed cabaret on Friday or Saturday night at Witchetty's Bistro.

One memorable night was a writers' cabaret and the theme was writers 'coming out of the closet'. I conned a friend of mine, Barry Skipsey, to organise a wardrobe to be put on stage and I made my entrance from inside that cupboard. That night was a real turning point. There had been a couple of acts on before me, a local poet and a singer/songwriter, and when my turn came I stumbled out of that wardrobe and read aloud two pieces I had recently written. These were a shopping list and a letter to my mum. I was rewarded with guffaws from my artistic buddies and knew then that I had an ability to be funny on stage.

I rarely missed an opportunity to perform at Witchetty's after that. If it was Mother's Day, we'd put on a Mother's Day cabaret. If it was St Patrick's Day, we'd put on a St Patrick's Day cabaret, and even way back then when I was performing Christopher was left holding the baby.

Christine Dunstan and I were chatting one night.

'You should write your own show and put it on in the main theatre. Araluen will be happy to produce it.'

Bloody Nora, I had never been so excited in my life.

Remote Control was the name of the show, and I co-wrote it with my sister-in-law Genevieve, who also played two or three cameos in the final production. An Italian restaurant in town called Puccini's boasted two of the most gregarious and talented waiters, Russell and David, and we roped them in as well to complete the cast of four.

Remote Control was a comedy centred on a woman who had become so addicted to her television that she had entirely lost her grasp on reality.

I definitely based an element of the show on my own weakness for television. Up until about 1998 Alice Springs had only had the ABC, and I'd been gorging on the box since the arrival of commercial TV. We played one night only to a full house of 500, and I think I went to bed that night happier than a human can be.

Shortly after *Remote Control* was when I took myself to Melbourne. I'm pretty sure everyone thought I was off my rocker. Chris was supportive, but I think a bit confused, as I headed off to there for a week to check out stand-up comedy. I slept on the floor of the girlfriend of a dental buddy of Christopher's, which gives you some indication of how few people I knew in Melbourne.

Honestly, I felt like Heidi down from the mountains. I was a young country girl who'd left behind a husband and three babies and travelled over 1,800 kilometres to watch live comedy for the first time. To make things even daggier, I had a letter of introduction in my handbag from the Araluen Arts Centre that I required people in the business to sign as proof that the $600 had been well spent.

While I had heard that Melbourne was the capital of comedy I was gobsmacked on my first day by how prevalent the comedy industry was. There seemed to be posters everywhere, and every second person was able to give me directions to a comedy venue. What had happened, you see, was that I had unwittingly arrived smack in the middle of the Melbourne International Comedy Festival.

That first Melbourne trip was where I performed my first ever open mike spot, and I spent the other five nights inhaling everything and anything comedic on offer. I remember the last performance I witnessed. It was at another renowned comedy pub called the Prince Patrick, and throughout the night there had been over half a dozen acts on stage.

The final act was a bloke who took all his clothes off at the end of his set. I was more than a little bewildered by this and then the country bumpkin in me really came to the fore when he stuck what appeared to be a small rocket up his arse and lit it. All of this took place to rapturous applause from the audience, and I went home that night still trying to work out what I'd missed.

Jane, the girl I was staying with, was a uni student at the time, and she lived in a share house with some blokes who were students as well. The next morning over breakfast I heard one of the guys talking about a bucks' night he'd been to out in the suburbs the night before.

'Yeah, it was incredible. This stripper turned up and stuck a rocket up her arse and set it on fire.'

I gathered then that what I'd witnessed was a fine example of the emperor's new clothes. Either that or there was a warehouse sale of arse rockets somewhere in the city.

I really was seriously bitten by the comedy bug after that Melbourne trip, and vowed to get as much experience as I could by grabbing any opportunity to perform that came my way. My first paid live gig in the Territory was in Tennant Creek later that year. I had been asked to perform at a preselection dinner for the Country Liberal Party, and that was one of my early successes.

My old schoolfriend, Jasmin, was living in Tennant Creek again by then, and fortunately for me she was the full bottle on Territory politics and helped me write a script that parodied most of the heavyweight pollies of the day.

My pay cheque was $100, and I was booked for two more political functions on the strength of that night. Very exciting, although a couple of days later it didn't sound nearly as thrilling when recounted by a five-year-old. Henry was at pre-school at the time, and had point-blank refused to join in with the morning talk from the day he started. He was a very shy boy and preferred to live in a world of his own. In fact he didn't talk much at home either, preferring to leave that job to Biddy, who didn't draw breath from dawn till dusk. But this Monday morning he had some news to tell, and he was hell-bent on telling it.

'Miss, I've got some news to tell this morning.'

'Really, Henry? How wonderful.' And I looked on with about five other parents, waiting to hear more.

'My mum went to Tennant Creek and got a hundred bucks.'

CHAPTER 9

GETTING INTO IT

The next few years were chaotic and happy. Our house was a heaving wave of drop-ins and visitors, foster kids, dinner parties and Friday night drinks. I love my solitude now and find it kind of unfathomable how much chaos I used to invite into my life. These days Biddy particularly often moans about how boring we've become. 'Remember when there were always people over? Why can't we have a party house like we used to?'

I reckon it's because I'm currently out of town for more than half the year and the social animal in me is more than sated by the comedy circuit. Bad luck for everybody else, I guess, but the most likely knocks on my door these days are either the gas man or the Jehovah's Witnesses. The kids range in age from teens to their mid twenties now, and the place has filled up with their own hangers-on.

I remember an eight-year-old Henry not batting an eyelid one morning as he walked to the kitchen table with his Rice Bubbles, carefully stepping over eight sleeping Austrian backpackers that I'd brought home in the middle of the night. They were architecture students who were at a gig I'd been emceeing twenty kilometres north of town in a dry river bed.

* * *

Thanks to my isolated circumstances I really believe that I should win the prize for unusual gigs. Tourism is an industry second to none in Alice Springs, and once local tour operators got wind of a comedian living in town I was offered all kinds of jobs. I've dressed as a belly dancer and performed in a harem out bush for Toyota executives, I've done stand-up from the back of a ute for a couple of hundred visiting detectives, and I actually got completely lost once trying to find a station in the outback where I had a lunchtime gig, and was rescued by two Japanese tourists.

'Molly's bash' probably beats them all for gigs in the middle of nowhere. Every year Molly Clark hosts an outdoor concert at her homestead on Old Andado Station. Old Andado is about a five-hour four-wheel-drive trek, and the homestead sits on the edge of the Simpson Desert.

'Molly's bash' raises money for the Pioneer Women's Hall of Fame, and Molly is the quintessential pioneer woman. After the death of her husband decades ago, Molly stayed on in her corrugated-iron house at Old Andado, despite everyone presuming that she'd pack it up and call it quits.

The first time I emceed 'Molly's bash' I wasn't prepared for what was in store for me. The generator had broken down and the toilets were out of action. I'd been feeling queasy on the trip out there and hoped it was just from bumping around in a four-wheel-drive for half the day.

No such luck. By the time I arrived at the gig I had a full-blown stomach upset and nearly froze in fear when I found out there were no amenities.

So there I was, about to perform for three hundred people or more, and I needed a toilet yesterday. I headed out into the red rippled desert and had no choice other than to keep going until I couldn't make out the audience with my naked eye. I figured if I couldn't see them, they couldn't see me.

I remember thinking at the time how I'd heard comedians complaining about the green room at various venues. Not big enough, no fridge, only one toilet and not enough chairs. I surveyed my green room in this wide open space and would have thought it was funny if I hadn't been so sick. I would have given anything for a bush to hide behind but there wasn't one in sight. I guess that's the desert for you.

Only one other time have I been hideously ill while performing. Albert was only a couple of months old and I had scored a fairly well paid gig in Tully, Queensland. Having only just weaned Bert, I was a bit worried about leaving him so soon but I went ahead with the trip anyway. I figured it was only one night away and we really did need the money.

The first leg of the trip was a flight to Uluru, where I had a two-hour stopover and then caught a connecting flight to Cairns. I actually started to feel unwell on the way to the Alice Springs airport but didn't say anything to Chris and decided to hope for the best. By the time I arrived in Yulara I knew for sure that I was heading for a bout of mastitis. By the time I arrived in Cairns I was hot and cold with fever and in serious need of a chunder. Somebody was there to pick me up and drive me to Tully, and for the life of me I don't know how I got through that three-hour car trip.

We arrived in Tully with about two hours to spare before the gig, and I made my way to my room, swallowed some Panadol and lay down. What happened next was a nightmare. I woke up delirious in a pitch-black room. I had no idea where I was or what time it was. Something was making a very loud ringing sound and I *really* wanted it to stop.

The ringing noise kept going, and after a long time I realised it was the phone.

'Hello.'

'Fiona? It's Nick from the function room. You've just been introduced at the dairy farmers' dinner and no one can find you.'

I fumbled around in the dark for my dress and nearly fainted as I did up the zip. My right boob was twice its normal size. In agony I put on my make-up and made my way to the hotel dining room, where I was booked to perform for forty-five minutes.

I'd love to say that I soldiered on and gave a fine and funny performance, but to be honest I don't think I strung a cohesive sentence together that night. I knew I'd made a terrible mistake and should have stayed in my room regardless of how out of pocket I'd be.

The problem was that once I'd got on that plane, cancelling the gig not only meant that I would lose the fee but that I would also be up for the cost of the airfares.

The venue was a tiny hotel/motel dining room with about sixty dairy farmers squeezed into it, and I was sitting on a stool about a foot away from the front table. I was wearing a very tight gold satin dress, and by now my right breast had taken on a life of its own and was throbbing mercilessly and leaking so much milk that one half of my torso was dripping wet for all the room to see.

I remember telling the audience that they were right to shoot cows with mastitis and the audience looking at me like I was some kind of lunatic.

This gig and other gigs like it are what are known as corporate gigs. Corporate gigs are when a company or social club employs you to entertain them during one of their major get-togethers or fundraisers. Corporates are usually dinner gigs, and comedians love them and hate them. We love them because they pay tenfold the money we can earn in a comedy club and we hate them because they're risky. You can win or lose, but the stakes are always higher.

In the early nineties I relied heavily on corporates, but still being relatively unknown in Melbourne and Sydney I tended to get these gigs in Alice Springs, Darwin and occasionally Cairns.

My first corporate in Cairns was after a bloke called Ben spotted me on *Hey Hey It's Saturday* and rang to see if I was interested in being the guest comedian at an upmarket hotel in Cairns. Local businessmen and women paid a sum of money for a three-course lunch and a guest comedian.

The fee was $1,000, and I felt more than a bit chuffed with my contribution to our finances as I boarded the plane, but as usual I was beside myself with nerves by the time we touched down in Cairns.

Never in my life have I had a more appalling introduction than the one I got that day. And never before have I met a more horrible little man than the one who ran the show and emceed the lunch.

'Ladies and gentlemen, please make welcome to the stage our guest comedian for this month. She's from Alice Springs. Now, the bad news is she's a woman, but the good news is she's not a gin!'

Vile, vile, little man that he was, the gig actually went very well, and I was booked by two businesses in the room for two other corporate gigs later in the year. Within a week the little creep rang again to see if I was available for a similar function the next month.

I could still kick myself for saying yes, and it serves me right, I guess, for not boycotting his gig on principle, but it was the thousand bucks that won out in the end. Only the day before, Chris had met with our accountant, who had informed him that my career was costing nearly as much as it was paying, and I was determined to turn some profit.

I headed to Cairns again, and again the gig went well. I only started to smell a rat towards the end of the day. I loathe talking money, but it was time to leave and I still hadn't been paid. 'Sorry to bring it up but do you have my money?'

'Oh, Fiona, I'm sorry, I forgot to bring my cheque book. Just jot down your bank details and I'll transfer it tomorrow.'

That little bastard never did transfer my money, and when I finally rang him on his mobile it had been disconnected.

Years later I found out from a comic in Sydney that it was a rort he'd had going for a long time. He'd book a comedian and pay them the first time and then fleece them a month later, only to change mobile numbers and start all over again.

I have had some fantastic experiences on the corporate circuit, but it's the horror gigs that always make for better stories. One corporate experience in Darwin almost went so horribly ugly that I still shudder when I think about it.

It was a dinner at the casino at the end of a conference for a big company, and afterwards I was invited by the managing director to join a party in his executive suite for cocktails on the balcony. He seemed a lovely old bloke and had been telling me at the dinner how disappointed he was that his wife was too sick with cancer to make it to the conference. He showed me photos of her and of his children and his grandchildren, and I thought he was nothing less than charming.

A while later I knocked on the door of his suite. The door was open and I walked on through to the balcony only to find there was no one there. In fact, there was not much of a balcony and it didn't seem much like an executive suite either.

'Hello?'

'Hello, would you like a glass of port?'

His voice was coming from the bathroom.

'No thanks, where is everybody?'

And then he came out of the bathroom and my panic really set in. His fly was undone and he'd turned into Mr Hyde. 'Do you want some port on your nipples?'

I took a couple of seconds to plan my exit. At that moment he was standing too close to the door that had shut behind me when I came in. He was an old man and I knew I could outrun him, but I needed him to come a few steps closer towards me before I made a run for it. Finally he did and I bolted. Aaaargh! The rotten old goat had checked out by the time I got to reception the next morning, and I guess reporting him would have been useless anyway. I'd been openly chatting with him downstairs and waltzed freely into his room. Aaaaaargh! The filthy old bastard, and idiot me, indeed.

* * *

My career was all over the shop in the early nineties. I worked when and where I could. I did a couple of seasons in Adelaide at Comix under the mentorship of Dave Flanagan and occasional spots at comedy clubs in Melbourne and Sydney, but it was always a negative financial exercise and I lacked the opportunity that other comedians have in the city to hone a set by simply doing it night after night or at least week after week.

Daryl Somers was a great ambassador for the Territory at the time and kindly gave me a few leg-ups, and I supported him on an Australian tour to launch one of the Northern Territory Tourism campaigns. Not long after that he asked me to do a live cross on *Hey Hey It's Saturday* from the Camel Cup, which was sharing its twentieth anniversary with *Hey Hey*. This went quite well, but not before I'd made an almighty dickhead out of myself the day before.

A camera crew from *Hey Hey* had come up to Alice on the Friday to scout for filming locations and get ready to shoot the race the next day. I was to meet them at about 2 p.m. on Friday at Blatherskite Park, the racetrack just out of town where the Camel Cup is held each year. Jasmin had recently driven down from Tennant Creek and caught a plane to Sydney and left her brand new bright red sports car at our place.

We had a daggy Ford station wagon at the time, or rather, the 'white car', and as I headed out the door for my terribly important meeting with a terribly important film crew from Melbourne I decided that it would be a far smoother look to turn up in a red sports car than a family wagon. I climbed into Jasmin's beautiful car and looked at the gearstick with just one small concern. I didn't know how to drive a manual.

Already sold on the sports car option, I made a plan to drive very slowly in first gear all the way and then put it into neutral at the front gates of Blatherskite Park and simply glide into the car park.

About an hour later I finished the three-kilometre trip and was thrilled to be stepping out of the car just as the producer noticed my arrival.

The crew and I had a great afternoon. We rehearsed my segment and they met with the powers that be from the Camel Cup, and then suddenly there was a panic from the cameraman, who needed to get some wide shots of Alice Springs before the sun went down. My stomach lurched when I heard the producer say to him, 'You go ahead in the hire car and we'll get a lift back to town with Fiona.'

About an hour later it was home time.

'Wow! Great car, Fiona.'

We kangaroo-hopped all the way. I was beetroot red and muttering some nonsense about needing to get the gearbox fixed. I don't think I fooled anyone for a second.

* * *

The other television atrocity was a spot on the *Midday Show* a few months later. Heaven knows how I talked my way into that, but somehow I was in the green room at Channel Nine, had just met Ray Martin, and was about to do three minutes of comedy on national TV.

I was so incredibly nervous I wondered why on earth I'd done this to myself. I had my old childhood friend Julia Kennedy with me for moral support, but by the time I went on I was nearly physically sick. All of a sudden I was being introduced, and there I was doing stand-up on television for the very first time. The set was only three minutes, but to me it lasted a fortnight and then some. I started out okay, kind of stumbled over my lines at the halfway mark and then the worst possible scenario played itself out. I had completely forgotten what came next. Apparently it only lasted for a few seconds but those few seconds were filled with unmitigated terror from which I didn't recover for the remainder of my spot.

Bombing on stage is the calculated risk that a comedian takes every time, but to do it on live television is truly awful. My immediate objective was to get out of that studio and as far away from it as quickly as possible. Poor Julia had done her best to console me but had to get back to work. I stood and waited for a cab by myself, and as soon as I was safely in the back seat and heading for the city I let myself burst into tears. After a while the cabby pulled over to the side of the road and turned off the engine.

He was a lovely Middle Eastern looking bloke and he turned to me and said, 'You are weeping, why are you weeping?'

Albert's christening.

The 'early years' in Alice Springs.

The day we moved over to the Old Eastside in Alice Springs.

'Freddy', one of our foster babies, with friend Amy Dawson.

Right: The kids and me filling in time while Chris ran the Sydney Marathon in 2000.

Bert and Tess at home in the land of 'Do as you please'.

Above: Backstage at Araluen.

Left: At Standley Chasm on my very first weekend in the Northern Territory.

Left: Rehearsing for my first gig at the Todd Tavern piano bar in about 1983.

Below: My first publicity shot, taken by Barry Skipsey in my backyard in the early 1990s.

Taken at the 'After Party' of *Hey Hey It's Saturday*, filmed in Darwin the day before I turned thirty.

Michael Horrocks directing Andrea Powell, Damian Callinan and Darren Casey in the final read-through of *Life at the Top*.

Top: New York! New York!
En route to Montreal in
2006.

Left: Onstage at the
famous Hollywood Improv.

Right: My spot at the
William Shatner Gala
in Montreal.

Dave Hughes, Meshel Laurie and me before the Melbourne International Comedy Festival Gala.

Onstage at the Opera House in 2010 performing my *Greatest Hits* show.

I couldn't bear to relive the experience and figured it was a confusing explanation anyway.

'My husband left me.'

'Oh, that is very bad. You come with me now to my home and my wife will make you some food.'

'No, really, thank you, I'll be fine.'

He dropped me off in the city and refused to let me pay the fare. I still have the picture in my head of him waving me goodbye in Macquarie Street.

* * *

Chris and I started fostering in 1990, and our first charge was a one-year-old Aboriginal boy called Terence who came to us on weekends and holidays for a couple of years. Terence had two different primary foster families in the time that we knew him, and we supplied them with respite every other weekend and for longer stints when they needed it. Terence also came to us when his first foster family returned to the USA and another one had to be found. He was a magnificent baby and every one of us fell in love with him on sight. His marshmallow cheeks were as soft as his hair and he was little for his age but as brave as a ten-year-old.

Terence had been born very premature and up until he was about two years old he was fed solely by a gastrostomy tube: you attach a funnel to the tube every mealtime and pour a bottle of milk directly into his stomach. He used to make my mum and me laugh when he saw the bottle coming and he'd kick his little legs with the same excitement as a baby who was actually going to taste the milk.

Terence had been born so premature that he didn't have the sucking mechanism that babies instinctively have, and without the tube he would have been unable to thrive. He had a younger sister in Adelaide who was born even more premature than him and would never walk or talk, and it was at this baby's birth that Terence's mother had died.

I believe our family wouldn't be who we are today if it hadn't been for Terence. I've never loved a foster baby more than I loved him. In fact I ended up loving him as much as my own kids.

Henry had not long started school at the time, and Biddy and Tess were still babies themselves. Even though it was physically more demanding to add such a fragile little person to our family, it was emotionally one of the most peaceful times of my life. And that's what got me hooked on fostering. The peace that it afforded me was amazing.

I don't think I'd be alone in acknowledging that images of famines and war leave me feeling uncomfortable and guilty. Whenever I had a foster baby I excused myself from being tormented. I didn't even watch the news as long as I was tucking up a little waif or two at night who had nowhere else to go.

Terence won many hearts, and one of the saddest and happiest days with him was the day he had his gastrostomy tube removed. He was with us at the time because he was yet again between permanent homes, and getting rid of the tube marked a significant day for Terence. It meant that he was now able to live with his relations safely in a bush community and would not be coming to us anymore. To this day I have never laid eyes on that gorgeous little boy again.

About eight years ago Alice Springs played host to a corroboree called the Yeperenye Festival. There were thousands of Aboriginal kids from nearly every bush community in Central Australia. The concert was spectacular.

I knew instinctively that somewhere in this crowd of thousands was a fourteen-year-old Terence. He was here somewhere, I just knew it. It was like a physical pain in my chest and I desperately wanted to find him somehow, and then just as suddenly I let it go. What would be the point? Terence would have no clue who I was, and I would no doubt be a blubbering idiot and make fools of the pair of us.

As people spoke of the Stolen Generation I did let myself have an almighty private sob in the dark and I understood that I know only a smidgeon of their pain.

Damien was our next long-term visitor, and he came to us having left hospital for the first time in his life at three years old. This little boy stayed with us for a few months, and I have to admit to not becoming attached to him in the same way I had with Terence. I felt a fair amount of guilt over this, which still stabs at me from time to time.

Damien's mother was a teenager addicted to petrol sniffing, and he was born with an enlarged heart and at three was unable to walk and needed twenty-four-hour oxygen.

His grandfather Hector was a great bloke who lived a traditional life out bush and would come in every month or so and take Damien out to the backyard and play with him for hours on end. Hector would never come inside but rather stand at the back door and wait for me to pass him his grandson.

One afternoon Damien was in the bath when Hector arrived and we persuaded him to come in. Hector roared laughing at Damien having the time of his life in the bath and then spent about half an hour in there teaching my kids the Arrernte words for 'water', 'hot', 'cold', 'grandfather' and 'yes' and 'no'.

Henry loved Hector because he'd shown him how to make a sundial out of small rocks in the driveway.

Damien could not walk or talk, and used to roll his tongue to communicate and shuffle around on his bum from room to room. Like any toddler, he was up to no good most of the day and I was furious with him once when I found him pulling off the flywire of an antique meat safe. I picked him up and plonked him in the corner of the kitchen and was pissed off with him for the rest of the day.

About a year later I was at my mum and dad's place for Christmas. Damien had gone back to hospital at least six months prior to this and I was having a coffee with Genevieve on Boxing Day when she spotted his death notice.

'Hey, Fiona, didn't you foster this little boy?'

I remember hiding away in Mum's laundry and crying. I kept thinking about the stupid meat safe and trying to fathom how that could have made me so angry. I have a thousand regrets when I look back on my forty-eight years on the planet, and little Damien and the meat safe is way up on top of the list.

The boy who broke my heart the most was Mitch, a white boy who had been abandoned by his mother and left with her ex-boyfriend who, although no blood relation to Mitch, had been the only family he had ever known. He had, to his credit, stuck by Mitch, but had at times left him alone while he went to work. This had come to the attention of Family, Youth and Children's Services and they had no choice but to remove him and find him a permanent foster home.

Mitch stayed with us for about four months in the interim, and what struck me most about him was how unused he was to being hugged or kissed. He was like a burly truckie trapped in a two-year-old's body. By this time I'd had my fourth baby, Albert. He and Mitch were born within weeks of each other.

It took Mitch a long time to let his guard down with us, but eventually he was nearly as tactile as Bert and the two of them lived much like fraternal twins and ate, slept and played together. He was a beautiful-looking toddler, with blond hair and blue eyes, and I thought it was criminal that he was not able to be adopted by anyone. Even though his mother had abandoned him, she still refused to give up parental rights, which pretty much sentenced Mitch to a lifetime of foster care.

I worried on Mitch's behalf every month that he grew older. The harsh truth of long-term foster care is that the earlier a bond is formed, the stronger it is. I wanted someone to scoop him up while he still had dimples where his knuckles were supposed to be.

When we started fostering we agreed that we were only suited to emergency short-term placements, and I had promised that I would never renege or guilt trip Chris out of the deal we had made. I backed out of this arrangement during this time and begged Chris to let us keep Mitch permanently. Very unfair of me, but he wouldn't budge anyway.

And then some fantastic news came Mitch's way. Welfare had found his grandmother and aunt in Queensland and they were ready to take him straightaway. They hadn't seen Mitch's mother for years and didn't even know she'd had a baby. It was great excitement all round and we packed him up to start his new life in Queensland with his aunty and three cousins and a grandmother living just around the corner.

Unfortunately there are very few happy endings in the world of foster care, and Mitch was no exception. I found out later that he was put into care again after only a few weeks with his aunt. She was a single mum herself and found him too much to take on after all. I don't know what happened to him after that.

Tess was my right-hand man all through the fostering years, and I doubt I could have done it without her. She had an innate sensitivity to our little ring-ins, and I remember adoring her particularly one afternoon with Maurice.

Maurice was only with us for a day and I don't remember his particular circumstances. What I do remember is that Maurice was blind, and had a cleft lip and palate. Tess was about four years old at the time and spent the whole day playing with this little one-year-old who could only get around flat on his back, steering himself with his legs.

Halfway through the afternoon Tess looked up at me and said, 'Mum, do you fink him's got a funny face?'

Before I could answer her she announced, 'Coz I don't!'

It became fairly impossible for us to keep up with fostering once my career kicked into gear and I was away from home more and more. Mary-Agnes was only a baby when we had our last foster kid, and I really think it's a shame that she hasn't had the benefits from it that the others have had. I really think it changed who they were. You can only tell your kids so much about social justice and the crap that goes on in a sometimes big ugly world, but when they actually have to move out of their beds in the middle of the night to make room for someone else, or cheer on a four-year-old who's learning to walk, or be doused in lotion for the head lice and scabies that have come for a visit, then suddenly there's kind of not much need to say anything at all.

* * *

In 1992 I had a regular gig at Toddy's backpackers every Sunday night. There are a number of backpacker hostels in Alice Springs, all in healthy competition with each other. The manager of Toddy's, a gregarious bloke called Peter, came up with the idea of a barbecue and outdoor entertainment on Sunday nights. Barry Skipsey and I were employed to sing songs and tell stories. Barry, a singer/songwriter, took charge of the singing and, lo and behold, I took charge of the storytelling.

I thought it was a great way to make a buck. We were meeting people from all over the world and getting free beer and a few laughs at the same time. It wasn't so much a performance as hosting a campfire get-together each week. Some Sunday nights were easier than others, mind you, depending on how many English-speaking backpackers were in.

On one of these nights I met Allan Grilliot, who was about twenty years old and six foot five and came from a farm in Hutchinson Kansas. I remember connecting with Allan early in the evening when I asked him if he had any brothers and sisters. He said he did and then pulled out his wallet in the way that people do when they're about to show you a snapshot of their family.

Allan didn't have a photo of his family, though, but rather a list of the names of his six siblings. At first I thought he must be a bit dimwitted, but then I realised he was just a very funny guy. I asked him where he was heading to after Alice and when he told me he was catching a bus to Adelaide, I couldn't resist giving him names and numbers of my family.

My sister Sarah picked him up from the bus station and showed him the sights of Adelaide and then she and Genevieve invited him to come to Warooka with them for the weekend. They arrived on Friday night and took what was possibly the first Kansan in history to the Warooka pub. I rang home to see how it was all going and Dad answered the phone. 'Yes, he's a lovely fella. Big hit at the pub tonight. Everyone wanted to meet him.'

I called the next day to check in again and Mum answered the phone. 'The footy team is down a ruckman so Allan's going to play. Of course, he doesn't know the rules and I don't know where we'll find footy boots big enough for him.'

I called again that night to see how the match went and Dad answered the phone. 'Yes, he was the man of the moment. Everyone wanted to shout him a beer in the clubhouse afterwards. He played with bare feet, did you hear?'

One more call the next morning and I'd heard it all. It was Mum this time. 'Well, we've all just been to mass. Allan did the readings.'

I think my sister Sarah still keeps in touch with Allan. He did eventually go back to the US. I'm surprised he didn't stay on and become the mayor of Warooka.

* * *

Bit by bit I started to weary of trying to carve a national career for myself in comedy. I had plenty to keep me busy in Alice Springs with my radio gig, the odd corporate gig and my column in the paper; and besides which I was pregnant with the next love of my life, Baby Bertie.

My fourth baby, Albert was born at a relatively uncomplicated time of our lives, and with the other three being so much older there was nothing much to do but enjoy him. The medical profession had relaxed their views somewhat on multiple caesareans and so I also enjoyed the prospect of maybe another couple of babies down the road.

By now a lot of our brothers and sisters were also having families. We had moved to a much bigger house on the old Eastside, and it was on this side of town that I made some astonishing friendships with a group of women that we still all collectively refer to as the Witches of Eastside.

The Witches of Eastside was formed quite by accident. I'd met a woman up the road who had a couple of kids the same age as mine and I invited her over for a glass of champagne one Friday night. The next Friday night she returned the favour and invited me and three other women. The Friday after that the drinks were at my place, and between the four of us we roped another four girls in on the action and the Witches of Eastside were born.

At first it was just a rollicking Friday afternoon session with kids everywhere and eight women getting to know each other better. In fact the name, Witches of Eastside, was coined a year or more later by one of our disapproving husbands.

Some of us had had prior friendships with one or more in the group, and initially our Friday night get-togethers were not much more than a friendly catch-up to mark the end of the week. But very gradually and over a period of some time it was almost as if someone was putting truth serum in the champagne and the talk turned from general banter to some amazing revelations of heartaches and secrets.

The Witches of Eastside were an eclectic mix politically, economically and socially, and I guess if nothing else our common ground was husbands and children. Some of us were millionaires and some of us panicked if it was time to buy school shoes, but every Friday for two years we would gather at one of our homes and throw food at the kids and get down to business. Old and young wounds were opened and dressed by the rest of us. We all had life pain, some more than others.

Alcoholism, neglected childhoods, sexual abuse, domestic violence and marriages on the absolute edge of collapse were the order of the day, and I don't know how many of each other's problems we solved. But bit by bit the Witches of Eastside gatherings slowly evaporated.

It hadn't all been tears and hand-wringing though. We laughed way more than we cried, but whatever the mood it was intense, to say the least.

Our husbands all knew each other in some way. Some were friends independently of us and some were enemies. The blokes had one thing in common (with the exception of one or two), and that was that they were suspicious of our weekly talk fests. One husband deemed it very dangerous. 'All this talking that goes on on Friday nights!'

Maybe he was right or maybe it was going to happen anyway, but over the course of that time two marriages imploded and some others came frighteningly close.

The last time we were all together was at the funeral of one of the ex-husbands who had suicided in a very violent way. Trust me: this poor bloke was a danger to himself long before the Witches of Eastside ever popped a cork. About five of us were sitting in a pew and got the giggles when we saw the placard that his ex-wife had placed in front of the coffin. A favourite saying of the deceased's had been: 'The man with the most toys wins!'

There in front of the coffin for all the church to see was: 'The man with the most toys still dies.'

He would have laughed at that.

I still see some of the Witches of Eastside socially, and some of them are still very close friends of mine, but we're not the Witches of Eastside any more. We're just a bunch of women who remember us.

* * *

In 1995 Chris and I went on our first overseas holiday. What was most special about it was that neither of us had ever left the country before.

Jasmin offered to have all the kids, which was an enormous gesture considering baby Bertie was only nine months old. We accepted in no time flat.

I'm a pain in the arse to travel with, as I'm way more interested in a good time and sleeping than anything else, while Christopher prefers to be up at dawn and cram a week's sightseeing into a day.

Our first stop was Rome and we both nearly lost our minds. Rome is a big, busy city by anyone's standard, but when you grew up in a town of three hundred people and then spent your adult life in Alice Springs, the City of Love can take some getting used to.

We were walking through the city and I couldn't shut up about how mad it all seemed to me. 'This city isn't working, Chris; there are too many cars and way too many people.'

'Well, Fiona, maybe it's Rome show day!'

Smart-arse.

We checked into our hotel and Chris was looking out of the window with his binoculars and started yelling, 'Timbalino! Timbalino!' His brother Tim was meeting us in Rome and he had just rounded the corner near our hotel.

The three of us spent a couple of days in Rome and took in the Vatican, where the lazy philistine in me really outdid herself. I went to the Sistine Chapel and forgot to look up.

Eventually we embarked on the part of the trip that I was most excited about. We were on a train heading towards the town of Arezzo in Tuscany, where we would be staying in a villa for a week with my old childhood friend Michael Patrick Kennedy and his Parisian wife Marie-Helene. Also waiting for us at the villa were Genevieve O'Loughlin and her new husband Vinnie Lange. Both couples were mates and they all lived in Paris.

Tuscany was superb, and we had a fabulous week.

The villa was huge and it was everything I ever imagined a Tuscan villa to be. We had a four-poster bed, a Tuscan view, a swimming pool, and in the words of my grandmother, 'Home was never like this.' By day we toured Florence, Sienna, Assisi or Arezzo and by night we would have an evening game of bocce and then spill into the dining room and eat home-cooked dinners that we took turns preparing. More often than not a guitar or two would come out, and I particularly remember a very raucous rendition of 'You Can't Always Get What You Want'.

Chris took a thousand photos, and I made one picture in my head that I'll never forget. We were sitting in a piazza in Arezzo when a wedding party turned up in a Rolls-Royce to have photos taken in the square. The bride was remarkably beautiful, and yet she had one of the biggest noses I've ever seen on a beautiful face. She had her hair in a bun and a long-sleeved empire-line gown, and she struck a pose for an individual photo like she was in a fashion shoot for *Vogue*. The groom was more than a dish himself, and he stood back and watched with a cigarette that he appeared to have forgotten about dangling from the corner of his mouth. He couldn't take his eyes off her and I couldn't take my eyes off either of them.

Later that afternoon we went to a chapel in Arezzo that housed some very famous frescoes. Everyone else had gone in ahead of me and I was dawdling outside having a last-minute cigarette. When I did enter the chapel I was struck by the silence inside. There was a group of visiting nuns on one side studying a wall of frescoes, a couple of other tourists dotted about, and my gang gathered around what appeared to be a crypt jutting out of one wall of the chapel.

I joined them but couldn't really see anything. I was the shortest of our group and the lid of the crypt was just above my eye level. Chris motioned to a little step on the floor and whispered to me, 'He's a monk who died six hundred years ago.'

I obligingly stepped up to see what I presumed would be the lid of the crypt with maybe a cross on it and the dates of the monk's life and death. But, oh no! It was a glass top, and there inside was an embalmed dead monk looking like a cross between Freddy Krueger and Frankenstein's monster. I let out a piercing scream and I remember the horrified looks on a few faces as I fled the building, but honestly it was one of the worst frights I've ever had.

Now let me tell you that spiders, crabs, worms and snakes are all things that I have phobias of. Chris has been so frustrated by my arachnophobia that he once suggested I get cognitive behaviour therapy to deal with the panic. Once, on the way to the shops, I actually 'lost time' when I was faced off by a huge huntsman on the dashboard of the car, and after my appearance back in the lounge room completely out of breath and making spider mimes with my fingers, Chris eventually found the car four blocks away, with the keys still in the ignition, the engine running and three kids in the back seat.

I am a fearless woman on some counts, but after that afternoon in Arezzo I've added embalmed dead monks to the list.

We had a week in Paris and then a week in London ahead of us so we said goodbye to the villa and caught a train to Paris. Sadly Chris and I had a fight on the train and we weren't actually on speaking terms when the train pulled in to the City of Romance. I don't know why, but we always seem to argue more on holidays than at any other time. He was exasperated when he found me in a smoking carriage at the back of the train with my nose stuck in the equivalent of an Italian *New Idea*, while all around me were the cascading waterfalls of the Swiss Alps in summertime.

'Fiona, would you just have a look at what's out there?'

'I already did.'

The magazine was chock-a-block full of Fergie in a pool with a bald guy and I didn't need to know how to read Italian to know that she was in a bonanza of trouble.

We both cheered up in no time back at Genevieve and Vinny's place. If the Tuscan villa hadn't been gloriously clichéd enough, the Paris apartment of my brother and sister-in-law topped everything. It was very beautiful and boasted three bathrooms and five bedrooms, and absolutely everything was painted white.

The Musée d'Orsay was their next door neighbour and they were about a five-minute walk from the River Seine. I was ever so slightly jealous. Well, to be honest I was a green-eyed monster for a good twenty-four hours, but it did pass and we had another fantastic week. I particularly loved a dinner party we had at the apartment two nights before we left.

Genevieve O'Loughlin is one of my dearest buddies, and she went above and beyond the call of duty the day we left for London. I had been a bit disappointed with myself on the tourist circuit in both Paris and Italy. I often joke about being a philistine, but I started to worry that I might really be a bit of a simpleton when it comes to the appreciation of art. While the O'Loughlins can spend a whole day in an art gallery or a museum, I can't seem to last much longer than an hour before I'm looking for the canteen. I've always had a pretty short attention span, but there I was at the Musée d'Orsay staring at a Gauguin and wondering why on earth it didn't move me somehow. I tried Monet on for size after that and was equally frustrated. The next day Tim, Chris and I headed off to the Rodin Museum, and it was there that I had a bit of a breakthrough.

'The Thinker' is the first sculpture you come across at the front of the museum, and since it didn't do a whole lot for me I went and sat on the museum steps to give Tim and Chris forty minutes or more to be in awe of it. When they were finished they headed towards me, and Tim exploded laughing. I had no idea but apparently I was striking nearly the exact same pose as the famous sculpture.

We headed inside and joined the queue that slowly wound its way through all the many sculptures on display, and at some point I was mesmerised. It wasn't a Rodin sculpture. It was a beautiful bust of a little girl sculpted by his mistress, Camille Claudel. Her head was tilted upwards and she was so lovely she made me cry. She reminded me of Tess, and for the first time in my life I was looking at a piece of art that I didn't want to take my eyes off.

I told Genevieve about it when we got back to the apartment, and later that day she took me to the Louvre to see another sculpture exhibition and I was enthralled again. This time it was a bust of an aristocratic baby boy. They were selling replicas of the sculptures and, even though I couldn't afford the $600, I made up my mind to buy one. Sadly I was too late. The last baby boy had been sold.

We headed for London the next afternoon, and before we left the apartment there was a bit of a panic as to the whereabouts of Genevieve. She'd gone out that morning and hadn't come back and it was getting pretty close to departure time. All of a sudden she burst in the door with a still slightly damp sculpture of the baby boy. She'd gone straight to the manufacturing outlet which was miles across town and brought my baby back to me.

We had to be so careful with it until it set properly and even then I didn't let him out of my sight the whole way back to Australia. At Heathrow he had to go through the conveyor thingy and I got a few odd looks when I saw a security guy shove a bag too close to him.

'Look out for my baby!'

I'm not an unforgiving person as a rule, but that baby sits on a table in pride of place at home and I've told all the kids that if anyone breaks him they'll need to find somewhere else to live.

I loved London, but at the same time as we cruised the Thames, gawked at the palace and shopped at Harrods, I was overcome with aching arms for Baby Bert.

A girlfriend of mine had lost her fifteen-month-old after a heart operation not long before this and I cried so much for Julianne while I was in London. I couldn't imagine how much her arms must have ached.

The day before we left for home the blokes headed to Cambridge to check out where their cousin Patrick O'Leary was temporarily doing veterinary work. Meanwhile my Aunty Carmel who we were staying with and I took a train to Windsor and had lunch and browsed in a classic English bookshop, where I bought myself an antique edition of *Uncle Tom's Cabin*. In my whole life I've never had Aunty Carmel all to myself and I loved every minute of it.

As we left the next day I was more than content with the holiday being over, and then I turned to Chris and saw that he was crying. I'd only seen him cry a few times, and it broke my heart.

'What's the matter?'

'What if I never get back here?'

Poor Chris. He'd worked twelve hours a day and most weekends for nearly a decade and all he could see was more of the same in front of him.

Little did he know. Within the next ten years he would be producing my first show in Edinburgh, going on to accompany me in London, Hong Kong and Scotland many times over – and New York and Canada was on our unknown horizon as well.

* * *

The year 1996 was tough. Christopher had been running a private dental lab for nearly ten years and for the better part of our married life had worked a seven-day week. He would take a short break every Christmas for the annual pilgrimage 'down south' to be with our families, but outside that he was pretty much tied to the lab.

For years he would get up as early as 5 a.m. and work until about seven, come home for a quick breakfast, be back at work by eight and go through till dinner with about a half-hour break for his ham and cheese sandwich. For as long as I've known Chris, he has had a ham and cheese sandwich for lunch just about every single day. I've told him if he ever puts tomato in that sandwich then I'll know he's having an affair. Often he would go back to the lab for a couple of hours after dinner as well. After nearly a decade of this he was close to burn-out.

One big issue we had for a long time was a long-held resentment that we had both harboured towards each other on the subject of babies. Chris felt that he hadn't been consulted on the family planning agenda, and I felt that if it wasn't for me taking the reins we wouldn't have had the kids at all. The truth lay somewhere in between, but one night after I had put Albert to bed, Chris confided to me that he didn't think he could handle the responsibility of having any more kids.

I was furious and heartbroken. We argued for hours that night and for a long time afterwards we backed off into our own corners in an emotional stand-off.

While Chris has been at times very uptight during my pregnancies, he's one of the most loving and tactile dads you could come across to all his kids, especially when they were little.

One thing we had both missed out on was the mad excitement some couples share when a baby is on its way. Chris harboured the worry and I harboured the guilt with every single pregnancy.

A few months after the baby argument I suggested that we go to some kind of counselling. We had reached a stalemate and neither of us looked like backing down. I knew that as much as I wanted another baby I never, ever wanted to buy another pregnancy test with my heart in my throat. If we did have another baby it would have to be what we both wanted.

The counselling was gruelling and painful. Chris and I have at times had a very volatile partnership, and neither of us held back in front of the poor woman from Centrecare who met with us each week.

And then a bomb went off in our faces. I found out I was pregnant. A few very painful days followed and before I knew it I was plunged into morning sickness and we both retreated to our corners again to lick our wounds.

Bit by bit, it was the excitement from the other kids that brought us around, and by the time I was ready to have Mary-Agnes every O'Loughlin was chafing at the bit to get their hands on our new baby.

* * *

We stayed at Christopher's brother Tim's house the night before I went in for my fifth caesarean, and for me that night was happy and emotional. I had a bath and watched my belly being kicked from the inside while I listened to Chris and Tim playing the guitar and singing Bob Dylan and Paul Kelly songs.

It was a really lovely night but I couldn't sleep. At about 2 a.m. I hauled myself out of bed and opened a brand new journal that one of the Witches of Eastside had given me and wrote a letter to the baby inside of me.

Dear You

It's Thursday night, 29th of July. The night before you are born.

We are at Uncle Tim's house, you, me, Dad, Henry, and Bert.

Biddy and Tess are in Alice Springs and very excited to hear who you are in the morning.

I know who you are already. I can't wait to hold you and kiss your face. I've loved you since I first knew that you were coming.

I don't know if you're a boy or a girl but I know who you are little you.

Part of me is sad tonight, most of me is happier than I've ever been.

But I'll miss you. You are probably my last baby and I'll treasure every kick and nudge.

I never want to forget what it felt like to have you inside of me.

You're asleep now and I think I'll join you soon.

I want to save tonight and that's why I'm writing to you.

I know that tonight is one of the very rare times in a person's life that is nearly perfect.

Mostly life is so far from perfect that these times are our glimpses of heaven and all God's promises.

I'll see you tomorrow.

Mum.

What I didn't know at the time was how important that letter would become to me over the course of the next year.

* * *

Mary-Agnes's birth was the first caesarean I had while not being under general anaesthetic. I was terrified, but I knew it was my last chance to witness one of my own births.

Unfortunately this wasn't the only difference between Mary's birth and the other four. For the first time in my maternal history I came face to face with the bastard that is postnatal depression. If I hadn't been through childbirth before I might not have recognised what it was but even in hospital I sensed something was wrong with me.

After every baby there was a magical time for me, and I think it's true with most mothers and their newborns. It usually happened in the middle of the first or second night. You're breastfeeding your newborn and they're staring right into you and it feels like there's no one else in the universe but you and your baby. It's actually an ecstatic physical rush and that's when you fall in love. I waited and waited for days to get that feeling and it never came.

What really frightened me, though, was what was going on in my head, and this is very difficult to explain. I had the most morbid thoughts imaginable. A nurse would come in and I would imagine her corpse. I saw corpses of just about everyone, even my new baby. I had an obsession with my and everyone else's mortality.

On the morning I left the hospital I noticed one of the nurses had put a postnatal depression booklet on the end of my bed. I hadn't said anything to anyone about the images in my head but after I read that booklet I managed to convince myself that the symptoms it described didn't have anything to do with me. And in a way that was true. I didn't feel particularly depressed. I could smile at visitors and chat normally, and I loved holding the baby and snuggling into her.

I went home and for the first few weeks nothing got any worse. But nothing got any better either. What happened to me is nearly impossible to put into words. I functioned quite well, and I loved my baby, but there was an invisible wall between me and everything else, and my morbid thoughts continued.

The mornings were the worst. I would wake up and slowly be overcome with a feeling of dread. It would start in the pit of my stomach and then crawl its way slowly through the rest of me. It was the same feeling as waking up and then remembering something terrible had happened the day before. The problem was that nothing terrible had happened, but I felt something would. We were all going to die and for some reason that was my foremost thought, day in and day out, and believe me it was exhausting.

Mary-Agnes developed reflux after a couple of weeks of being born and she screamed for most of the day. She was the first baby I'd had that I couldn't settle, and I nearly lost my mind with tiredness. For some reason the only thing that would temporarily soothe her was the sound of the vacuum cleaner. I used to turn it on and put it next to her cot, and that would give me about twenty minutes peace. I blew two vacuum motors before she was three months old.

One thing I was determined to succeed at was breastfeeding. Before Mary, I used to joke that I breastfed all of my kids for four months if you add it up, and that was pretty much the case. I went through three or four bouts of mastitis that first year, but nothing was going to stop me breastfeeding this one.

So we all plodded along, the baby screamed from morning till night, and the mother was a nut case who thought about death and dying all day. But life went on, kids went to school, and Chris kept up his punishing routine. Then one day the camel's back was broken by a very unlikely straw.

I was feeding Mary in the TV room and noticed a newsflash come up on the telly. It was something about Princess Diana having possibly broken her leg in a car accident. I shushed everyone and didn't get off that couch again for the rest of the day. Personally I hadn't been a huge fan of Diana's since the Bashir interview, but I could barely breathe when the news came in that she was dead.

In my head of course I was convinced that my morbid merry-go-round finally had a point to it. We *were* all dying, and what better proof of that than this cherished woman being crushed to death in a tunnel?

Chris walked into the kitchen later that night to find me on the floor, sobbing my heart out. I hadn't told him anything of what had been happening in my head, and he was more than a bit confused to see me bawling my eyes out on the kitchen floor.

He just stood there for a while, and then I remember him asking the question, 'And . . . you're sure . . . you're . . . you're sure you're just crying about Princess Diana?'

I made an appointment to see a doctor the very next day, and within twenty-four hours I was taking the antidepressant Aropax. Within a week whatever part of my brain that had gone on holiday was back at work and life was nearly normal again. My doctor said that the Aropax wouldn't give me a high, but would more just make me who I was supposed to be. I still disagree with that prediction. I was never that nice. For the six months that I took antidepressants I was an absolute delight to be around. I think Chris decided to make hay while the sun shone and I remember not batting an eyelid when he brought visiting dentists home for dinner, and I even remember telling him he should go to the pub more often for a couple of beers after work.

I don't think it was all the drug's doing, though. I was deliriously happy to be well again, and Mary became the focus of my world. She still cried an awful lot, but something in me changed. I had always expected my babies to sleep through the night and have at least a two-hour afternoon sleep. Mary-Agnes just simply didn't want to fit into this age-old plan, and I decided to throw away the rule book and take my lead from her.

So lucky, lucky Mary-Agnes had the only hippy infancy out of the lot of them. She was breastfed when and where she wanted until she was nearly two, and slept in our bed until she was seven and a half. I don't know which path was the right or wrong one, and I figure I'll wait until the first O'Loughlin kid steals a car, and then I'll have my answer.

CHAPTER 10

THE PERFORMING LIFE

In 1999 the only regular performing I did was to play improv once a month at Witchetty's Bistro. I'd formed a troupe with three American guys and two Australian girls and we called ourselves The Laughing Stock. I loved playing improv, and thanks to the networking of the Alice Springs American community we had a very strong following and played to good houses once a month.

I also really enjoyed hanging out with my new American buddies Butch, Garth and freakin' Daryl, as we called him, and their families. Butch was a one-time stand-up comic from Texas and he taught me loads about the techniques of improvisational comedy, but more importantly made me laugh till I cried, and kind of replaced Scott Casley in the role of having a comedy peer in town to throw ideas around with. Butch was also a house husband and had a little girl the same age as Mary-Agnes.

So while Mary and Aly played, Butch and I would talk for hours about all things comedy, and during that year the wannabe stand-up in me slowly started to come back to life. It hit me between the eyes one night while I was watching the Melbourne International Comedy Festival Gala on TV.

As the special went on, and more and more comedians took to the stage, the knot in my stomach got tighter and tighter. I was blinking back tears and I guess the best way to describe what it felt like is to say that I was that kid watching all the other kids playing in the playground where I wasn't allowed to join in. I turned off the television and let myself feel whatever it was that was hurting so much, and it was an awful, awful, steaming, shitload of regret.

I wanted to do everything over and try harder and be better. I wanted another chance at stand-up. But first I wanted to cry about it and I locked myself in the bathroom and bawled myself stupid for hours. Broken dreams must run a close second to broken hearts, and I indulged my grief with enormous gusto, and then just as suddenly I stopped crying and made a plan.

I was going to write a show and then throw my hat in the national comedy ring by touring with it. So there!

Within a day of making this plan I rang Araluen and booked the main theatre for a Saturday night in three months time. I was snookered now, and that's pretty much the way I've always operated. Give myself no chance to escape and I'll do it. I decided on Araluen first as a way of running in the show before I took it anywhere else.

My little sister Emily was twenty-two years old by now, and had just finished a three-year course at the Centre for

Performing Arts in Adelaide. We had performed a couple of ridiculous songs together recently at Mum's sixtieth birthday and I rang her to see if she was interested in writing and performing in a show with me. She jumped at the idea, and straight after Christmas 1999 she moved to Alice Springs and we worked on the show that had the title *Fiona and Her Sister (and some guy)*.

The 'some guy' element was filled by Emily's then boyfriend Sam Willoughby, who played guitar and sang with Emily at the Oxford Hotel in Adelaide every Thursday night.

The show was first and foremost a vehicle for my stand-up but it also included a half-hour series of sketches with Emily and me, and sometimes Sam, playing a variety of characters. Emily and I wrote the sketches over a month around my kitchen table and Sam contributed as well and also helped me write some song parodies.

I didn't know it at the time but *Fiona and Her Sister (and some guy)* was to be the show that launched phase two of my ridiculous career. In that first year we performed the show in Alice Springs, and then after a few rewrites we took it home to the Yorke Peninsula and put it on in the town hall in Yorketown.

We all drove down from Alice Springs for the show, Chris and the kids included. Christopher had backed the show unreservedly from its inception. I guess he had a stake in my personal happiness, but more importantly he really thought it was funny.

Another man who showed unwavering support was my dad. I will never forget making a picture of him in my head, unstacking chairs and lining them up in the Yorketown Town Hall.

The town hall is very similar to many in rural Australia. Red crushed-velvet curtains, a polished wooden floor and a damp dusty smell that just one whiff of can transport me backstage and back in time. The town hall was host to every school concert we performed in as kids, and I remember vividly being backstage as a ten-year-old, with clogs on my feet, a green vest and pantaloons, about to partner Columba Cairney in a stellar tribute to the windmill. The play was called *Play Day in Happy Holland* and was long considered to be a credit to the Sisters at St Columba's.

I remember being very jealous of Mary-Anne Williams and my sister Cate, as they both scored solos that year. Mary-Anne sang a song about the eel; Cate had a solo about an altercation with a goose.

We did a lot of world travelling on that stage with the nuns. I remember being in the choir (which was not optional for anyone at St Columba's) and singing 'How are Things in Glocca Morra?' and wondering where the heck was Glocca Morra, and what the hell did it have to do with us?

But I do digress.

I was back at the Yorketown Town Hall nearly thirty years later, and there was my dad, a farmer in his seventies, arranging the seating in the hall for four hundred or so people from the district to come and see a show that his daughters had driven fifteen hundred kilometres to put on, as if it was the most natural thing in the whole world. I was so grateful for my gentle, generous dad and I'd never loved him more.

Another great show of support was from Ivan, Tim, Peter and Judith, who had made their way over from Adelaide to be in the audience and at one point I remember being spurred on by the sound of Pete's belly laugh.

It was a big success for a couple of reasons. The sketches were strong, and my stand-up had finally come into its own. Emily and I were pedantic about how good the sketches needed to be. We played to the truth of me being more than a decade older and took it in turns to be each other's straight men. We were Mariah Carey, we were Nimbin-born folk singers, we were English backpackers, traditional Irish dancers, pregnant New Zealand aerobics instructors and alcoholic neighbours. I've never felt safer with anyone else than Emily on stage. She can ad lib to perfection and I take my lead from her in character, particularly when accents are involved. Ever since she was little, Emily has been able to mimic a horde of accents to perfection, whereas I can hold an accent once my ear has harnessed it but find it hard to locate them on my own.

My stand-up had evolved to a point where I found my old routines unrecognisable. I think for a long time I was afraid of my stand-up because deep down I didn't really endorse what I was rabbiting on about on stage.

I love telling a story, and always have, and yet my early stand-up reflected very little storytelling. I was frantically trying to write set-ups and punchlines for years without realising that some of the strongest material I had was sitting right under my nose.

For *Fiona and Her Sister (and some guy)*, I threw out every joke I'd ever written and started again from scratch. I told jokes and stories that were based in truth. I talked about big family car trips and leaving the baby in Liquorland and fighting with my husband. I talked about stuff I knew about and I finally had a particular voice for a particular brand of stand-up comedy.

I knew now that we had a product and it was a show worthy of a national audience, but I also had to find a way to showcase it.

We went to Melbourne next, and for old time's sake hired the main room at the Star and Garter and performed *Fiona and Her Sister (and some guy)* for one night only.

Chris, Sam, Emily and I stayed in a hostel very near the Star and Garter and I remember seeing the saddest scene at a train stop on the short walk to the venue. I was running late and everyone had gone on ahead. I was crossing an overpass and heard screaming from the street below. I didn't really have time to stop but I leant over the railing to see what was going on.

There was a young woman screaming at a boy who looked about seven or eight years old. She seemed really threatening and the boy was kind of cowering by a rubbish bin.

I guess I presumed she was a junkie by the look of her – scrawny and dirty, with long blonde matted hair blowing across her face, as she just kept on and on at the boy. I felt so sorry for him and I wanted to help. He was trying not to cry and I was trying not to yell at her to leave him alone, when she suddenly stopped and squatted on the ground, cradled her head in her hands and started sobbing. About a metre away from the boy a man I hadn't noticed before appeared with a baby on his hip and sat down next to her and gently rubbed her back.

Then the sad boy moved in and they all huddled together. The man noticed me and looked up and stared at me for ages, and I just stood there and stared straight back. The whole picture looked so bleak and hopeless. Maybe it wasn't as bad as it looked. Maybe the mother couldn't find a hairbrush that morning and maybe the boy had spent their train fare home on a packet of footy cards. But I doubted it. I was pretty sure I was looking at a family in agony and I didn't know what to do. So I turned away and headed for my gig, and put a new snapshot in the photo album in my head. If I had an exhibition of the pictures in my head I don't know what I'd call that one. But it would never be for sale.

* * *

Having left behind nursing and fostering kids, I'd felt a weird kind of guilt about the self-indulgence of comedy and its ultimate worth, and something about that family hit me. Life can be so hard and sore that funny really matters. If fucked is the Yin then let funny be the Yang. Surely, that's not too much of an ask. I can still see that guy staring at me that day and I hope that whenever I'm on a downer somewhere, he's having a laugh.

The show at the Star and Garter wasn't ever going to be a financial success, but having already run it a couple of times in regional areas I was keen to put it in front of a city audience.

By now *Fiona and Her Sister (and some guy)* had been subjected to six or seven rewrites and there was no exception after Melbourne.

Finally it was as ready as it was ever going to be and we registered for the Adelaide Fringe in February 2000.

* * *

The Adelaide Fringe is an international festival, and second only to the Edinburgh Fringe – which is the biggest in the world.

Christopher put up the $8,000 for the registration and venue hire, I moved into Emily's rental house in Goodwood about a week before opening night, and the fireworks began. I guess we were both more than a bit nervous but the fights we had that week were astounding. The fundamental difference between Emily and me as performers is our vastly different tactics as an opening night looms.

At some point, rightly or wrongly, I prefer to walk away. The 'Que Sera, Sera' factor kicks in and I figure once we've done all we can the rest is in the lap of the gods.

My baby sister, on the other hand, will rehearse right up until the box office opens. Emily was professionally trained in theatre and as far as she's concerned it's never too late for one last rehearsal to get it right. She'll fret about costumes, obsess about warm-ups and run a show half a dozen times or more on the afternoon of an opening night.

I could have explained all of this a lot better by simply acknowledging that I'm lazy and Emily isn't but that's not really the lasting impression I want to leave you with.

The arguments went up and down the hallway for days.

'Fiona, what if the show is crap and no one laughs?'

'Then the show will be crap and no one will laugh.'

'Don't act like you don't care.'

'I care, Emily. My arse is on the line too, but you can't get guarantees. There are none.'

'What are you talking about?'

'You should have been a typist.'

'God you're a bitch.'

'Performers don't get given guarantees, whereas a typist gets lots of guarantees; you can guarantee yourself exactly what you're going to type if you're a typist. You should have been a typist.'

'We're going to be the laughing stock of the Adelaide Fringe, Fiona.'

'Good! It's a comedy.'

'Maybe I should have been a typist?'

'I don't think, on the whole, you'd have been as happy as a typist as you are as a performer.'

'Well, at least if I was a typist I wouldn't have to put up with your bullshit.'

We actually opened at the Adelaide Fringe not speaking to each other, but the show worked and people came, and we were on our way.

In Adelaide during Fringe time all sorts of spaces are converted into venues to cater for the hundreds of shows on offer. People perform in anything from cinemas to cellars, and Emily and I were actually allocated a horse stable.

It was behind the Stag Hotel in Rundle Street and seated about sixty people. That's sixty people in fold-up chairs on a cobbled stone floor in a windowless barn that smelt suspiciously of rats. I was really horrified when I first saw our venue, but after it was swept and hosed out and the stage and the lights went in I had to agree with Emily. It had character.

Opening night was such a relief that we headed straight to the Stag to celebrate, and most of the audience came with us. That's because most of the audience were either relatives or mates, with the guests of honour being Denis and Deirdre Taheny from Warooka.

About a week or more into the three-week season of the Fringe I started to really let go of my anxieties and enjoy every minute of it. I had been worried about leaving the kids, worried about my show not being up to standard alongside other national and international acts and worried that we wouldn't make a return on our money.

It had all been a lot of angst for nothing and all of a sudden I felt like it was okay. I had a right to be here. Nobody seemed to think of me as a country bumpkin and I was selling tickets faster than any other independent show in town.

* * *

Emily and I are as quick to forgive and forget as we are to fight in the first place, and one of the great advantages of collaborating with a sibling is being able to dispense with the post-mortem of a falling-out. We were closer than ever by the end of that first festival and I remember having a celebratory lunch at Cate's house on the last Sunday of the Fringe.

Cate and Phil had renovated a house with a gigantic kitchen in Magill and had filled it with six kids. We referred to their place as 'The Function Centre'. Tahenys had always loved a kitchen gathering, and finally there was one big enough for us all.

I pulled up out the front of 'The Function Centre' and Dad was carrying some rubbish out to the bin. He was in a very chipper mood.

'Have you seen today's paper?'

I hadn't yet, but he was referring to an article summing up the success of that year's Adelaide Fringe, and I was named alongside Paul Kelly and Robyn Archer as examples of the talent that had come from former South Australians. It was the icing on the cake after a four-and-a-half-star review from the *Advertiser*, and I drove back to Alice Springs with Chris and the kids as happy as a pig in shit, as the old saying goes.

* * *

I think I have mentioned already that I have had since childhood a pathological propensity to lose things. As an adult I have managed to misplace more than a dozen handbags, many a driver's licence and, at one particular low point, a small child. More often than not the lost is inevitably found but it is without doubt a debilitating way to live.

My great friend Jasmin has understood this failing for years. When we were sixteen, Jasmin found an antique brooch that my grandmother had left me on the floor under my bed at boarding school. She said to me, 'Fiona, I'm not going to give this back to you because it's beautiful and you'll lose it, I know you will. I'm going to keep it and when you have a daughter and she turns eighteen, I'll give it to her.'

Sure enough, Jasmin still has that brooch and Mary-Agnes will have it in five years from now. All I can say is that it's one less thing I have to worry about.

While I lose a lot of things, generally everything works out in the end, which is probably why I nearly went mad one night at Heathrow Airport. I was heading home from the Edinburgh Festival a couple of years ago and was travelling alone. I swear I was almost obsessive-compulsive about checking and rechecking the whereabouts of my passport and plane ticket. Sure enough, as I stood in line to board the London–Kuala Lumpur leg of my trip, I put my hand in my bag for the hundredth time and my passport and ticket were gone. While I certainly wasn't calm about this, neither was I engulfed in panic.

Someone will help me, I thought. Everything will sort itself out and I had plenty of time. My plane wasn't leaving for an hour or so.

When I reached the Malaysian Airlines counter it dawned on me that maybe this little hiccup in my journey was pretty damned serious. The girl at the counter didn't bat an eyelid when I confided in her.

'I'm on your 8.30 flight to Kuala Lumpur and I've lost my passport and ticket.'

'Then you're not on our 8.30 flight to Kuala Lumpur.'

'Pardon?'

'If you don't have your passport or your ticket, you're not going anywhere.'

Suddenly the panic set in. I was stranded. I had only $2 in my pocket and had to find that passport.

'Where do tickets and passports get handed in?'

'Generally people hang on to their passports and tickets, but maybe security?'

She gave me directions to security and I ran all the way, hoping hard.

I was attended to by a much more sympathetic bloke than the Malaysian Airlines chick, but no ticket had been handed in.

'I'd say if someone found it they'd hand it in to Malaysian Airlines. Why don't you go back to them and check?'

'Thanks.' I was at least grateful that he showed me more concern than Bitchface.

She actually smiled when she saw me and seemed to enjoy telling me that nothing had been handed in. I had an overwhelming urge to smash her in the face and once again raced the length of the terminal to the guy from security.

'Nothing, love. Keep trying, though.'

By this time I was frantically running back and forth, tears streaming down my face, I had just heard the final boarding call and knew pretty soon I'd have to give up, ring the kids, disappoint them, and surrender myself to a charity for the homeless for the night. I had no access to any money. I had deliberately left my credit card back home for fear of losing it, and had spent my last traveller's cheque on duty-free stuff in Scotland.

Bitchface rolled her eyes as I reached her counter for the seventh time that night. Just as she started shaking her head we both overheard the businessman at the next counter.

'I found someone's passport and ticket on the bus from Terminal 9.'

I screamed with joy and grabbed him and my ticket and thanked him over and over.

Bitchface actually seemed personally annoyed by my happy ending.

'You're a very lucky woman.'

'And you're a horrible person, and I hope for your sake that one day if something really horrible happens to you, then someone . . . a lot nicer than you . . . will be there to look after you.'

And off I went, knowing that my little speech was ineloquent but also knowing that Bitchface was right . . . I was a very lucky woman.

I remember one night when Jasmin was visiting, Henry, my eldest, was in a foul mood with me because I couldn't find his birth certificate and he needed to take it to the motor vehicle registry. He'd walked out of the living room and slammed the door behind him. I heard Biddy ask nobody in particular, 'Why doesn't Mum ever know where anything is?'

Jasmin explained it to her: 'Biddy, there's a part of everybody's brain that tells them where their car keys are and whose birthday it is next and what time they're supposed to be somewhere, and your Mum just can't use that part.'

'Why can't she?'

'Because that's where she keeps all of her favourite lines from the *Young Ones*, the theme songs from about fifty American TV shows and Earl Spencer's speech from Princess Di's funeral.'

* * *

The Montreal Festival is the festival that feeds the North American market for the next crop of sitcoms or comedy superstars. It's a surreal environment, and unlike the Edinburgh and Melbourne experience in many ways. The Montreal 'Just for Laughs' comedy festival is more of an 'expo' for comic talent than anything else. It's almost a convention for agents, managers and producers; the comedians are relegated to the bottom of the pack.

Only the likes of Billy Connelly and Joan Rivers perform whole one-woman/one-man shows. The rest of the hundreds of comedians on offer are squeezed into 'showcases' in venues of greatly varying size and quality all over the city, performing for a mix of local comedy connoisseurs, talent scouts, network executives, producers and the like.

It is unmitigated joy to be inside a comedy festival. Imagine organising a dinner party, and if you're anything like me you wouldn't dream of peeling a potato until you had secured the acceptance of the 'life of the party' friend. Everybody has them, those special, hilarious favourite mates that can be relied on in any situation and are simply always fun to be around. So now imagine a hundred of those people in one room.

In a room of comedians no one bothers with the disclaimer 'only joking' after an offensive quip or an irony-laden insult. There is an unspoken shorthand in conversation, and for me the relief of actually being more silent than I have ever known. I had always been the clown in the classroom and the loudmouth at the party, and now there were plenty of others to take up the slack.

I shall always remember that first night in Montreal at the bar in the famous Delta hotel. I had finished my first twelve-minute set in God-knows-what venue and then it was on to the Delta Bar where comedians drank, amused each other and themselves, and the agents got down to business.

Agents and producers who had spent the evening at the smorgasbord of 'Just for Laughs' showcases were doing deals with each other by way of yelling over the crescendo of opening night. The accents were mostly American and the clichés abounded.

'Hey! I saw your guy tonight! Very edgy, very new. Hey! Harry! Have your people call mine!'

'Thanks Phil, yeah, we've got the buzz.'

'The buzz' was what happened every year. Some new comic who rose up from the pack got talked about the most, and whoever was 'the buzz' was quite possibly the next Ray Romano or Seinfeld. Or maybe not.

I remember a familiar face that belonged to none other than Dom Irrera, the legendary Italian American comic. I had met Dom on a couple of occasions and he reminded me again in an instant of his ruthless humour.

'Hi, Dom!'

'Fiona!' (smooch smooch) 'Do you know Deidre?'

I had indeed met Deidre before, and without doubt she is one of the finest of Irish stand-ups.

'Hello, Fiona.' (smooch smooch) 'And have ye not met Eddie?'

'Well, no,' said I. 'Good to meet you, Eddie.'

And as Eddie and I shook hands the great Dom couldn't resist.

'She's terrific, Eddie, but whatever you do, don't judge her by her act.'

Dom sounds exactly like a New York gangster to my Australian ear, and I remember him thrilling my son Bert during the Melbourne festival. Bertie was about eight at the time and had tagged along with me, and his eyes lit up when this funny American man gave him his full attention.

'Hey Bertie, I'd hate ya to take the way ya mom's raisin' ya all personal like. Ya know, she's real nice to people she hardly knows.'

One evening about two months later, Bert started screaming in the living room. It sounded like his throat had been slit, and I dropped a colander of spaghetti in fright and pelted in to rescue him. As it turned out he was hollering for joy. He was watching a rerun of *Seinfeld*, and making a guest appearance was none other than Dom Irrera.

'Mum! It's him! On *Seinfeld*! The funny man in Melbourne who said you were a crap mother!'

* * *

After Montreal I headed for Los Angeles, as I had received about four or five invitations to meet with various American networks. There had been an ever so slight 'buzz' around the forty-year-old Australian woman with all the kids, and though the notion of a development deal with an American network was a long shot, it was a shot I would never have forgiven myself for not taking.

Many mistakes, hiccups and humiliations lay ahead as I boarded the American Airlines flight to LA, but I was blissfully unaware of this as I settled in to seat 15B and arranged my carry-on luggage neatly under the seat in front of me.

'Hello, Fiona,' welcomed a very gay LA voice from 15A.

I nearly jumped a foot in the air. Who the hell could know my name on my virgin plane trip from New York to LA? Let alone be sitting next to me?

'Hello?'

'Well, of course you don't know me,' he dazzled with the brightest of teeth. 'My name is Steve, and I'm a casting agent with NBC. (Imagine the voice of Jack from *Will and Grace*, if you will, dear reader.) 'I saw two of your sets in Montreal – lovely! And will be going to your showcase at the Improv on Thursday night, very excited! Quite a nice buzz around you, dear.'

I have no recollection of the small talk I made with this man for the next half hour or so, but before long an uncomfortable silence had settled in and I made my way to the lavatory to collect myself and gasped in fright when I saw my reflection in the bathroom mirror.

You see, my last night in Montreal had been spent having a girls' night in with fellow comedian Judith Lucy. We whiled away the hours after raiding our managers' mini-bars, laughing and talking and becoming firm friends indeed. Consequently, I had packed and dressed for my trip to LA in a furious rush and with an impressive hangover and after flying from Canada to New York I then spent the hour or so stopover catching up on some much-needed sleep. Unfortunately by the time I'd met Mr NBC with the dazzling teeth it had been some time since I'd powdered my nose, so to speak.

No kidding, I had a mascara line a foot long running almost down to my neck, and a lipstick smudge that made me look like the crazed Bette Davis in *Whatever Happened to Baby Jane?* and all of this was capped off beautifully with a headband that had long since left its post and was holding the majority of my hair in some weird tangle at right angles to my head. I stayed in the bathroom for as long as I could get away with and then spent the rest of the flight in a desperate depiction of sleep.

Los Angeles is ugly, sad, desperate, beautiful and wondrous all at the same time. The 'have nots' work tirelessly for the 'haves', hoping one day to cease being a 'have not' themselves. Sunset Boulevard is filled with wannabe actor waiters, waitresses, strippers, bellboys and even the occasional star. I found the strip to be a weird and aesthetically very unappealing place.

It was a surreal to the point of frightening experience, and never before or since have I felt so out of place in any environment. We checked in to our hotel, The Standard on Sunset (where I've since seen paparazzi shots of the likes of Lindsay Lohan and Britney Spears with their limos) and I think I must have looked a lot like Ma Kettle would have as I took in my surroundings.

The foyer of the Standard doubles as a nightclub, so one checks in at the reception desk to the beat of throbbing music and strobe lighting. I noticed Drew Barrymore and her posse in beanbags in the corner, and had barely got over the sight of that before I became aware of the terrarium behind the reception counter. A huge glass box jutting out from the wall housed not turtles or fish or foliage, but a real live near-naked model lying on her tummy flipping through a magazine.

Nice work if you can get it, I guess. There was a different model in that box for an eight-hour shift every day of the week and I couldn't help but notice the Monday night model was a bit lardier than the rest.

Speaking of which, it dawned on me after we checked in to our rooms and had a drink by the pool that I was quite possibly the fattest person in LA, not to mention one of the oldest. What on earth was I doing here? A middle-aged housewife from Alice Springs who had only ever harboured a dream of landing a gig in a Melbourne comedy club. The incongruity of it all overwhelmed me and I had a very restless sleep wondering what the next day had in store for me. Oh, if only I could rewind the clock. Strap yourselves in, it gets worse.

I had a meeting with a network at 4 p.m. and so I spent the morning at the hairdresser's, shopping for a dress and finding a tanning salon. The dress was exactly what I wanted, as I was aspiring to get the look of Lucille Ball and was delighted to find a fifties-inspired navy blue and white polkadot frock with gorgeous three-quarter-length sleeves, a huge bow and metres of skirt. Being only five foot tall and somewhat apple shaped, I'd hazard a guess that I probably resembled Lucy's best friend Ethel more than the icon herself, but I had also acquired new high heels (very high heels) and felt as though I'd done all I could.

I guess it was the fake tan I could have done without. I've always been a huge fan of counterfeit colouring, and I remember Cate and I bronzing up on the morning of Sarah's wedding. 'You know, Fiona, if fake tan had been around when we were younger, we could have made completely different choices.'

No offence to either of our husbands, but she did have a point. God knows how many times we sweltered on the sidelines at pool parties waiting for the sun to go down. Shorts and tank tops had never really been an option for the Taheny girls. It's not so much that we were white or Nicole Kidman alabaster, but more of a pale pink that deepens to a frightening aubergine as the temperature rises. My nickname at boarding school was 'Blancmange'. Oh, how I envy the L'Oreal liberation that my own gorgeous girls have benefited from.

So it wasn't the fake tan itself that was new to me that morning in Los Angeles, but rather the method of its administration at the tanning salon opposite The Standard on Sunset.

'Yes, madam, booth number three is available now.'

The young bronzed Adonis behind the counter handed me a shower cap, booties and a towel, and I made my way down the corridor to booth three and eventually worked out the procedure. Stark naked, sans the cap and booties, I chose the lightest of the three shades, pressed the button and was sprayed from back to front, and started laughing myself stupid at the sight I must have been. I have no idea why I found the whole experience so gut-bustingly hilarious – but what a shame I couldn't have kept a straight face.

When I emerged, the tan was quite nice and dark, and looking in the mirror back in my hotel room I realised why the Adonis had been smirking as I paid for the new look. There were bright white lines all around my eyes where the tan hadn't gotten into my crow's feet. Fuck! And Dammit! I hit the panic button and scrubbed my face until it was red raw. Tears, soap and mountains of make-up later I was with my manager Andrew and my agent Cara at the Disney Studio in San Fernando Valley, on time for that oh-so-important meeting.

My heart thumped and my feet trotted precariously behind my minders in my new heels as we made our way to reception and then through to casting. Lots of smiles, bottled water and handshakes were exchanged before I finally sat on my first ever casting couch in Los Angeles.

Unfortunately I sat in the middle of the couch with my manager and agent (who were a little larger than me) either end, and had left myself with no options of armrests to disguise my nervousness, and I had sat far too far back into the couch as well.

My feet were about a foot from the ground and I felt powerless, ridiculous and all too well aware that in my polkadot dress with the massive skirt and bow, and my legs sticking out at right angles to my hips that, even without there being a giant rabbit in the room, I was indeed giving a splendid impersonation of Alice in Wonderland.

Networks in the United States leave no stone unturned in their quests for sitcoms. Meetings with casting agents and the pitching of shows go on every second of the day, and hundreds of TV shows are piloted with only a minimal chance of ever making it to the screen.

And there was I, on that couch, in my polkadot dress and my burning face, exchanging very early dialogue with a network to determine whether an idea was even viable enough to proceed to a development deal.

Sadly, I did none of the talking. The three or four network executives beamed at me from time to time amid the banter that went on over the top of my head.

'Okay, so she's Australian with five kids. What would bring her character to America?'

'She's married to a diplomat?'

'She'll need to be married to an American, there's no room for more than one Aussie accent.'

'What about her kids?'

'She inherited them!'

'Like from a dead sister?'

'Maybe they were living in the States all along. *She* just happens to be from Australia originally?'

''What if she and her husband are starting up an Aussie theme park?'

'Like that crocodile guy?'

'No, again, too much Aussie.'

'Why can't she be American? Say from Montana? Coming to the big smoke for the first time?'

'I don't know. Can she do an American accent?'

To this day I can't separate any of the next four meetings with networks in LA because they followed such a similar vein. Except maybe for the final hurrah, which was NBC.

'Well, thank you so much again for coming in.'

'We'll be in touch.'

'Sooooo lovely to meet you.'

'Please let us know when you're back in LA.'

'Bye then.'

After that it was back in the hire car – and finally time to enjoy the drive down Sunset Strip in a yellow sports car. The sun was actually setting, which I quickly made a memory of, and then I fiddled with my sunglasses, which seemed to have shrunk since lunchtime. I took them off and noticed that while nearly identical to mine they were somebody else's. Mine had no D&G lettering on the wings.

'What's D&G stand for?'

'That'd be Dolce & Gabbana. Where'd you get them?'

Somewhere in the NBC studios was a casting agent with my $11.95 sunnies from the Shell Mount Gillen Service Station in Alice Springs.

* * *

If my trip to Los Angeles afforded me anything it gave me the chance to play the Hollywood Improv. The Hollywood Improv is the Mecca of stand-up clubs. It's what the MCG is to cricket, Madison Square Gardens is to baseball, Covent Garden is to opera. Unfortunately and not surprisingly Fiona O'Loughlin, middle-aged housewife from Alice Springs was blissfully unaware of this until it had been pointed out to me by my agent two nights before I played there.

So there I was, at the famous Hollywood Improv, not on stage, but in the audience. My gig at the Improv wasn't until the next night, but I had found my way there to get a feel for the place in the desperate hope of allaying some of the nerves that still render me nearly physically sick to this day. What happened that night was confusing and heartbreaking to say the least.

I had happened upon African American night, which from memory was a Tuesday night ritual at the Improv. The place was packed and I was getting more excited by the minute. In the world of laughs the African American comedy community is to my mind one of the finest. Whoopi Goldberg, Eddie Murphy, Bill Cosby; too many to name and too good to be true. I wondered which next superstar I might have the privilege of seeing live at the coalface of stardom in Hollywood. I could see the future and hear myself bragging about it to my as-yet unborn grandchildren: 'I saw him live at the Hollywood Improv in 2001.'

What happened next still hurts my heart and I will never understand it. An all-male line-up is not unusual in the world of comedy but the order of the day from the comedians that night seemed to be an unrelenting tsunami of misogyny. I had never really come across a form of comedy where I couldn't find something to laugh about. My own style is narrative and sometimes dark in its themes but I appreciate every flavour of joke-meistering there is. From the absurdism of Sam Simmons to the glorious intuition of Damian Callinan to the unbridled joy of Judith Lucy's scathism.

I've never needed to be politically or morally in sync with a comedy performance to be entertained. I'll find a joy in its wit or its rhythm or its irreverence. Just about any genre of comedy, so long as it is well executed, will do me just fine.

But that night at the famous Improv it seemed I was the only person in the room not getting the joke. Women were referred to by the male comedians as whores and hoes and collective pussy, and I looked around at the hordes of both male and female audience members in hysterics and realised I had absolutely no compass to navigate the humour. In other words, I simply didn't get it. Whores and hoes were words that were by no means new to me, and I had heard a thousand jokes in my travels that were solely at the expense of women and sometimes beyond the pale when it came to graphic language.

I was long enough in the tooth by now to not bat an eyelid at any swear word. Words don't frighten me at all and nor do themes but the difference on this night was that the relentless onslaught against women appeared to be entirely devoid of irony.

Irony is a basic ingredient of stand-up comedy. Without it is akin to making omelettes with no eggs. I simply couldn't find the irony at the Improv that night, and before I knew it I couldn't find my breath either. Suddenly feeling like I was bearing witness to a pack rape, I fled the venue and stood in the car park and cried an exhausted and bewildered cry.

I pulled myself together and looked up at the massive murals on the exterior walls of the Improv. Jay Leno, Ellen DeGeneres, Richard Pryor and David Letterman all smiled down at me. I didn't smile back at any of them, and hailed a cab back to the hotel where I fell into a tormented sleep that was about to be broken by an equally tormented reality at about 3 a.m.

* * *

There was knocking on my door. 'Fiona, everybody's okay, but you need to call home. Chris has been in some kind of car accident with the kids.'

Some kind of accident? Poor Chris had been involved in one of the most bizarre accidents anyone could dream of. He and all the kids were driving back from Adelaide and were about twenty minutes outside of Alice Springs in the very early hours of the morning when Chris, after not understanding what he was seeing for a second or two, suddenly realised that there were two Aboriginal men lying asleep on his side of the road in line with his front wheels head first and their feet towards

Alice Springs. They were only twenty metres in front of the car and there was no time to brake. One of my husband's best assets is his lightning reflexes, and resigned to the fact that he was probably going to hit them he veered enough to avoid running over their heads, all the while doing everything he could not to put his own precious cargo at risk.

He heard the sickening sound of human bodies thumping the underbelly of the car and screamed like he never had before, waking everyone in the car.

'Dad, what's wrong?'

'I've just run over two men.'

Moments later, while Chris was on the phone to emergency services, and running towards the two blokes, he saw the miracle of one of them sitting up and the other one standing. The ultimate toll had been the broken right femur of the man sitting.

Still, it had been a shocking experience, and after trying to make sense of the whole nightmare he was informed by a local doctor that the drama could be attributed to one of three scenarios that I guess he will never have the answer to. It was either a consequence of drunkenness, attempted suicide or murder.

So there I was in an LA hotel having been filled in on all of this many hours later. Everyone was safe and sound but I wanted to be home like never before, and I cried again, and I cried for a long time. I cried for the fear that my husband and kids had gone through and I cried for the two men on the highway, and recalling my earlier cry that night at the Hollywood Improv I realised that black America was absolutely none of my business. I had enough to cry about in my own backyard.

My showcase gig at the Improv the next night was pretty disastrous. I opened with my golden oldie sure-fire line: 'I've got five kids, I know that's an awful lot of kids in this day and age but my husband and I are going to keep trying till we get one we like!'

It went down like a lead balloon.

I didn't really care that much, to be honest. I was flying home the next day, and I couldn't have been more ready. I had my last laugh in Los Angeles in the ladies' toilets straight after my performance. Sitting in a cubicle I was eavesdropping on some critiques of my show by a couple of women at the basins.

'Wasn't she awful?'

'I agree. What on earth is funny about not liking your kids?'

'No irony there at all. That was her problem.'

* * *

'Five kids! And an international comedy career! How do you juggle it all?' It's a question that I've been asked more times than I care to remember. For a start I can't juggle oranges let alone teenagers and jokes, but I have had some bad days. Very, very bad days if I'm honest, and forty-eight hours or so in early February in 2003 was a period of time that quite literally brought me to my knees.

It started in Melbourne when I was recording a pilot for a panel type show at Channel Ten. I'd flown over from Adelaide, where Chris and I and the rest of the kids had said our final goodbyes to Henry, who was having his first ever night at Sacred Heart Boarding School. My eldest baby was leaving home, and I fought back tears the whole flight from Adelaide to Melbourne, and Chris and the other kids apparently cried at least as far as Port Augusta on their long drive back to Alice Springs where I would join them in two days time.

I barely slept that night in my hotel room, and all these years later I still have the simple text from Henry from his lonely bed in a dormitory of strangers: 'Night Mum.'

I'd like to say it was purely the grief of my firstborn leaving home that interrupted my sleep repeatedly that night at the Como Hotel in South Yarra but I was also distracted by an insatiable itch to my head.

The next bleary-eyed morning and all was revealed as I dressed and readied myself for yet another disappointment in the world of television. Oh my God! I had head lice! I'd seen enough head lice in my time to recognise those vile parasitic humiliations immediately, and I was well and truly panic stricken. My timing was as disappointing as the massive blind pimple emerging from the inside of my left nostril, which was incredibly painful but fortunately invisible to the outside world. But this was the very first time nits had made their way to my own head.

If I was ever to congratulate myself on the few life skills that I possess it would most definitely be for my ability to problem-solve in the face of complete chaos, and while I was due in hair and make-up at the television studio in less than an hour I flew out of the hotel and hailed a cab to Oxford Street in the search of, believe it or not, a wig shop.

'Yes, hello, can I help you?'

'Look, I'm so sorry, I don't have cancer or alopecia or anything really serious, but I need a wig, kind of immediately!

A wig that pretty much looks exactly the same as my own hair, but could it not be real hair? Like from a real person's head? Because I do have slight obsessive compulsion and somebody else's hair would kind of completely freak me out. I'm talking too much, aren't I? It's just that I'm in a really, really, really big panic and I need a wig as close to my own hair as you've got, kind of . . . now!'

Ten minutes and $200 later I was in a cab with a head of synthetic hair to rival Jennifer Aniston's. (Seriously, I wore that wig on stage for the next eighteen months or more.) And another ten minutes later I was in the make-up chair at Channel Ten, and all was pretty much right with the world, except for the blind pimple up my left nostril, which had begun to throb incessantly.

The make-up artist was a lovely woman whom I'd come across before in my travels on various TV shows and we both agreed (especially me wholeheartedly) that my hair needed nothing doing to it but she did notice that one of my nostrils seemed a bit inflamed and red and set about concealing it with some manner of what looked to me like the Spakfilla that my husband buys from Mitre 10.

The TV pilot was a show called *The Chatroom*. I never made it past my audition, however, as my performance was as painful as my nose and as humiliating as my head lice. Once again I flew back to Alice Springs with another disaster under my belt, and by now a new life form growing from within my left nostril. I had actually been in so much pain on my last night in Melbourne that I had a doctor come to my hotel room. He held my head so far back as he studied my inner honk that I was afraid my wig would fall off right there and then, but I was now able to add a nostril abscess to my head lice; surely two of the least sexiest maladies a modern woman could endure. He started me on a course of antibiotics and charged me the obligatory call-out fee, which resulted in my hair and nose having cost me a combined and formidable $430 including the prescription costs and taxi fares.

I was ready for home. But here lies one of the greatest hardships I have in juggling career, family and an isolated location. Home is never quite where the heart is for me when I first walk in the door after yet another trip away. It's nobody's fault, but simply the reality of my choices. I walk in the door and the house looks like a bomb has hit it. Chris has three businesses in Alice Springs and works on average a ten- to twelve-hour day. He's not a cook, and I haven't really raised any of my children as housekeepers. Probably out of guilt I always see it as my job to put the house back together and sort the washing and start cooking proper meals as soon as I return.

But this day I simply wasn't in the mood, and speaking of moods, mine was as black as thunder. Take-away containers, wet towels, spilt cat litter, footy socks, dress-ups, and even a melting Cornetto ice-cream on a newly covered couch. My mental health was hanging by a thread, but even then I had the good grace to not go ballistic, and took the option that I've taken my whole life when the world has become too much. I ran a bath and got in it until I was calm.

Sadly for me that day, not even my most tried and true remedy went smoothly. The bath was bubbly and beckoning and I was centimetres from legging into it when I tripped on a cream lamington and went flying through the bathroom arse over tit.

That was the last straw for me, and I went rampaging through the house like a wild thing looking for small prey. 'Who in God's name left a lamington on the bathroom floor?'

We were renovating at the time and the back end of the house had been demolished. One of the poor builders got way more than he bargained for, as I was wearing a bath mat as opposed to a bath towel and hadn't even noticed him in my quest to find offspring and murder them then and there.

I don't know where everybody fled to, but I was literally screaming through the house and yelling to myself. 'I'm too old to be slipping on lamingtons on bathroom floors! Are you listening to me, little pigs? . . . Little pigs? . . . Little pigs? And more importantly, what is the thought process of someone not only eating a lamington in the bathroom but then deciding, That's enough of my lamington now, I think I'll just leave it right here! On the bathroom floor.'

'Are you okay, Mum?'

It was Bert, the only one brave enough to show his face. I was still too sore and furious to show even him some mercy. 'Go and clean your room!'

'Uhm . . . I don't have a room.'

That actually made me laugh, and all of a sudden I started to feel better. I was home, and I'm used to mess, and I had a gorgeous bath waiting for me.

'Where is everyone?'

'Mary's next door, Biddy's at the movies, Dad's in the shed and Tess is on the roof.'

All was well with the world, I had my head lice treatment merrily exterminating those nasty nits in my hair and I lolled in the bath for at least half an hour before my serenity was interrupted by the most frightening sound of screaming and crashing that I'd ever heard. Tess had fallen through the bathroom skylight, and I couldn't believe my eyes. A pair of teenage legs were dangling above my head, right through the ceiling.

Chris, Bert and a builder or two had come running at the almighty noise.

'Oh my God, Tess, are you all right?'

'Yes, but I can't hold on much longer. Can someone help me down?'

Bert had run off for a ladder while Chris and I just stared agog at this most unusual sight.

'Fiona?'

'What?'

'She's got pretty good legs, hasn't she!'

We all recovered from the shock of that afternoon and I was too tired to do anything but order a take-away and watch some TV before heading to bed. The next day loomed like a monster, as I had the Comedy Channel arriving from Sydney at nine-thirty to film me in my natural environment (God help them). I had every intention of being up and at it at the crack of dawn to put the house back together, but I was so buggered I slept through the alarm and we all woke at eight.

Not the end of the world generally, but school starts at ten past eight in Alice Springs and it was Mary-Agnes's very first day. Two milestones in a matter of days. My oldest baby had gone to Adelaide and my youngest baby was about to start school. I held her little hand and handed her over to the system as near as I've ever been to breaking point.

'Goodbye, gorgeous face. I'll miss you all day, I promise.'

'Goodbye, Mum. I love you lots.'

I didn't make it to the car park before I broke down completely, and was spotted by one of the most devoted and caring mothers on campus. She gave me a big hug and said she was exactly the same when her youngest started school.

'Do you know what you need to do, Fiona?'

'No, Marian. What did you do?'

'You need to take yourself to the movies or out for coffee and cake and be extremely kind to yourself today.'

'That's a great idea, Marian.'

Oh, how I wish I could have followed Marian's kind, but impossible, suggestion. I didn't have the energy to tell her that I had exactly forty-three minutes to put my face, home and hair together and would have to worry about my grief at a later date.

CHAPTER 11

BIG ISSUES

Since the very beginning of writing this book – and with two fingers I might add (insert an applause break here if you are so inclined) – I have had a nagging worry of how in hell's name I was going to deal with a big issue.

As per usual, and having been born under an extremely lucky star, the answer was right under my nose all along. The answers to most of my life's conundrums have pretty much always been right under my nose, and unfortunately nine times out of ten that's the last place I look.

The truth of the matter is that there has been an absence of truth since the very first page, but in my defence I didn't know it at the time. I certainly had my suspicions for a while but it has only been now, after all these years, that I have come to understand that I am undeniably an alcoholic.

I'm actually crying as I write this, sitting at my kitchen table, the house is unusually empty, just Doug the dog and myself, with Paul Kelly unknowingly serenading me from the stereo blaring from the next room as I weep the wettest, fattest tears I've ever cried. But I'm happy, it's a strange happy that I've never really felt before. I don't believe people are capable of ever crying from happiness alone, though. Ironically, happiness is often a trigger for regret. So if there was a recipe for the cocktail of my tears this afternoon I'd say at a guess it would be about one quart of joy with a double shot of heartache, a dash of disbelief and a twist of hope.

I've just had a weekend that utterly changed me, and if you will follow me one last time I need to backtrack a bit to fully explain.

* * *

'Fiona, we need to have that chat about *Dancing with the Stars.*'

My manager Andrew and I were standing out the front of the Melbourne Town Hall on a Tightarse Tuesday during the Melbourne Comedy Festival. I pulled my best scowly face and drew hard on my cigarette.

'I hate reality television.'

'You watch a lot of it.'

'I know I do, I'm addicted to it, but I'm still ideologically opposed to it. It robs artists and actors and real writers.'

Andrew sighed, smiled and smoked.

'Sweetheart, are you ever going to get over *Life at the Top*?'

'Probably not. And it's Channel Seven!'

'Well, it's up to you, the offer's there. Talk it over with Chris and we'll chat again about it tomorrow.'

I stubbed out my cigarette with the sole of my black boot. I've never performed in anything but black boots. 'Tell *Dancing with the Stars*, yes, I'm gonna do it.'

I really believe I have a guardian angel. And for her sake I hope I'm her only client. I've kept her very busy over the years. Something instinctively nudged me towards signing up for Australia's ninth season of the show. A lifeline, about my ninth lifeline I guess, and I grabbed it with both hands.

* * *

I don't know many things for sure, but I do know that prior to throwing my hat into the national ring of stand-up at the Adelaide Fringe in 2001 I was not a drunk. Alcohol had never controlled me. I had been drunk more than I care to admit, but getting plastered was never something I had actually set out to do. People, conversation and fun were always my motivation socially.

Ever since I was a kid in windy Warooka I wanted the moon. Sometimes how much I wanted and not even knowing what I wanted was a physical ache. Why wasn't everything ever enough? Why wasn't I like everyone else? From Easter eggs to laughing with Mrs Kennedy to closing time at the pub. Why could I never be satisfied that tomorrow was another day and the end of one thing isn't the end of it all?

What a dangerous arena the world of stand-up was for someone as insatiable as myself to step into; a world where the fun never ever has to stop, if you don't want it to. I had found my Magic Faraway Tree and I inhaled everyone and everything about that Adelaide Fringe.

And I defy anyone who takes pot shots at the city of Adelaide to not gulp at its intensity on a balmy night during the Fringe Festival. Rundle Street literally buzzes and brims with masses of punters and performers filling venues, cafes and restaurants, and spilling down to the Garden of Unearthly Delights. Adelaide can be a stuck-up Protestant bitch when she wants to be but in the last three weeks of summer she's a gregarious magnificent whore.

For the first time in my life I exposed myself to daily alcohol. In my head, I had no other choice. I suffered from such debilitating nerves before I stepped on stage (and still do to this day) that I never fathomed the possibility of going on without a double brandy. Emily's and my show *Fiona and Her Sister (and some guy)* was such a surprise hit that we couldn't resist celebrating every night. It would have been near impossible to resist as there wasn't one night during that whole festival that we didn't have at least a dozen relatives or friends in the audience.

This was also the first time in my life that I drank on a hangover. I had never been able to look at a cigarette, let alone a drink, the day after the night before, but at the age of thirty-six I had begun a dangerous dance that over the next nine years would spiral horribly out of control and could easily have cost me my life.

Before I go on with my spectacular decline, I really have to insist that my memories of my nine wicked years of excesses are far from all doom and gloom. The belly laughs comedians enjoy in the company of each other are unparalleled, and by far one of the most delectable perks of the job. If science is correct, and the endorphins released from laughter really do lengthen your life, then Daniel Kitson and Lawrence Mooney alone have bought me at least ten more years. Sometimes I actually feel real guilt about the privilege I've had of so much laughter in one lifetime.

I nearly split my sides at my beloved English friend John Moloney when he articulated the absurdity of our profession after many drinks at the Melbourne Comedy Festival one night in the Peter Cook Bar. He picked up an imaginary phone and started to talk to an imaginary person from Centrelink on the other end.

'Yes, hello. Um, I would like a job, please . . . yes, I'm prepared to work between twenty and forty minutes a day. I'd prefer evenings, of course, as I need to sleep most of the day. I will need to swear quite a lot while I'm working. Obviously I'll choose my own uniform and quite often I'll be drunk. And if I should begin not to enjoy myself during my work I will need to reserve the right to tell everyone to go fuck themselves and leave my job early. Obviously in such instances I should still like to be paid and of course also retain the right to turn up to my work or not the next day, depending on my mood.'

Laughs, laughs and more laughs. From roadshows around Australia, Canada and New Zealand to festivals in Hong Kong, Edinburgh, Montreal, Adelaide and Melbourne, I grafted more and more comedians to my heart and threw myself into a party nearly every night of the one hundred or more days of the year that I was on the road.

Poor Chris. At times it must have been truly awful for him. Well, actually, I know for a fact that it was. Of all the things we've shared over the years belly laughs had been few and far between the two of us. Deep resentment on both sides of our polarised lives gathered enough momentum for us to nearly call it quits. Particularly once I began to make real money, the same old argument went around and around and the record was well and truly broken.

'So you travel the world and I just have to rot away in that dental lab?'

'Sell the damn dental lab and come with me?'

'I have to work!'

'So do I!'

The truth was that by now some of the kids had started boarding school in Adelaide and we needed both incomes. I couldn't afford to stop gigging even if I'd wanted to. My drinking hadn't yet had any disastrous effects on my professional life, but deep down in a place I was reluctant to visit in my soul I knew that I was in trouble.

I recall gagging in the physical agony of a hangover on a tour while attempting to brush my teeth one morning in a hotel room in Launceston. I stared right through my reflection in the mirror and spoke out loud to the hateful witch that was myself staring back at me. 'You are so sick. You are so sick.'

It was a mantra I was to repeat many more times over many more hangovers. As always hell turned to hilarity time and time again. Only that morning a few hours after my chat in the mirror, myself and about four other comedians sat around a table in a café, having just ordered breakfast before heading on to the next show in Hobart. We were all bemoaning our hangovers, and Tom Gleeson wondered out loud what could be the worst possible scenario a person could find themselves in, in a hung-over state. I think Fleety jumped in first.

'Going hiking with your dad.'

'Helping your grandma move into a nursing home.'

'Helping your grandma move into a nursing home in Karratha.'

'Going to a dry Jehovah's Witness wedding in Broken Hill.'

'Being a Jehovah's Witness in Broken Hill and going door knocking in forty-degree heat.'

My phone started ringing, and I stepped outside to talk to Chris. Half an hour later I returned to the table just as everyone was finishing their breakfast. 'I've just found out what's the worst possible thing someone can be put through on a hangover.'

'What?'

'Having your husband call you from Alice Springs and read out loud every word of five kids' report cards.'

Laughs all round.

Stand-ups had become another family to me, my carnival family if you like. We talked about everything and anything and eventually I started to confide my dark secret to those closest to me. Dave Grant and Charlie Pickering were the first to know, and offered unwavering support, but while it was a temporary relief to offload, there was only one person who would eventually pull me out of harm's way. She of course was far too busy at the time living between the two worlds of bright lights and Central Australia.

My beautiful friend Lulu Cain who I've been so close to since the Trevelyan Street era also knew how desperate my life had become and I am forever grateful to her for having the patience and the love to simply wait with hope for me to come out from under my own cloud of chaos.

My times at home in Alice Springs conversely became more peaceful. My nursing knowledge, as trim as it was, recognised that I could seriously injure myself physically with my level of alcohol consumption, so I literally withdrew myself from as much social interaction as I could get away with while I was at home, and laughingly referred to Alice Springs as the Betty Ford Clinic. My madness in believing that alcohol and stand-up were inseparable continued, but I stopped drinking at home with surprising ease unless we were entertaining, and I made sure we did precious little of that.

I threw myself into housework and cooking and, since my kids have rarely given me anything but joy, I was more than happy indulging in their company and little else. The only downside to this perceived solution was that it enabled me to retreat further into denial.

'I rarely drink at home,' I remember announcing to some astonished comedians a couple of years ago in Edinburgh.

'Jaysas!' marvelled the Irish comedian I was slurping with. 'Not one pub in Alice Springs?'

Of all the camouflages a problem drinker can have, the world of stand-up has got to be one of the handiest. While there's lots of comics that don't drink, there's lots that do, and even besides that there's a camaraderie of shared misbehaviour that we find ourselves in, especially during a festival. Comedians sharing the experience of the same festival are almost in an exclusive bubble where we exist in a world without normal consequences.

'Hey! It's the festival!'

I couldn't count the number of times I've used or heard that phrase in reaction to my own outrageous behaviour or someone else's.

As I said earlier, not all of my experiences are going in the shame box. Sometimes, drunk or sober, unforgettable funny really happened, and when I'm an old lady in a nursing home I will still reel with laughter at an episode that occurred during the Melbourne Comedy Festival in 2007.

* * *

Mark Watson, a Welsh comedian who I believe to be one of the most perfect stand-ups ever created, was doing a twenty-four-hour show at a performance tent down by the Yarra. I'd seen some of his thirty-six-hour shows in Edinburgh a year or so earlier and, as nuts as it sounds, it is a record-breaking and groundbreaking experience that incorporates everything from stand-up to improvised songwriting to live internet interaction with punters around the globe. It captivates some of his audience enough to bring sleeping bags and pillows and remain for the entire performance.

This, of course, is an impossible feat if you are a performer yourself in the same festival, but Chris and I were riveted in Edinburgh and had to drag ourselves away for sleep at the six-hour mark. By the time I wandered past his show in Melbourne at midnight one Saturday Mark was about halfway through his marathon of mirth and I decided to pop my head in and see what was going on. By now Mark and I had become buddies after touring with the Melbourne Roadshow the year before.

Mark encouraged fellow comedians to swing by and either heckle or join him on stage for any manner of madness, but he was in the middle of what seemed to be a lengthy dialogue with someone in the audience so I headed to the back of the tent to see if any fellow comedians were about.

'Fiona, I've got an idea.'

Adelaide-born Mickey D and I had been giggling backstage for a few minutes trying to come up with some sort of surprise attack for Mr Watson while he was on stage. Mickey was well plastered and I'd had more than a few glasses of personality myself, but even I was shocked at his suggestion. 'Let's kit off and run across the back of the stage.'

'You've got to be kidding.'

'Trust me, Fi, it'll work. We'll hold hands and skip across the stage and back again. The audience will see it first and he won't know what's going on.'

'Skip across the stage holding hands?'

'Yeah.'

'In the nude?'

'I promise I won't look at anything.'

By now Mickey had his back turned in the darkness and was nearly undressed.

'Okay, but I'm keeping my boots on *and* my cap.'

'Yeah, no worries. Keep yourself nice by all means.'

Before I knew it the deed was done. Me, one of the oldest ladies in comedy, hand in hand with the wickedly young and chubby Mickey D, romped deliciously across the stage to the delight and disbelief of everyone in the audience.

Mark Watson barely batted an eyelid.

'Yes, ladies and gentlemen, I do believe what we all just saw was in fact real.'

I swear I'd never felt funnier, more liberated or joyously ridiculous. That is until the next morning when I woke up to my daily delivery of a hangover and gut-wrenching self-loathing.

The mental torture of my hangovers was every bit as painful as the physical consequences. I spent my daytimes during festivals in tortured snatches of sleep, reprieved only by urgent bathroom visits and as much water as I could manage to swallow down paracetamol or aspirin or both. I was also intensely agoraphobic and could only take calls from my management, sometimes Chris and my sister Cate.

The morning after my naked romp Cate rang.

'Cate!'

She recognised my tone; she'd heard it many times before.

'Oh Fiona, what's wrong?'

'I've really done it this time.'

'What? What's happened?'

'I don't think I can even say it out loud. Oh my God! I am such a fucking idiot!'

Cate was left hanging for some time as it suddenly dawned on me that someone could have been filming Mark's show! Anyone with a mobile phone could have downloaded it on YouTube! There could have been a reviewer there. It might end up in the papers. Oh, oh oh, no! The kids! Mum and Dad! Chris! I rolled around the floor still clutching my mobile phone.

'Fiona! . . . Fiona! . . . Are you there?'

'Sorry, yeah, I'm still here. Oh my God, Cate! I'm dead this time.'

'Fiona, can you please just calm down and tell me what happened?'

'Well, last night after my show, I had a few drinks at the Peter Cook bar and then . . . Arrrgh, sorry Cate, I don't think I can talk about it.'

'Fiona, it can't be as bad as you're thinking it is. You're always like this when you're hungover. Just take a deep breath and tell me about it. For God's sake, it's not like you killed anyone.'

'No, it's nothing like that.'

'And it's not like you took all your clothes off in front of hundreds of people.'

'Well, actually it is a bit like that.'

Suddenly the hell switch turned off again and we roared laughing until we couldn't breathe.

We were interrupted by the hotel phone. I answered it only because I had been warned that a lawyer from NBC in America was going to ring me with a few questions regarding my visa application. I had just signed on to be part of *Last Comic Standing*, a television show that I would be shooting in Los Angeles in about a month's time.

Coincidentally the voice on the phone was American, but it was my sister Emily pretending to be some kind of journalist. She introduced herself as a Marjorie someone and then launched in to some questions.

'Have you ever appeared naked before an audience that was either photographed, taped or filmed?'

'Fuck off, Emily.'

I hung up on her and had another laugh and my day improved from there.

The news spread like wildfire at the festival.

'Fiona O'Loughlin and Mickey D got naked at Mark Watson's twenty-four-hour show!'

'No way!'

'I can't believe I missed it.'

'Get out! Completely naked?'

I bumped into one of my best comedy friends, Anthony Menchetti, before my show the next night. He grinned.

'Fiona, is it true?'

Corinne Grant congratulated me wholeheartedly.

'Good on you! Hilarious, God I wish I was there!'

By now I had had my daily medicine of three or four drinks as I always did before my show, and that, cocktailed with the fury of adrenaline that accompanies me before any performance, had started to make me feel normal again. In reality I was doing nothing more than starting the merry, tragic dance all over again, but besides all the highs and lows of my daily and ritualistic rollercoaster I at least had the time on stage for my show, which I looked forward to the most. Strangely, it was the only time in a twenty-four-hour period where I felt truly safe and at peace. I was paying an exorbitant emotional price for one hour of sanity, but hey, I was nuts at the time.

Ardal O'Hanlon from *Father Ted* fame was always just vacating the backstage as I was entering, as we were sharing a venue and his show was before mine. I loved my brief chats behind the curtain with him.

'Oh, Ardal! I drank too much again last night and ended up running across a stage stark naked. Do you think that might be my rock-bottom moment?'

'Oh Fiona, I doubt that's anywhere even near your rock-bottom moment.'

'Yeah, you're right. I did keep my boots on.'

'Well, there you go then, you're a class act. Have a great show.'

Andrew my manager had just ducked in backstage, as he often did before I went on.

'Who's a class act?'

'I am.'

'Okay, class act. Would it be possible for you to do me a favour tomorrow?'

'Anything you wish, Mr Manager.'

'The lawyer from NBC is going to ring you again regarding a background check for your US visa. Would it be okay if this time you didn't swear and hang up on her?'

'Oh my God! I thought it was Emily.'

* * *

Edinburgh 2007 was a wall-to-wall experience of highs and lows. Professionally, I performed a one-woman show twenty-seven nights in a row (barring one night off) and was rewarded with five-star reviews and a near sell-out season at the Gilded Balloon.

Personally, I was barely able to function, and had the added stress of being accompanied by my two youngest kids Mary-Agnes and Albert, and my mother Deirdre.

I had desperately wanted to bring Bert and Mary, who were thirteen and ten at the time, because I had really started to feel the heartache of 'losing' precious moments as all of my kids started galloping towards adulthood. Mary and Bert have been the two who have been motherless the most, as prior to turning professional I had effectively been a 'stay at home mum' for most of Henry's, Tess's and Biddy's childhoods.

The 'bear cubs', as we call Bert and Mary, had well and truly earned a trip overseas, and much to the disapproval of my mum I showered them with video and digital cameras and pretty much anything else their little hearts desired to create a magical and unforgettable time in Bonny Scotland.

We certainly had an unforgettable time, but the magical moments were few and far between with Mum and me. I'm happy to say though that, even to this day, I only ever have to ask Bert and Mary the simple question: 'Best day ever?'

And 'Arthur's Seat!' is the immediate response.

I managed to get one day right during that Edinburgh Festival, and I will be forever grateful.

I don't remember enjoying our previous excursion to Arthur's Seat all those years ago because that day I had one of the worst hangovers of my life. God knows what we'd gotten up to the night before, and maybe it wasn't so much the severity of the hangover as the requirement to actually leave my apartment and participate in life during daylight hours – not something I was accustomed to do during a festival in any city. And it wasn't just the lure of a drink or ten that I was drawn to after a performance. The performers' bars are in a sense still part of a comedian's working day.

'How was your show?'

'The audience seemed happy but I definitely phoned it in tonight.'

'Phoning it in' is an expression we use if we feel more like we've performed on autopilot rather than being truly present.

'How was your show?'

'Shitty audience, so I pulled the parachute on my new stuff and went back to old rope.'

'How was your show?'

'I had a heckler. He got thrown out at the twenty-minute mark, but then my timing was just all over the shop.'

'How was your show?' . . . Honestly, comics can talk for hours about the ins and outs of the craft and, even if you don't drink, an early night during a festival would be 2 a.m. Some of us don't finish gigs until eleven, and even then we often have guest spots on other shows that can start as late as midnight. The debriefing that goes on is really no different to any other profession. Our day simply starts later and ends later. It is a truly nocturnal existence.

Mary, Bert's and my Arthur's Seat day was unmitigated joy. They climbed up hill and down dale like billygoats while I either followed them or simply lay back on the moss that is the Celtic lawn with the warm sun on my face and inhaled everything about this delicious part of the world and my two youngest children. I wondered why on earth I drank when days like this were possible without a hangover. We laughed and rolled down slopes and even found a stream of fresh water that we gulped from with the cups of our hands. This was the type of countryside that I had been dreaming about when I was their ages looking out of that school bus driving through the Peesey swamp, and until my dying day it will remain one of the happiest days of my life.

'Why is this so good, Mum? I never want to leave.'

'I think we're Aborigines, Mary.'

'I don't think we're Aborigines, Mum.'

'I know, but every single one of your great-great-grandparents were Irish Celts. We're fullbloods. And even though this is Scotland, it's very close to Ireland. And it's still Celt land. I reckon we're like Aborigines from the city going bush to the land where their blood comes from.'

'Can we climb to the top again?'

'Yes we can. One more time.'

My mother seemed incredibly out of sorts for most of our Edinburgh trip, and while she's no stranger to a late night herself and to this day loves nothing more than a drink and socialising, I think she was truly shocked at the hours I kept, and deep down I think she witnessed first hand and for the first time how very hard I played, and I imagine her grumpy exterior was masking an inner fear for me and the lifestyle I was hell-bent on leading.

We were relatively short with each other for most of that month. I was disappointed that she wasn't more actively taking charge of the kids while I slept off my late nights, and I guess she was disappointed that I wasn't interested in seeing the sights of Edinburgh.

* * *

So yes, I have regrets.

My professional regrets are less personal but have been more publicly embarrassing. My lowest moment was waking up in the Brisbane hospital to discover that I had gone on stage at the Queensland Performing Arts Centre so loaded the night before that I literally fell down dead drunk on stage in front of more than three hundred people. Before the Brisbane fiasco, or 'the incident' as my sister Cate delights in referring to it as, I had skimmed very close to the edge on at least five occasions in live stage shows, and three or four times on television. When I say skimmed close to the edge, I mean that I had had too much to drink before my appearances, but had either denied it the few times I was challenged or simply somehow got away with it.

The problem wasn't so much that I had a skinful before a show, but that at times I had drunk so very much the night before, and sometimes right through until morning, that the 'rabbit foot' of my double vodka before hitting the stage was enough to top me up again.

By 2008 my binge drinking had gathered enough momentum for me to be hospitalised three times via an ambulance for alcoholic poisoning. At one stage I was diagnosed with bipolar disorder and I dined out on that wholeheartedly for weeks. I was so excited that it was a mental illness! Far more showbiz and much more fashionable than 'drunk'. Sadly, it turns out that although I do experience higher highs and lower lows than a lot of people, so does about twenty per cent of the population, so it was back to the drawing board.

I ache with guilt over some of my travels because I feel like I've left a stain on some of the most wonderful cities in the world. New York! Drunk! Montreal! Drunk! Singapore! Drunk! London! Drunk! Edinburgh! Drunk! Toronto! Drunk! Obviously not drunk around the clock, but I created chaos and shameful memories that are large enough in my mind to overshadow the joy. The picture gallery in my head of some of these cities has bleak shots that I reluctantly revisit occasionally and are definitely at the very back of the album.

Still, even in some of my darkest times, funny continued to accompany me, although on occasions it was only funny in hindsight.

I doubt I'm alone among other comics in that I live and breathe my show from the moment I wake up, hungover or not, until it's time to hit the stage again. I relive every line in my head, agonising over why one gag worked and the next one didn't. Which story is the best to end on? Should I try the new material I'd just worked on, or play it safe?

I have never thought of my audience as a room full of separate individuals. Less than a minute in on stage, I gauge the bums on seats as one cumulative personality. Like any person that you can greet for the first time, I wonder every night backstage who I am about to meet.

I'm pretty sure it's an unusual thought process, but it's the way I have always related to my audience. It has never been me and them, but rather he or she and me. I perform one on one, and one on one only. One night in Broken Hill a couple of years ago a lovely elderly woman came backstage to introduce herself and thank me for the laughs. 'Do you know, dear, and this may sound strange, but I couldn't help but feel tonight that you were talking exclusively to me.'

And as a matter of fact, I was.

Sometimes I have said more than I intended to on stage, and have inadvertently hurt the feelings of some of my brothers and sisters, Chris or the kids. I haven't had that problem since I committed myself to performing sober for the rest of my days. It's bad enough when you've imbibed too much alcohol in a social situation and woken up regretting telling your dinner party guests that your last caesarean section left your pubic hair looking a lot like a goatee beard as they shave just about an inch past your bikini line, let alone waking up and remembering that you told three hundred strangers that you'd rather eat a Toblerone than have sex, which, quite frankly, you find 'icky and embarrassing' as, after all, you 'have to take your pants off!'

I was twice nominated for the ultimate prize in Australian Comedy, that being the much coveted 'Barry Award', named in honour of Mr Humphries himself, and I was also once nominated for a Helpmann Award for best live comedy stage show. All three times I was thrilled to the back teeth for the nod, and then wholeheartedly disappointed at my name not being announced on the night of the awards. I am glad that I never took home either trophy. It would be have been tantamount to 'drug cheating' at the Olympics. I have learnt, and learnt the hard way, that nothing is worth saying to the paying customer unless it is said sober . . . well, obviously with the exception of Peter Cook and Dudley Moore.

For two seasons of back-to-back Adelaide, Melbourne and Edinburgh festivals my mum had been the butt of many of my jokes and anecdotes, and to her credit she took it all in her stride and with very good humour.

Of all family members, female comics tend to talk about their mothers as much as if not more than about their spouses. I don't know why this is the case exactly, but I guess mothers are relatable-to for nearly everyone in the market for a laugh and can be the perfect foil for a daughter to highlight the contrasts of our generations and tickle the funny bone of our collective memories. I'm always assured of this at the end of a gig by strangers approaching me.

'My mother used to say exactly the same thing!'

'My mother used to lose her mind at Christmas as well.'

'I think we had the same mother.'

Poor Mum. As with all my routines, they are based in truth but always painted with a much broader brush for the sake of the laughter that is my life's fuel. The closest she has ever come to complaining was when she rang one Boxing Day to see what I was up to. My mother and I speak almost daily on the phone and always have.

'I'm on the computer today trying to write my new show.'

'Oh that's nice. Do you think you could lay off your mother for a while?'

'You know it's not the real you exactly that I talk about on stage?'

'So you've told me.'

* * *

I walked into the studio for my first rehearsal for the 2009 season of *Dancing with the Stars* having no idea that I was stepping into a period of incredible change personally and professionally. Kerrie Kerr, our segment producer, had met me outside, and I was certainly a little nervous as I climbed the stairs to meet my dance partner Craig Monley for the first time. My nerves were nothing of concern to me, however, as I was used to being in situations that took me out of my comfort zone as my career had progressed, and the 'out of the ordinary' had become 'the ordinary' time and time again.

In a way, I was used to 'pinching myself' and having my own private giggle at me for talking my way all the way from Warooka to the wonder of wherever I found myself on any given day. Never has the privilege of working with the people I've worked with or met been lost on me. The only way to describe this is to blatantly name-drop, but I can see no other way around it, so please forgive me if, well . . . if I sound like a dickhead.

From being interviewed by Colin Cochrane in Canada for a documentary he was filming about improv, to having an early dinner with Paul Kelly in Edinburgh before our shows, to sitting backstage and laughing with Jerry Lewis in Sydney or hearing that Lyle Lovett had dedicated a song to me at Hamer Hall . . . always my steady exterior belies my inner and utter disbelief that I have been somehow allowed inside this world.

Essentially it can't be different to any trade or profession. If I was a hairdresser, and loved it with an absolute passion and was trusted with the same scissors as the hairdresser I most admired on the planet, then wouldn't I be as happy as a hairdresser as I am as an artist? I think so. Performance is generally a less tangible job than most, but at the end of the day we want our tiles to be laid well and admired by those we laid them for; we want our operations to be successful and our patients to be well pleased and grateful; we want our restaurants full and our food to be complimented. Simply speaking, we offer a service, and love to be asked for more. I think by now I might be being a bigger dickhead than when I was name-dropping, but I think you get my drift.

I had no idea of what lay ahead with *Dancing with the Stars*, especially on a physical level. I hadn't for a second thought that learning to dance would be all that hard. I'd always been able to hold a tune in a jam session, and as far as I knew I always tapped my feet in rhythm. I didn't even mind the odd spin on the floor at weddings and twenty-firsts. Nothing to be worried about, really, apart from two million people watching.

Learning to dance is a bit like learning to walk. I didn't pay much attention to Craig for the first fifteen minutes or so of us meeting, as the cameras were rolling for the 'behind the scenes packages' that make up a large whack of every episode of the show and after the initial introductions he had me literally step my way through the very basics of a waltz for an hour or more.

It wasn't until we physically 'took up hold' to walk through those same basic steps together and then gradually begin dancing/walking to music that I was overwhelmed with inadequacy. Besides being one of the kindest, most generous human beings I have ever come to know, Craig Monley is a goddamned Adonis! I had forgotten entirely what a young man felt like and he is made up of nothing but muscle and good looks. A blond-haired, blue-eyed, buff Aryan is the best way to describe Craig.

Meanwhile, I felt like a bag of potatoes in an unmade bed in comparison. Middle-aged women have a thousand tricks to hide the wobbly womanly weary truths of a life half-lived, but being in the arms of a young fit man rendered me naked, and I wanted that dance floor to open up and swallow me whole.

This poor boy was going to have to suffer ten weeks or more of this and that's before the show even started!

I made up my own lyrics in my head to go with the music: 'This isn't fair/this isn't fair/Fred Astaire and a polar bear!'

Craig and I became very good mates in no time, but 'taking up hold' at the start of each training session left me incredibly embarrassed every time for a month or more. Fortunately, each day found me less and less self-conscious and keener than ever to learn. Apart from the early shame when he held out his hand to take my paw, I have never enjoyed myself more on a professional level than working with Craig and our producer Kerrie for *Dancing with the Stars*.

I was also unusually healthy for me at the time, as I had just finished a tour of New Zealand and had put in action a plan I had used once before to combat my drinking, and it had worked a treat. I simply told the basic truth at the start of the New Zealand tour: 'I'm going through a bit of a battle with the booze at the moment, fellas.'

'You on the wagon, O'Loughlin?'

'Not completely, but I'm trying.'

There has been a long-held misconception that my 'carnival family' had been leading me astray for years, when in fact the opposite was true. As 'eclectic' a family as comedians are, we look out for each other and neither judge nor interfere with each other's sobriety or weaknesses. I think the others actually watched my back for the duration of our three-week tour, and never once did anyone encourage me to party. I encouraged myself one night in Auckland towards the end of the tour, but apart from that I steered myself home after every show and, though hard to do at times, it was made a lot easier by having been open with the others in the first place.

I had used the same plan once before, and I'll be forever grateful that I did. In 2006 I had the honour of being the only international guest on a road trip through Canada with the Montreal 'Just for Laughs' comedy festival. I only knew one of my fellow comedians at the start of that tour, an LA-based Canadian comic called John Wing, but, having an innate trust in any fellow joke-meister, I quietly filled every one of my five tour buddies in on my struggle, and barring one night off in Toronto and another night to celebrate the tour I was blessedly able to experience touring across the most beautiful country in the world without my nasty hangover companion.

I could go on forever about the joys of that tour and the friends I made, but I have to resist heading off on another tangent or this book will simply never see the light of day. Having said that, I must tell you about one memory I made and have forever imprinted in the album in my head.

I was having breakfast in a hotel in Saint John in Nova Scotia on the first morning after arriving. The hotel dining room looked out to the ocean. A huge fishing trawler was docked so close that I could watch three or four fishermen beginning their day, and God bless one of them who actually smoked a pipe and had a beard to complement the scene. I really did pinch myself as I tucked into a Mexican frittata with the joy ahead of at least twenty Canadian cities to see and then, like an old friend tapping me on the shoulder, I noticed the music that was playing in the restaurant.

Bloody joy! One of the most satisfying moments of my comedy life had been put to my favourite song 'From St Kilda to Kings Cross' by Paul Kelly, on the other side of the world.

* * *

Mary-Agnes, when she was only eleven (and I was really in the depths), wrote this piece – which I discovered far later. She certainly wanted me to find it – and understand it – far, far sooner than I actually did. I have printed it out and will keep it on my person forever.

ALCOHOLICS

By Mary O'Loughlin

There is no cure to this bad, life ruining disease, there is only absence. Alcoholics need to learn that their life is being taken over by alcohol, and that humans are much stronger than alcohol, which means they can live without it.

About Living with an Alcoholic

By Mary O'Loughlin

My mum is an alcoholic (although she denies it) and I hate it. Last year mum told me that she would give up drinking for a year so then she might be a normal drinker again. I knew it was too good to be true, so to make her try and keep the promise I made her a locket with 'I love you' on one side and 'promise' on the other. It only lasted until Christmas. Mum doesn't go out drinking all the time, but when she does, she gets really, really, drunk. Every time I see her drunk I cry,

but I don't know exactly why. Either I need help, Mum needs
help, or we both need help.

* * *

Even in an AA meeting my intuition steered me towards the
comedy in the tragedy. I was under no illusion. I was where I
belonged, among the broken and the defenceless in this room
of rock-bottom, but the comedian in me never ceases to observe
the absurdity of humanity. It was my first meeting, and I was
advised that it isn't customary to 'share' on this, my debut at
Alcoholics Anonymous.

'Hello, my name is Sarah! and I am an alcoholic.'

Polite clapping ensued, and I joined in while stifling a giggle
at the same time. Applause for the self-confessed drunk at an
AA meeting. Why ever not?

*'Well done, Sarah! Good on you! You've fucked up big time!
Round of applause.'*

My internal dialogue kept up a steady pace throughout
Sarah's monologue of her journey through to sobriety.

'I first realised that I had a problem with alcohol about a
year ago.'

*'For heaven's sake, you look eighteen! I doubt you'd even know
whether you were a vegetarian yet, let alone an alcoholic.'*

'My boyfriend and I went out to Bojangles Nightclub and
we got very drunk.'

*'Been there, done that, sweet child, three hundred and seventy-
four times, give or take a hangover or two.'*

'We had a terrible fight and then went home, and the fight
got worse and I threw the phone book at his head.'

'Well, the Alice Springs phone book is hardly an encyclopedia. It's not like you live in Hong Kong where a phone book could really do some damage.'

'Luckily for him it missed his head, but it was my wake-up call to finally do something about my drinking.'

'Good for you, Sarah. Nip it in the bud. Meanwhile, thanks to your skills as a raconteur I've never needed a double scotch more.'

Time for a joke, I decided, or I was sure my head would explode. I leant over to the gentlemen on my left, who had kindly winked a welcome at me at the beginning of the meeting.

'Excuse me,' I whispered in his ear and he leant forward.

'Is there a higher level? I think I might be in the beginners class.'

* * *

Celebrations are frequent in a family as big as ours, with milestone parties always within spitting distance on our continual calendar of conviviality. This night was special, though. Mum and Dad were joined by all of my brothers and sisters, a fair whack of the original cast of their wedding party fifty years ago, and some forty other friends and rellies. We were actually unusually restrained with numbers, for a Taheny bash, but Cate was single-handedly catering a sit-down reception, and the venue was the barn at our beloved 'Cletta'.

We started with drinks on the verandah before we headed over to the newly floored and roofed barn, and I stood apart from the crowd and felt momentarily grief stricken that I couldn't join in in the way that I once would have: champagne all round, and the booming voices of much loved men, and the laughter and cracking conversations of much loved women; this was always the part of the party that I loved the most. The beginning! The heightened excitement of all that lay ahead; the night literally an unborn pup, and the knowledge that all that lay ahead for now was laughs, laughs and more laughs.

Years of habit had me aching for a glass of bubbly just like the one Genevieve was holding and the one my brother Richard was handing to one of my aunts. I slipped inside the house and stood behind the door in the dining room and allowed myself a pocket of time and privacy to feel sorry for myself and get a grip at the same time.

'One quick cry is all you're getting, Fiona. Yes, the old you would be holding the floor already out there on that verandah, and the old you would be as tingly as the Yellowglen you were holding, but the old you would have already downed a less-than-dignified amount by now, and then the night would slide as steadily as your feet and you would wake up tomorrow with a hangover from hell and a heavy heart again. So shut up and get back out there.'

'You okay, love?'

My Uncle Anthony and his wife Arlene had happened upon their absurd niece behind the door, and I quickly wiped my eyes but gave an honest answer.

'This is my first sober family party. I'm scared.'

Arlene gave me a hug that was nearly as good as a shot of tequila.

'You're going to be okay, I promise.'

The only word I can use to describe that night is splendiferous. Richard had decked out the barn so elegantly and awash with candlelight that his sexuality briefly came into question. Cate delivered on three courses that would have gotten her through to a semi-final of *Masterchef*, and my brother Justin's wife, Joanne, orchestrated a seamless montage of photographs that beamed continuously against the whitewashed wall of the old building we were squeezed into. Mum and Dad were seated in a wedding reception re-enactment accompanied by all of their remaining groomsmen and bridesmaids.

And my brilliant daughter Tess pulled together a compilation of music from the fifties and onwards that was jam-packed with nostalgia.

It was a 10 out of 10 party. Dad delivered a stunning speech that had us laughing and crying, and yet we still had one last card to play, and it was an ace up my sleeve. Craig and Sriani from *Dancing with the Stars* were waiting in the kitchen for me to give the signal. Just when a party couldn't be going better, in burst two of the world's top Latin dancers and performed a *paso doble* right there in a barn in little old Warooka, South Australia. I have never seen my mother look as pretty as she did at that moment, and had never delighted in the giving of a gift more.

Nights like Mum and Dad's fiftieth wedding anniversary are like the gifts we get in life every so often that make everything perfect, if only for a while. I grabbed that winter night with both hands because I knew it would pass, but for probably the very first time in my life I didn't fight or rally against the inevitable end. The end came as it always had, and inevitably had passed, as it always would.

I stood apart from the crowd for the second time that evening before I took myself to bed, and felt awash with gratitude that the old Fiona hadn't been invited.

Cate and Emily were tearing up the dance floor, and Craig and Sriani were looking on in great amusement with my oldest friends Joanne Hayes and Mary-Anne Williams. My showbiz world had intertwined with my familial world, and I was content.

George Kokar sauntered over and took a seat next to me.

'You going okay?'

George was our local GP, but our family friend first, and had known me since I was a kid. I was very touched and I understood that he was not asking that age-old question in a perfunctory way.

'I really am, George. I was scared of tonight. But I'm okay.'

George is a funny, gruff, generous, cryptic, genuine bloke.

'I'm glad. Life's a funny thing. Some people drink too much. It can shit your liver . . . but none of us get out alive, you know.'

* * *

Writing this has actually exhausted me with the memory of it all, but it is not my intention to whine about my lot. At times it has been a massive struggle physically and emotionally, but I have had experiences throughout my career that I never could have believed possible as a somewhat odd little girl from Warooka.

I've walked through Central Park with my husband, with the thrill of Montreal only days ahead of me. I've toured thirty cities in Canada and sat in a luxury bus laughing with Jerry Seinfeld's buddy Tom Papa, with the Snowy Mountains in the background. I've held hands and taken a bow with the great

William Shatner and been told by him that I had 'some great lines'.

I've played the Sydney Opera House and the Massey Hall in Toronto. I've flown over mountains in Kabul in a Hercules on my way to entertain our troops, laughing myself inside out with Lehmo.

I've had breakfast at the famous Beauties in Montreal with Biddy, afternoon tea at the Shangri-La Hotel in Hong Kong with Henry and a pizza slice with Tess at Mariella's on Eighth Avenue in midtown New York.

I've lain in the mild summer sun of Scotland on top of Arthur's Seat while Mary-Agnes and Bert raced around me on a day they still refer to as 'the best day ever'.

There's been some lowlights as well that are probably worth mentioning; I've accidentally said the 'F' word in front of the Queen, tipsily asked Shane Warne in an Edinburgh nightclub why he never text messages *me*, and I once lit my cigarette from the original Olympic flame on its 2000 visit from Athens.

But I have laughed longer and louder and harder than I ever thought possible, grafted more comedians to my heart than I ever believed I could have made room for, been continually loved by my family and my friends, and become prouder of my magnificent kids than any mother can be. I've still never owned a camera or taken a photo that was good enough to frame, but the album in my head gets bigger by the day and I hope you feel like you've at least flipped through it after reading this book.

ACKNOWLEDGEMENTS

Thank you Chris, Henry, Biddy, Tess, Bert and Mary-Agnes for all the time that this book has taken me away from you and for everything you have given me to write about.

Thank you Matthew Kelly from Hachette Australia for your tireless work as an editor and campaigner for this book. Also thank you to Katy Stackhouse for first suggesting I put pen to paper. To my friends who gave me feedback as I wrote, especially; Anna Worden, Jasmin Afianos, Denise Pursche, Mary-Anne Williams, Meredith Campbell, Jason McIntosh, Mark Screaigh, and MaryAnne Kennedy. Thank you all so much.

Thank you to Andrew Taylor, Jeff Green, Nadia Galea and everyone at Andrew Taylor Management.

Thank you Mum and Dad and lastly my brothers and sisters, Genevieve, Richard, Cate, Justin, Sarah and Emily. You are my tribe and without you I would have no story to tell.

If you would like to find out more about Hachette Australia, our authors, upcoming events and new releases you can visit our website or follow us on twitter.

www.hachette.com.au
www.twitter.com/HachetteAus